Market Structure, Bargaining Power, and Resource Price Formation

Market Structure, Bargaining Power, and Resource Price Formation

Walter C. Labys
West Virginia University

LexingtonBooks
D.C. Heath and Company
Lexington, Massachusetts
Toronto

Library of Congress Cataloging in Publication Data

Labys, Walter C   1937–
  Market structure, bargaining power, and resource price information.

  Bibliography: p.
  Includes index.
  1. Mineral industries—Prices.   2. Mineral industries—consolidation.
3. Commodity control.   I. Title.
HD9506. A2L23   338.2′3   78-19541
ISBN 0-669-02511-9

Copyright © 1980 by D.C. Heath and Company

Published simultaneously in Canada

Printed in the United States of America

International Standard Book Number: 0-669-02511-9

Library of Congress Catalog Card Number: 78-19541

To Alf

Contents

List of Figures

List of Tables

Preface and Acknowledgments

Commodity price behavior has once again come to the forefront as an international economic issue. Much of the discussion related to the call for an international economic order stems from a dissatisfaction with existing patterns of mineral prices and trade. Although much of this discussion has centered on problems of short-run price fluctuations such as those related to speculation, equal attention has been given to problems of long-run price movements such as those related to supply-demand balances. This latter problem is particularly critical for international commodity markets involving resources of a nonrenewable nature, the fuel and nonfuel minerals. Today, a multitude of questions have been posed regarding not only the determinants of price formation but also the levels of prices considered equitable from an economic and social point of view.

This book attempts to answer several of the more important of these questions. The approach normally followed in analyzing commodity price formation is that of microeconomic theory. However, a number of factors influencing minerals markets make the application of this theory to mineral price analysis difficult. Minerals markets, for example, are influenced by the presence of monopolistic competition as well as by institutions' such as producers' organizations and cartels. To overcome such problems, a framework is proposed that I believe is suitable for analyzing mineral price formation. Although the framework centers on supply and demand conditions, it reaches beyond them to include market structure, bargaining power, and market implications. The results obtained from applying the framework confirm its usefulness as well as aspects of its limitations to be pursued further.

The first half of the book features the development of the framework. Because of the comprehensiveness of the framework, not all aspects of it could be used in the mineral case studies. However, it is general enough to be applicable to a wide range of commodities. The commodity case studies related to international mineral price formation occupy the second half of the book. These case studies are directed to the four minerals of most importance to developing countries and international trade: copper, tin, bauxite, and iron ore.

The study will be of interest to commodity economists, resource economists, development economists, and policymakers. Academics will find the analytical framework and commodity examples valuable for teaching an introductory course in mineral economcis. It can also supplement courses in microeconomic theory, resource economics, industrial organization, and market and price analysis. Mineral economists in government and industry can use this approach for making mineral market surveys and for analyzing investment decisions. Development economists will appreciate the interpretation of market implications and the evaluation of bargaining power between host governments and mineral investing firms. Finally, I hope that graduate students and other research workers will find insights and results to employ in their own work.

The idea of the book was a consequence of research to determine the economic value of natural-resource commodities. That is, do market prices reflect intrinsic resource value? The major stimulus to expand the scope of my research effort on the topic came from Marian Radetzki, and I am extremely grateful to him. He not only provided a critical analysis of the work in its early stages but also encouraged me to incorporate ideas from his seminal paper on the topic, "Market Structure and Bargaining Power: A Study of Three International Mineral Markets." References to it are thus found throughout the text.[a] Much of this work was also stimulated by research I carried out at UNCTAD (United Nations Conference on Trade and Development) in Geneva during the summers of 1977 and 1978. This involved work on the study of the environmental component in the social evaluation and pricing of natural resources. In this respect I am deeply grateful to Jack Stone and to Alfred Maizels. Peter Dorner also was helpful in inviting me to present some of my material at the Wisconsin Seminar on Natural Resource Policy.

Finally, a number of persons should be thanked for their assistance in reading and correcting preliminary drafts of the manuscript. These include: John Tilton, Chris Brown, Gress Hickman, Connie Shelton, Bruce Bancroft, Lu White, and Paul Wielgus. The views and opinions expressed are mine, however, and I take full responsibility for them.

Help in preparing this manuscript was given by the secretarial staff of the College of Mineral and Energy Resources, West Virginia University.

[a]I am grateful for permission by Dr. Marian Radetzki to quote from his paper: "Market Structure and Bargaining Power: A Study of Three International Mineral Markets," Mimeographed, Institute for International Economic Studies, Stockholm, 1976. This paper appeared subsequently in a reedited and abbreviated form in *Resources Policy* 4 (June 1978): 115–125.

1   Introduction

Background

This study deals with the complexities surrounding price formation on international resource commodity markets, specifically the minerals markets. Many persons are not aware of the recent problems and developments that have occurred in this area. To begin with, much of the discussion related to the call for a "new international economic order" stems from a dissatisfaction with the existing patterns of mineral production, processing, consumption, and trade. Essential to understanding these patterns is a comprehension of the role played by mineral prices and their underlying determinants. These prices normally have been explained in the context of balancing supply and demand, that is, allocating scarce goods among competing end uses.

However, there are a number of factors that inhibit the straightforward application of microeconomic theory in this regard. For example, many mineral markets possess structures that deviate from the given competitive norm; mineral exploitation is based on imperfect knowledge of the extent and grade of a deposit; mineral production and processing involves questions of income transfers and income distribution; and mineral consumption requires allocating demand between present and future generations. Because of problems such as these, it is not surprising that there is not yet any universally accepted theory about mineral price formation.

As recently emphasized by Bosson and Varon, perceptions of the role and determinants of price formation are presently undergoing a process of reevaluation and transformation.[1] What are some of the major considerations in this debate? First, the magnitude and conditions of recent changes in oil prices have drawn attention to the idea of the availability and cost of substitutes as a benchmark for pricing. Second, persisting inequality in the global distribution of income has drawn attention to price formation as a concept to facilitate income transfers. Third, there has been an increasing awareness that international market prices are difficult to determine for minerals. This stems from the fact that there are no "free commodity markets" of any substantial size for many of these commodities and that published price estimates are vulnerable to transfer pricing practices. As a consequence, it seems appropriate at this time not only to develop an approach useful for analyzing price formation but also to make specific applications to those mineral markets presently of greatest international importance.

1

Commodity Pricing

The analysis of commodity price behavior is normally divided between the long-run price, which can be termed the equilibrium or trend price, and the short-run price, which is associated with speculation and cyclical or random price movements. These different price movements serve different purposes in commodity market adjustments and require different analytical approaches for explanation, although the two are obviously related.[2] The concept of price formation studied here refers to the long-run price which is formed by the interaction of long-run supply and demand.

Here the process of price formation deals with a number of allocation problems at once: which goods will be produced, how (with what combination of inputs) they will be produced, and to whom (which users) they shall be distributed. For the case of mineral commodities, two other allocative questions need to be considered: How will consumption be divided between present and future generations? And how will the economic benefits of resource exploitation be divided among producers and consumers? In the case of developing countries that are among the major resource producers, the division of gains between the host government and foreign investors must also be considered. As a consequence, the microeconomic explanation of long-run price determination must be expanded to include trade-offs between conservation and income as well as the distribution of income among countries.

However, the difficulty of optimizing allocation in these two last situations precludes the direct application of microeconomic theory. Microeconomics assumes that in the absence of structural change, the production of a good can go on indefinitely. This is generally not the case for resources such as minerals, where deposits can eventually be exhausted. Of course, some minerals are recyclable and can be reused, but the theory of exhaustibility makes no distinction between recyclable and nonrecyclable materials. It is only concerned with the maximization of the present value of the future output of a mine.

A further assumption of microeconomics is that the market process is basically a bargaining situation. The number of participants and their knowledge about the market determine its degree of perfection or imperfection. Since future generations cannot be present in the bargaining process, there is no way for them to express their preferences. Thus, microeconomics has difficulties in allocating scarce resources among generations.[3]

Also essential to the above assumption is that the market should not become too imperfect. Otherwise the tools of analysis available become less useful for determining the prices that should result from a particular bargaining situation. Consider the concentration of consumers as well as producers. When they are in large numbers on both sides of the market, the structure is one of competition-competition, and prices can be determined. When they are only one or few on the supply side, the structure is one of monopoly-competition or oligopoly-competition, and some prediction of the price outcome is still possible. However, the market structure at the primary commodity stage of resource production is often oligopoly-oligopsony. Here, microeconomic theory also fails to help us with price determination and hence resource allocation, even in the present.

A final aspect of commodity pricing is the difficulty of obtaining knowledge about many of the prices that are being reached in the world arena. For example, mineral prices related to the primary or mining stage are often not quoted publicly. However, we do know that such quotations are available for agricultural commodities at the primary stage. This information seems to be a consequence of the generally competitive or free nature of the markets: large numbers of transactions take place daily between independent buyers or sellers and are recorded on official exchanges. In addition, this price information often stretches to each stage of marketing and distribution from producers through dealers to final consumers, sometimes including price margins. If we return to mineral markets, we find that their structure ranges from markets of a similarly competitive nature to ones which are highly integrated, both horizontally and vertically. Although market prices can be measured for the former, they are almost impossible to determine for the latter.

Problems such as this are considered particularly serious for the mineral resources.[4] To begin with, mineral prices rather than ultimate consumption reflect the gains to be realized from resource exploitation. Lack of useful accurate information about prices is a source of conflict and an obstacle to effective planning. In addition, the structural imperfections of the mineral markets which account for the lack of accurate information on prices have distorting influences on the price movements themselves. Finally, factors such as externalities often do not enter estimates of current market value, and this makes mineral project evaluation a difficult task. Any attempts to improve our understanding of price formation thus work to the benefit of both parties in the bargaining process, producers as well as consumers.

Goals for This Study

These brief observations suggest a need to develop a framework or methodological approach for mineral price analysis. In accepting this as the major goal of this study, we should realize the economic complexities of explaining mineral price formation. Mainly, we need to go beyond the typical microeconomic approach to include the study of market organization or structure and its implications. What is involved is the study of a multitude of factors including demand and supply elasticities, investment and supply costs, interindustry demands, substitution, technology, market concentration, bargaining power, administered price structures, rent, division of gains, and so forth. Obviously the complexity of the interactions involved calls for caution in developing and applying the framework as well as in claiming that one can begin to decipher all the elements of the problem.

Among other goals to be pursued, an attempt is made to include a behavioral analysis of interactions among the actors involved in the market, that is, producers, consumers, trading firms, governments, multinational mining corporations (MMCs), and international organizations. The commodities selected for applying the framework are those of most interest on world mineral markets as well as important for developing countries: copper, tin, bauxite, and iron ore. The implications of these markets for host governments in mineral-dependent developing countries as well as for foreign investing mineral firms are also considered.

This approach to understanding price formation is deemed important because the price behavior of these commodities has been little studied from a qualitative point of view in recent years. To this end, the institutional character of the approach should permit price-related policies to be analyzed more appropriately in a politicoeconomic context.

Notes

1. The importance of studying price formation in the present context is well brought out by the authors and frequent reference is made to their work in this study. R. Bosson and B. Varon, *The Mining Industry and the Developing Countries* (New York: World Bank and Oxford University Press, 1977).

2. As an example of the differences in approach and technique required, the reader is referred to my previous works dealing with commodity price behavior. The first of these analyzes behavior of a daily, weekly, and monthly nature: *Speculation, Hedging and Commodity Price Forecasts,* with C.W.J. Granger (Lexington, Mass: Lexington Books, D.C. Heath, 1970). The second analyzes price behavior mostly of an annual nature, including the underlying market structure: *Dynamic Commodity Models* (Lexington: Lexington Books, D.C. Heath, 1973).

3. A discussion of this problem appears in R.M. Solow, "Intergenerational Equity and Exhaustable Resources," *The Review of Economic Studies,* Symposium, 42 (1974):29–46.

4. See Bosson and Varon, *The Mining Industry,* p. 110.

2 Framework for Analyzing Price Formation

Introduction to the Framework

Chapter 1 indicated that existing approaches of microeconomics become inadequate when confronted with the complexities of analyzing price formation on international resource markets, particularly those of mineral commodities. Radetzki has extended the argument to include the several approaches employed: price theory, industrial organization theory, and theory of bargaining.[1] Price theory does have a lot to say about prices which emerge under conditions of perfect or monopolistic competition, monopoly and oligopoly, but it becomes relatively ineffective when perfect competition does not prevail on the other side of the market. For example, only a price range can be specified for bilateral monopoly; even less can be said for other combinations such as monopoly-oligopsony. A similar case can also be made regarding industrial organization theory, where the forms of market control found among producers on the supply side are normally compared only to a competitive norm on the buying side. Finally, bargaining theory which does provide insights into behavioral patterns related to two-person zero-sum games becomes ineffective in cases where mutual dependence arises, where more than two decision-making units operate on each side of the market, or where the sum consequent to solution is nonzero.

Nonetheless, certain facets of microeconomics do provide insights into resource markets and price formation. In particular, economic theory possesses a methodology which is generally directed to the following ends: (1) analyzing the way in which an economic system functions or provides a systematic account of such a system, (2) explaining why it operates and behaves as it does by linking that behavior with its underlying determinants, (3) predicting how the system will perform including its variation under specific circumstances, and (4) evaluating the performance of the economy based on its inherent conduct.[2]

Some suggestions as to how the preceding approaches reflect these insights are as follows: Price theory can help us to explain the underlying demand and supply conditions in a market as well as the related market structure and consequent price formation. Industrial organization theory can provide a link between market structure and price. That is, it can explain how resource production is brought into equilibrium with society's demands for goods and services through some organizing mechanism such as markets. It can also help to explain how variations and imperfections in this mechanism affect the success achieved by producers in satisfying society's wants. Finally, bargaining theory can help explain the evolution of the changing nature of the relationship between multinational mining companies who are foreign investors and host governments who attempt to develop their resource base.

The framework proposed here embodies these elements and makes it possible to deal with price formation for different commodities by focusing on certain properties that their markets have in common. As shown in figure 2–1, price formation is related to market conditions, market structure, and the impact which market structure has on the principal market participants.[3] *Market conditions* reflect the basic determinants underlying supply and

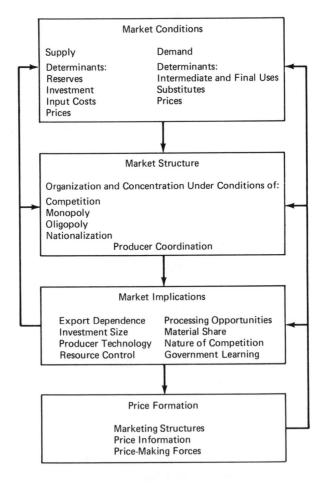

Figure 2–1. Framework for Analyzing Price Formation

demand. The study of mineral supply involves examining the supply process from exploration to mine development, extraction, and processing. To analyze mineral demand we must study not only the stages of demand but also the influence of substitution. *Market structure* is determined by the attempts among market participants to control market prices, demand, supply, investments, or rents through different bargaining strategies. At the international level this includes the behavior of multinational mining companies, attempts of host governments to nationalize firms, and movements toward producer organizations and cartels. *Market implications* relate to the impacts of the market on producers and consumers. Here we are particularly concerned with the division of gains in the market and how this has been affected by the evolution of bargaining between foreign investors and host countries. Market conditions, structure, and implications when integrated provide the backdrop for explaining *price formation*. Before proceeding to a complete development of each of these aspects of the overall framework, let us examine its general structure more carefully.

Market Conditions

Basic to the framework are the market conditions explaining supply, demand, and trade behavior for the mineral group of resource commodities. Regarding supply, these conditions begin with the stages of production: exploring for deposits, developing mines, smelters, and other conversion facilities, and processing the ores into primary materials. Underlying determinants include economic, geologic, technological, and institutional factors as well as considerations regarding risk and uncertainty. Also of importance are investment and supply costs.

Although market concentration and power relate specifically to the subject matter of market structure, they are considered first as they arise separately in supply conditions and demand conditions. A number of factors determine market power in supply, including economies of scale, control over technical knowledge, government policies, and control over the resource. In turn, the degree of market power generally determines the form of market organization, that is, competitive, oligopolistic, or monopolistic.

Market conditions relating to demand include economic conditions, production technology at the derived demand level, and changes in tastes. A first step in analyzing demand is to stratify it by levels: primary, intermediate, or final demand. Substitution processes are also important as a single mineral is often employed in a number of end uses. Market power in demand can be reflected in competitive as well as in oligopsonistic and monopsonistic buyer arrangements.

Market Structure

To link market structure to market conditions, each of the mineral markets will be described in terms of a flow diagram such as that shown in figure 2–2. This diagram links the various stages of the market system and traces the nature of price formation. Here the emphasis changes from supply and demand to the actors involved in the producing and the consuming countries. These can be functionally grouped according to sellers (producers, local processors, government and private intermediaries, and multinational firms) and to buyers (intermediaries, processors, wholesale-retail distribution industries, and multinational firms). One possible listing of participants in the market is: (1) independent or nonintegrated producers providing their own capital, management, and so forth; (2) integrated producers including downstream marketing and processing; (3) government-managed production and marketing enterprises; (4) producer cooperatives or state trading enterprises serving as a producer's agent to obtain remunerative prices; (5) government marketing boards performing credit, collection, storage, shipping, and other marketing functions; (6) private intermediate traders, brokers, and merchant firms specializing in international importing and exporting activities; (7) independent intermediate processors in exporting or importing countries; (8) multinational mining companies of a separate nonintegrated or conglomerate integrated type; (9) specialized trading organizations such as exchanges dealing in spot, forward, and futures trading; (10) financial companies such as banks and insurance companies providing finance for mining projects; and (11) governments of the producing and consuming countries in question.

Also essential to figure 2–2 is the chain of prices leading from producer to consumer. Determining the value of a commodity for a producing firm or a host government depends on the point selected in the overall market structure. The price at the production stage could depend on factors other than costs, for example, a bargain being struck between a firm and a government (royalties) or accounting and tax practices (transfer prices). Examining the price chain is essential for perceiving at what stage the main barriers to entry exist, where concentration is the strongest, or where the division of gains takes place.

The major determinants of market structure examined here include the numbers and size of firms in the form of buyers and sellers, barriers to entry, nature of product differentiation, extent of vertical integration, and multinational presence. The latter reflects the number of foreign firms or enterprises present in a country acting as sellers, although they sometimes are also buyers. Although market power is considered in relation to supply and demand, the interaction between power on these two sides is now brought together, including empirical assessments based on concentration ratios. Finally recent attempts to change market structure and power are integrated into the explanation. That is, increasing attempts by the developing producing countries to nationalize mineral industries and to form mineral associations and cartels.

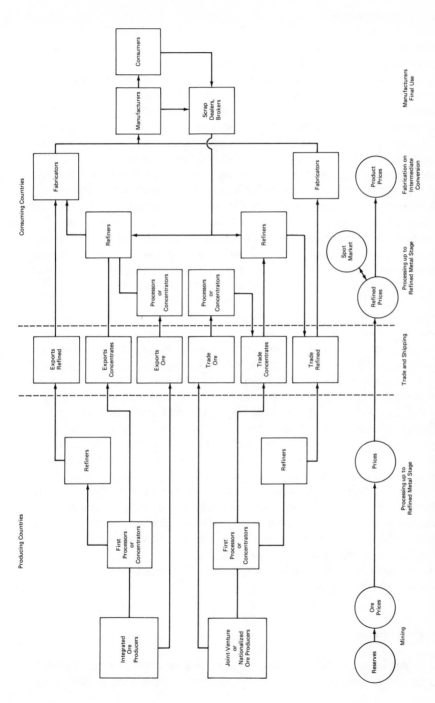

Figure 2–2. Hypothetical Market and Price Structure for Nonrenewable Resource Commodities

Market Implications

Market implications relate to the impact of market conditions and structure on the various participants in the market. The measure of such impact according to conventional theories of industrial organization are defined in terms of market performance. Given that the present study deals with international rather than domestic markets, it is extremely difficult to evaluate market performance. Because market performance is so important in analyzing the behavior of participants and subsequent price formation, an attempt is made here to examine performance in a very limited way. Attention is thus directed to the implications considered most critical in view of the problems of developing the world's mineral industries today. These problems relate to the dependence of the many producing nations on these commodities for their income coupled with the recent declining mineral investment and the associated impediments facing foreign mineral investors.[4] Essential to this dilemma is the changing nature of the division of gains or the bargaining situation confronting these two parties. By a bargaining situation is meant the conditions facing a mineral-producing country in its effort to alter market performance. These conditions are normally viewed in the context of the struggle between foreign investors in minerals and host governments in mineral-producing developing countries. These governments recently have attained success in elevating their share of profits in mineral extraction, and this trend has noticeable implications for market control and price formation.[5]

To analyze market impact under these conditions, we first examine the extent of the mineral export dependence of a developing producing country, the existing pattern of control over resources and production, the related influence of production technology, and the opportunities for increased processing. These are then expanded based on two criteria suggested by Radetzki.[6] The first of these concerns competition in the mineral market as well as in the market in which the mineral buyer sells his product. The second evaluates the share of raw material costs in final product prices. Given the static nature of these criteria, it would be useful also to examine factors of a more dynamic nature. Moran has suggested three such factors: the magnitude of the fixed mineral investment, the changing nature of risk and uncertainty and its relation to the obsolescing bargain, and the "learning" of the host government in its ability to gain managerial skills, to negotiate contracts and to increase industry control.[7]

Price Formation

Important for analyzing international mineral price formation in relation to market conditions and structure are the mechanics of the pricing system itself.

Clues to mineral pricing can be found in the marketing and distribution system for a commodity. For certain minerals, sales transactions take place through long- and short-term contractural arrangements or through a highly vertically integrated industry structure. In such cases, market price information is not readily available and one must search for other measures of value. Finally, basic price-making forces must be specified not only as they relate to market conditions but also to market structure and power, and to existing social and political institutions.

The many limitations involved in developing and applying the framework to explain price formation should be obvious. Most importantly, the economic framework provided is severely limited by the lack of information about the minerals of interest. There are also social and political factors involved that are always difficult to deal with. In addition, the nature of the markets differs so much from commodity to commodity that it is extremely difficult to develop a framework that will apply to several of them at once. Such problems should be kept in mind in interpreting what follows.

Market Conditions: Supply

The role played by supply in mineral price formation involves a number of complex interrelationships, including factors affecting supply, nature of investment and supply costs, and market power of producers. Interpretation of this interaction is further complicated by the need to decipher short-run as compared to long-run phenomena. Resources represent long-run supply, whereas reserves and extraction constitute the short-run supply of a mineral. There is also the problem of converting minerals as geologic resources to minerals as economic goods. As shown in figure 2–3, this conversion process embodies several sequential stages: (1) exploration, (2) extraction and mineral processing including the development of facilities, (3) depletion, and (4) market supply including primary and secondary sources.

Related to or explaining supply at each of the stages are the following: (1) resource development, (2) economic determinants, (3) geologic conditions, (4) technology, (5) institutions, and (6) uncertainty. Although these can explain the supply process itself, they need to be translated into conditions which determine the nature of the investment and cost structure of the mineral industry. Also of importance is the organization of the industry concerning market and price control as exemplified in bargaining power.

Elements of Supply

Resource Development. Production of a mineral commodity embodies the activities involved in finding it, in determining its size and physical characteris-

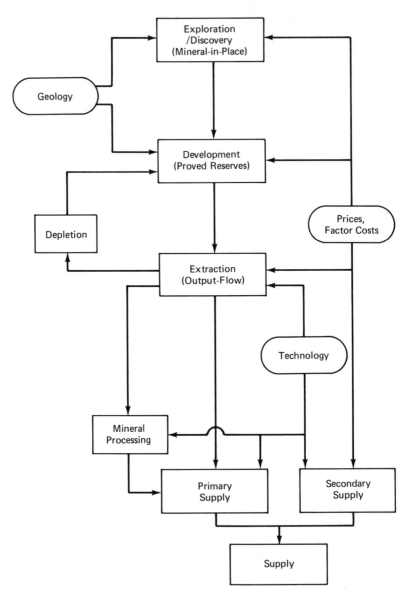

Figure 2–3. The Mineral Supply Process

tics, and in developing the deposit to the point where mining and processing can begin.[8] The first two of these activities are associated with exploration. Exploration in an elementary sense can be considered as an input similar to others essential to mining and processing. One attempts to optimize allocations among these inputs, making appropriate adjustments at the margins where inputs can be substituted. The fact that firms pursue exploration so intensively leads us to consider reserves as a form of capital stock. Koopmans shows that if exploration is unimportant, then a high discount rate could accelerate the rate of extraction.[9] If it is important, then a high discount rate could decrease extraction in the long run.

A major factor in determining the profitability of exploration is the realization that the location, size, and grade of mineral deposits are rarely known accurately and forms of uncertainty are involved. As suggested by Harris, one needs first to build models of mineral endowment which embody geostatistical techniques so that probabilities of discovery can be ascertained.[10] Such a model can subsequently be combined with an economic model which describes the development of exploration mining and transportation. Profitability of exploration and opportunities for discovery consequently would be related to final production costs and prices.

A more modest possibility is to consider exploration as a process of resource identification which offsets reserve depletion by adding to the knowledge of incompletely defined deposits. Here resources include identified and unidentified deposits as well as identified deposits that cannot be recovered at the present price and level of technology. In contrast, reserves constitute economically recoverable material in identified deposits, typically representing a ten- to twenty-year supply.

Apparent in this description is a relation between the uncertainty involved in the geologic discovery or deposit estimate and the economics of recovering or exploiting it. For a given deposit, the estimate would increase when a higher price or lower degree of certainty is accepted. Brooks has formalized this relationship through the use of a two-dimensional diagram, such as that shown in figure 2–4.[11] Measures of the degree of geologic uncertainty are shown on the horizontal axis, and all measures of economic viability or net present value of a deposit (cost-price conditions) are given on the vertical axis. The degree of uncertainty increases moving left to right as resources are classified as identified, hypothetical, or speculative. The costs that indicate the extent to which a mineral is economically recoverable increase in moving from top to bottom. Implied in this description is that the relation between exploration, resources, reserves, and prices is a relative one. Increased exploration can reduce geological uncertainty, while new technology of extraction can make some resources economical to mine.

Going one step further, the link between reserves and production has been generally assumed to follow the conventional "theory of exhaustion." In discussing reserves, it has been shown that the exploitation of mineral deposits over time leads steadily to their exhaustion, which may be defined as the gradual and sudden rise in the cost of exploitation caused by extraction. (Exploitation costs can be assumed constant up to final depletion, costs then rising so quickly that the quantity demanded is zero.) Since this is not the case

Quality of the Resource (economic dimension)	Degrees of Certainty about the Resource (geologic dimension)				
	Identified Resources			Undiscovered Resources	
	Proved	Probable	Possible	In Known Districts	In Undiscovered Districts
Recoverable under market and technological conditions	Reserves			Hypothetical resources	Speculative resources
Recoverable at prices up to 2 times those prevailing now or with comparable advance in technology	Paramarginal resources				
Recoverable at prices 2 to 10 times those prevailing now or with comparable advance in technology	Submarginal resources				

Totals: Potential resources = paramarginal + submarginal + hypothetical + speculative

Total resources   = reserves + potential resources

Resource base   = total resources + other mineral raw materials

Figure 2–4. Classification of Mineral Reserves and Resources

in reality, it is better to think of a gradual rise in the cost of exploitation over time, usually a consequence of mining poorer quality ores at a given level of technology. Exhaustion could be said to occur only at the point where the cost rises such that none of the mineral is demanded. This point depends not only on the quality of reserve levels but also on factors such as final demand for the intermediate product and prices of substitutes.

There is a substantial and growing literature concerning the economics of resource exhaustion.[12] To a large extent, it is highly technical, relying on the calculus of variations. Because a detailed treatment of this theory is beyond the scope of the present study, only the more salient conclusions that have emerged will be discussed. The theory of exhaustion points to the central goal of a mining firm. How much should the firm produce in each period of time until exhaustion of the deposits? If the resource is so abundant that exhaustion appears far in the future, then the firm would produce that output where price is equal to long-run marginal cost. Decisions on a particular year's output, therefore, have no effect on output in any other year.

Two extremes to this case can be cited. If the long-run cost curve is horizontal, assuming investment opportunities are reflected in a positive interest rate, then the entire deposit should be extracted as soon as possible, thus maximizing the present value of the difference between revenue and cost. Alternatively, if the long-run cost curve has a minimum and the rate of discount is zero, the firm would select that output conforming to minimum average cost until the deposit is exhausted.

Neither of these cases deal with the assumed situation of gradual depletion. As stated by Herfindahl and Kneese, the firm will select that sequence of output that reflects the impossibility of increasing the present value of total revenue minus outlays by transferring a unit of output from one period to another.[13] This follows only if the present value of price minus long-run marginal cost is equal in all periods of operation or exhaustion. What this reflects is that the onset of diseconomies of scale in mine operation attributable to declining grades of the deposit is a major factor in evaluating mine life. Although the ratio of reserves to production says little about final depletion, it does say something about the technological innovations that have influenced the rate of exploitation. Substantial quantities of deposits may remain unexploited, simply because no technology exists to exploit them at this time.

More recently, Heal has expanded the argument that a necessary condition for a deposit to be allocated efficiently is that its price, net of extraction costs, should rise at a rate equal to the rate of return on other assets.[14] When owners of a resource recognize it as a capital asset in their portfolio, they will hold it just as long as the return that it gives them (the rate of increase of net price) is no less than the returns available elsewhere. The mentioned necessary condition is implied by equilibrium in the asset market. Heal also has provided limited confirmation of this hypothesis by his finding that resource prices have risen equivalently with interest rates for zinc, lead, and copper from 1965 to 1973.[15]

A complicating factor recently confronting the theory concerns the impact of monopoly ownership of the deposits. Stiglitz has compared the rate of exhaustion in monopolistic markets with that in competitive markets.[16] He suggests that limitations in exercising market power may very well cause monopoly prices and competitive prices to be equal, although in some cases, monopoly will require marginal revenue rather than prices to rise at the rate of interest. With the monopolist's price now rising more slowly, he would expand output more slowly than his competitive counterpart.

Another complicating factor concerns the actual situation that minerals extracted in developing countries are produced mostly by foreign-owned corporations. Brodsky and Sampson suggest that since there are now two participants in the extraction process, there are also two returns of relevance.[17] For the foreign corporation the relevant return is the market price less the sum of the cost of extraction and royalty payments to the government, that is, net price. For the developing country, the corresponding return is that portion of the market price which accrues to either the government or to domestic factors of production, that is, returned value. The stated theory thus becomes modified such that the country should base its depletion on a comparison between the rate of interest that it deems relevant and the rate of growth of its returned value from the resource. The foreign corporation should base its depletion on a comparison between the interest rate and the rate of growth of net price. As will be shown later, this focus has implications regarding the relative bargaining power of firms and governments.

Economic Determinants. Determinants of supply normally classified as economic relate to the process of producing a single or joint output through acquiring and transforming several inputs. Most obvious of the identifiable variables in this relationship are the market price of the product and the prices of the inputs utilized. The latter prices are normally associated with the variable costs of production, those that vary with the annual rate of production. In addition, it may be necessary to include the fixed costs which are independent of the rate of output in the short run. Here we have primarily investment in fixed or quasi-fixed factors such as rental of leased property or a new mine facility. Depreciation costs associated with owning and maintaining a fixed productive facility such as a mine also enter.

To interrelate these various factors in explaining mineral supply, one can use the theory of the firm. In short, supply is hypothesized to depend on profit maximization subject to a given production function for the commodity of interest, assuming that the production and consumption decisions are separable. This can be conceptualized in terms of differences between firm or industry revenue and costs. Gross revenues or profits depend on the price, cost, and quantity of the mineral commodity produced and sold. Costs depend on the set of prices and services from variable inputs as well as fixed inputs. The production function will then depend on the inputs utilized together with any geologic and technological characteristics of the production process.

When the production function is substituted into the profit relationship and maximized with respect to the variable inputs, one obtains the demand for services of the variable inputs. Substituting the maximized level of inputs into the production function and solving for the level of production yields the resource quantity or supply as a function of the commodity price, the input prices, the geologic, technological, and other possible determinants. This is a conventional form of mineral supply function which is static in nature. Information is missing regarding the nature of short- and long-run supply adjustments, which depend on the distinction drawn between variable and fixed factors or between quasi-fixed and fixed investments. These dynamic considerations are normally explained in terms of lags. There are at least three lags to be considered: (1) an implementation lag, which is the time lag between a change in price and the reaction by decision makers; (2) a technological or developmental lag, which is the time required to place new mining capacity into full production; and (3) an exploration lag, which is the time between the decision to explore for new deposits and the utilization of the deposits in production.[18]

These lags affect output, depending on the time lag of the price response in each case. As shown in table 2–1, the response or reaction to a change in price takes from one to two years to implement. Sometimes the lag effect is difficult to perceive, particularly on downward price swings. For example, a price decrease will rarely lead to a discontinuation of operations at a particular mine, since it is costly to discontinue operations if price is expected to rise again. Mining will continue even though price is below the short-run breakeven point. However, if the depressed price exists or is expected to exist for one or two years, then mining firms are likely to discontinue operations and output will fall.

The technological lag, describing the time from investment in mine capacity until initial operation, has been shown to vary between one and five years. This can occur because of a sustained period of higher than normal prices reflecting a low supply condition or of expectations that future supply will be tight and concomitantly higher prices will exist. Most projects introduced to develop new capacity require at least two years of preparation, if not longer.

Among the factors affecting this gestation period are the capital and skill intensity of the mining operation. As pointed out by Brown, capital-intensive low-variable-cost mines would continue to operate at low prices as long as operating costs are being covered. Less capital-intensive high-variable-cost mines would be able to respond more readily to price. The essential ingredient in explaining response is the ability to use existing capital stock more intensively. But to extend capital stock such as in reopening mines is more difficult, accounting for the tendency of mines to remain operating even when prices are depressed below variable costs. This would help explain lags when prices decline.

It is worth noting that attempts to adjust capital quickly have succeeded, and these have often led to capacity expansion at a rate unwarranted by long-run demand. Also, attempts to adjust capital at different parts of the business cycle have not been symmetric. Upswings result in rapid accumulation of capital, but in downswings disinvestment does not occur and substantial

Table 2–1
Nature of Mineral Supply Response Lags

Period of Production		Period of Response to Price or Other Economic Signals	
Change in Output	Implementation Lag	Technological Lag	Exploration Lag
t	$t - j$ $j = 1$–2 years	$t - k$ $k = 1$–4 years	$t - r$ $r \geq 4$ years

excess capacity is the result. Also of importance to the gestation period is the infrastructure of the investment. If the mine is located in a remote region, a new town with facilities or a transportation network including harbors may have to be built.

The exploration lag is the longest and the most difficult to assess. The response between exploration induced by some price or profit signal and actual mine production is as long as the technological lag and most often longer. Where the lag is so long that it is a large fraction of the time horizon under consideration, then it no longer becomes relevant to include it in the supply analysis. Costs of exploration, nonetheless, can affect shorter-run supply costs.

Production depends not only on lags in price response but also on the magnitude or elasticity of price response.[19] As long as mining capacity is in excess, firms confronting higher prices can expand supply easily over the given range of output. As output approaches full capacity, however, price increases will not immediately lead to supply increases and lags occur. Pointed out above was the time required to expand capacity or to develop new mines. This implies that the price elasticity of response has to be low or near zero once short-run capacity has been reached. However, the elasticity will increase as capacity is expanded in the long run. This suggests that supply curves for minerals tend to rise only gradually until full capacity is reached, and then become very steep. Some examples of mineral supply elasticities obtained from econometric studies are given in table 2–2.

All that has been discussed thus far refers to primary supply. Because of the increasing problems of environmental disturbances as well as scarcity, the secondary supply of minerals is becoming increasingly important. The following three characteristics of secondary supply or scrap are the most important.[20] First, it is a stock derived from past production activities, and the stock accumulates as long as the rate of production is greater than the rate of recycling. Second, secondary materials generated out of scrap from production as well as movement of materials from the stock of existing products are generally independent of technological capabilities for recovery. And third, the amount of scrap usable depends on technical possibilities for recovery and related cost and market conditions.

Scrap materials are generally classified in three forms: *home scrap,* the material generated in the production of semifinished metal products and recycled within the manufacturing of new products and collected for sale to others; *prompt industrial scrap,* scrap created during the manufacture of new products and collected for sale to others; and *obsolete scrap,* scrap generated as a consequence of wear, damage or obsolescence of products. Once accumulated their utilization depends on cost-price considerations. Where the cost of collection and processing is sufficiently low that the cost-price ratio is less than one, the materials are immediately used. Where the cost-price ratio is greater than one, the scrap remains a stock.

Table 2-2
Price and Income Elasticities for Selected Resource Commodities

Commodity	Supply		Demand		Income Elasticities
	Short run (1 year)	Long run (3–5 years)	Short run (1 year)	Long run (3–5 years)	
Aluminum/bauxite	0	0.4	−0.13	−0.80 to 1.35	1.5 to 2.5
Cobalt	—	—	−0.68	−1.71	—
Copper	0.06	0.1	−0.3	Above −2.50	0.8 to 1.0
Iron ore	0	0.3	−0.1	—	0.7 to 0.9
Lead	—	—	−0.1 to −0.3	Elastic	0.1 to 0.3
Tin	0.19	0.44	−0.6 to −0.5	−1.25	0.1 to 0.3
Tungsten	—	—	−0.15	−0.3	—
Zinc	—	—	−0.55	−0.67	—
Petroleum	—	—	−0.4 to −1.0	−0.7 to −1.6	0.8 to 0.9

Price Elasticities

Source: J. Behrman, *International Commodity Agreements* (Washington, D.C.: Overseas Development Council, 1976); *Outlook for Prices and Supplies of Industrial Raw Materials*, Hearings before the Subcommittee on Economic Growth of the Joint Economic Committee (Washington, D.C.: U.S. Government Printing Office, 1974); World Bank, *Price Prospects for Major Primary Commodities* (Washington, D.C.: IBRD, 1975); and W.C. Labys and J. Hunkeler, *Survey of Commodity Price Elasticities* (Geneva: Research Division, UNCTAD, 1974).

The elasticity of price response also is important. For the case of prompt industrial scrap, response is fairly inelastic with all scrap being immediately resold over some rather wide price range. For obsolete scrap, much of this needs processing before recovery, and the price elasticity is slightly higher. There are several factors which suggest that price response is becoming more elastic: the impact of environmental regulations on costs of primary supply, the more demanding energy requirements of primary supply, and increases in royalty charges on primary supply in a growing number of countries.

Geologic Conditions. Essential to mineral supply are the surrounding geologic conditions such as modes of occurrence or variations in quality. In figure 2–4, the cost-price dimension of resource characterization was shown to be highly interrelated with the geologic dimension. As a reserve becomes depleted, costs of production and prices normally rise. When these higher prices exceed current extraction costs, this signals the capital gains value of future reserves. This normally leads to increased exploration, although it also can imply a slowdown in the extraction rate or the development of substitutes for the scarce resource.

Further interpretation of this relationship can be made by returning to figure 2–3. There the structure of the mineral-in-place, including the distribution characteristics of known and unknown reserves, is shown as an input into the development and the extraction process. The development of these reserves following discovery depends on several factors: the discovered reserve structure per se, the expected costs of exploiting remaining known and unknown reserves, the costs of factor inputs into exploration and extraction activity, and the expected market prices for the mineral.[21] The rate of extraction which follows depends on the structure of known remaining reserves per se, the costs of factor inputs into mining activity, and again the expected market price. Feeding back into reserve development and exploration is the rate of depletion of the mineral.

This entire process including mineral processing and related technology reflects a long-run supply adjustment, that is, ten to twenty years or longer. Geologic factors also enter short-run supply adjustment. Of importance here are ore grade, seam thickness, and overburden.

Technology. Depletion of mineral supply implies the loss of high-grade easy-to-find and readily accessible deposits accompanied by increases in extraction costs over time. Technological innovations have traditionally had the opposite and dominating effect, thus causing real costs to fall. Using the United States as an example, Barnett and Morse found that from 1870 to 1957 the index (1929 = 100) of labor-capital input per unit of mineral output fell from 210 to 47.[22] Pollution and environmental costs were not taken into account, but they are not likely to have influenced the decline in private costs noticeably.

There are a number of ways in which technology has affected costs. Generally speaking, it has helped to broaden the properties of more abundant, low-cost, available domestic resources by: (1) an increase in substitution potential, (2) a broadening of the recoverable portion of the resource base through the development of new resources, (3) an improvement in recycling levels, (4) the maximizing of recovery and utilization levels of by-products and coproducts, (5) the development of nondestructive approaches to mineral production and utilization, and (6) the ensuring of environmental quality.

Taking some specific examples of how technology has reduced costs, recent advances in survey and geochemical sampling methods have improved the efficiency of both exploration and recovery. New processing technologies have assured a greater recovery ratio. And upward trends in labor productivity have occurred because of increased use of mechanized equipment, automation, and more efficient operating procedures. Using the U.S. copper industry as an example, increased production from open pits, use of large-scale underground methods, and new capital equipment have led to an increase in productivity. During the 1960s and 1970s, the amount of ore mined increased by 70 percent and the average number of men working daily fell by 20 percent.[23]

Whether technology will continue to aid mineral supply as much in the future has recently been brought into question. With exploration now proceeding rapidly in developing countries, capital is being pushed in the exploration rather than the research direction. Other disincentives are that technological developments are not generally protectable by patent and that returns to innovators are not assured because of industry fragmentation. What these symptoms reflect is the limitations of technology in overcoming existing mineral extraction problems.

Institutions. The surrounding institutional framework is sometimes as important as technological or geologic influences. Financial institutions must be reasonably effective to provide the substantial capital flows needed to facilitate investment in new and improved facilities. Although price expectations for development may be of the right magnitude, present rising costs imply problems of increasing debt-equity ratios, of lowering liquidity or borrowing on such basis, and of increasing competition for capital.

Environmental institutions and laws are now having more than an imperceptible influence on mineral supply. Disruption of the environment through mining and processing activities is being affected by land reclamation acts with subsequent influence on costs, and surface and underground pollution are being countered by abatement laws. Sometimes linked to the overall environmental dimension is the social dimension; mineral investment and depletion are associated with decisions relating to income distribution or to intertemporal adjustments in the rate of depletion.

Government and other political institutions enter through the mineral policies adopted over time. For example, these policies can relate to price controls for natural gas or fuels. Although price controls might affect an industry favorably, over time they are likely to increase demand while inhibiting supply expansion. An alternative to price controls has been inventory control; it has been pursued in the United States through the minerals stockpiling efforts of the General Services Administration. And finally, the government is a large landholder and this involves it in questions of leasing rights and environmental quality.

Between nations, mineral supplies can be affected by policies concerning export taxes, export controls, or tariff barriers. Such measures are considered in the context of bargaining between producing and consuming countries where new relationships are emerging that reflect attempts by mineral-endowed countries to exert greater influence over the use of their resources. Supplies can also be affected by international institutions such as those involved with the UNCTAD (United Nations Conference on Trade and Development) integrated program for commodities (IPC). Policy conerns include export quotas, buffer stocks, compensatory financing, direct indexation, multilateral contracts, and other measures designed to stimulate investment and to promote diversification.

Uncertainty. Substantial uncertainty exists over the complete horizon of the mineral supply process. Starting with the mineral-in-place, the risks associated with exploration and limited probabilities of discovery have always plagued the industry. Even at the development and extraction stages, uncertainties exist in regarding geologic conditions such as variations in ore grade, thickness of seam and overburden, or related roof stability and water conditions.

Less than perfect knowledge also exists for the uncontrolled output and input prices which are realized over each period of the depletion horizon. For example, when a producer decides what quantity of a resource to put on the market, he normally copes with uncertainty by forming expectations about what prices are to be in the future. As the time horizon increases, the attempt to form expectations becomes more difficult. This is the case of investing in a mine that might not be productive for a number of years. Such uncertainty and the accompanying wrong expectations are very likely to be a cause of the frequent and wide price swings found in mineral price behavior. Concerning input prices, uncertainty arises because of changes in costs of labor, energy, and other factors between the time a project is begun and the time it is completed.

Investment and Supply Costs

Investment. The production of minerals requires exploration and development prior to production and then processing before utilization can begin.

Analysis of mineral supply thus requires examination of the underlying investment processes. Investment involves outlays on exploration, development, mining, and processing.[24] Required exploration comes at the beginning of the investment cycle and requires expenditures on geologic surveys, land and property rights, initial drillings, road building, and so forth. At the final stages of exploration but before a decision is taken to develop a deposit, a feasibility study is made. The next stage of the investment cycle is perhaps the most costly—the development of mines and mineral processing facilities. As mentioned, these may even require building of a town complete with medical, educational, and commercial facilities in addition to a transportation system. The final stage of the investment cycle sometimes comes after extraction has commenced. The geologic characteristics of a deposit are not fully known until after mining has begun, and this may require investment in further exploration as well as modifications of mining and processing equipment.

Concerning underlying motivations, investment in exploration and development is traditionally viewed as a systematic response to profit expectations. This response can be said to be divided according to the prices expected over the lifetime of the investment, the terms of the contract possible, and the prices accepted for delivery. Current and future price estimates upon which the decisions are made thus incorporate a number of signals of economic and geologic realities. Included are producers' and consumers' estimates of future supply and demand, present and future discoveries, and changes in costs of factors. Added to this should be the prevailing influence of government policies. Cameron holds these in high regard stating that most explanations of investment suffer because they abstract from the high level of mineral industry transactions costs, which are due partly to the pervasive effect of government policies.[25]

Investment can be judged as completed when deposits of uniform quality are found and subsequently extracted. However, when the deposits found show variations in quality, expenditure on exploration will be made to reduce costs of mining and processing. Herfindahl and Kneese point out that variations in allocation occur, when exploration consists of finding deposits of variable quality only up to a fixed limit.[26] Substitution between exploration, mining, and processing costs is still possible, but a choice is made such that deposits not mined now will be mined later. In short, a cutoff point in quality is reached above which exploration and exploitation are varied together. Only after all deposits have been found will the deposits below the cutoff point be exploited.

Within this substitution framework, exploration has been considered only in a general sense. Exploration outlays in fact are of many different types. Some of these come early in the investment cycle; others come later when finer distinctions are made. If the quantity of mineral output is small relative to the reserve-land base, then development would involve an optimum sequence and mix of exploration activities which would be repeated. If the volume of output is now large relative to this base, then an optimum sequence and mix of exploration activity is devised only once, followed by progressive modifications of the plan.

Supply Costs. Mineral supply costs can be best explained by first considering the time periods involved. The traditional view is that the long run is considered as a period long enough to permit variation in all of the inputs subject to control by firms in an industry. Relative to investment, its length is sufficient to permit the exploration and development of a deposit up to the point of production. The short run is viewed as sufficient to allow output to be varied but too short to permit altering a mine structure or exploring for additional deposits.

In both the long and the short run, costs of supply can be considered as an increasing function of the industry's rate of output. In the short-run, these costs rise because higher levels of extraction will require higher input prices in bidding labor, capital, supplies, and other inputs away from other industries. The extent of the rise normally depends on suitable mining and processing methods, the extent and nature of the mechanization to be used, and the tonnage limitation. Underlying these are the geologic and mineralogic aspects of the mineral to be dealt with, including the grade of the ore produced and the richness of its by-product metals content. With regard to the inputs themselves, labor is becoming increasingly important in production costs. Zinc labor costs, for example, comprise more than 50 percent of direct mining costs.

Concerning long-run costs, these are often seen as being determined by changes in resource quality and extraction technology. With resource quality declining over time, the tendency is toward extracting lower-grade deposits. Not only will greater amounts of energy be needed for extraction and processing, but there is the necessity of mining, transporting, and processing proportionally greater amounts of the material. Possibly offsetting this tendency will be improvements in the technology of extraction, as previously discussed.

Costs and Prices. Related to mineral investment is the question of desirable capacity levels and capacity adjustments. The relationship between costs and prices is important in assessing whether new extraction or processing facilities will be profitable. Bosworth has noted that prices must approach costs in the long run, since deviations between the two will not provide the proper capacity adjustment.[27] He proposes that the expansion of capacity depends on price incentives, even though the investment associated with a given change in capacity may be highly variable over time. For example, when costs are rising, price increases will have to follow in order to create investment incentives in the form of increased profitability. The results obtained by Bosworth in analyzing price-cost relationships for the aluminum industry are reported in table 2–3. As a measure of expansion incentive, the price-cost ratio is shown to

Table 2-3
Indexes of Supply Costs and Prices for Primary Aluminum Ingots, 1960 and 1965-1975
(dollars per ton, except as noted)

Year	Fixed-Mix Supply Cost			Market Price			Ratio of Market Price/Costs		Operating Income as percent of Sales[f]
	Operating Costs (1)	Capital Costs with 6 percent Return (2)	Total[a] (3)	List[b] (4)	Realized[c] (estimate) (5)		Operating Costs[d] (6)	Supply Costs[e] (7)	(8)
1960	320	113	433	516	n.a.		1.61	1.19	20.5
1965	300	102	402	464	445		1.55	1.15	18.2
1966	306	104	410	464	452		1.52	1.13	19.9
1967	313	107	421	473	n.a.		1.51	1.12	19.4
1968	329	117	446	483	447		1.47	1.09	18.9
1969	330	128	458	515	469		1.56	1.12	17.9
1970	335	131	466	543	507		1.62	1.17	15.9
1971	348	130	478	549	452		1.58	1.15	14.9
1972	365	139	504	500	433		1.37	0.99	14.1
1973	383	145	528	480	454		1.25	0.91	13.4
1974	497	162	659	644	675		1.30	0.98	15.3
1975	595	178	773	754	n.a.		1.27	0.98	14.9

Source: B. Bosworth, "Capacity creation in basic-materials industries," *Brookings Papers in Economic Activity* 2 (1976):331. Copyright © 1976 by the Brookings Institution.

n.a. = not available.

[a]Supply costs include full cost of meeting 1983 environmental standards beginning in 1972.

[b]The list price is adjusted to exclude delivery costs by multiplying an index of list price by an estimate of average factory price from the 1967 Census of Manufactures. The list price is obtained from *American Metal Market, Metal Statistics, 1975* (Fairchild Publications, 1975), p. 25.

[c]Price realizations are adjusted for delivery costs in the same manner as list prices but reflect some effects of discounting.

[d]Column 4 divided by column 1.

[e]Column 4 divided by column 3.

[f]Based on the summation of gross operating income (including depreciation) as a percent of sales for Aluminum Company of America, Reynolds Metals, and Kaiser Aluminum and Chemical Corporation. The estimates are standardized at 95 percent of capacity as described in the text.

have declined throughout the last half of the 1960s and in the first part of the 1970s. The relative increase in capital costs reflects inflation and pollution-abatement costs. Operating costs, however, are shown to have increased more sharply, and prices have tended to follow operating costs more closely than total costs. The hovering of the ratio about 1.5 suggests that the industry has not expanded capacity as much as necessary.

Supply Organization

Concentration. At this point it is necessary to advance from the motivations underlying individual suppliers to those explaining the interaction between suppliers. In other words, when given the goal of profit maximization and the constraints of the factors discussed, how does market organization affect mineral supply response? To answer that question, we must examine the extent to which the suppliers operate under competitive conditions. There are a number of arguments cited by Behrman which suggest why these conditions prevail in commodity markets.[28] Among the political arguments offered are: (1) the atomistic structure of buyers and sellers required for competition decentralizes and disperses power; (2) the fundamental economic problems are solved impersonally through the market place; and (3) with no barriers to entry, there is relative freedom of opportunity. The economic arguments include: (1) each firm is producing its output at minimum cost so that resources are employed at maximum efficiency; (2) the marginal cost of production equals the price paid by consumers so that utility maximization decisions reflect actual marginal costs of inputs; and (3) price equals average total costs so that there are no supranormal profits or rents.

However, Behrman as well as others have cast doubt on the appropriateness of these arguments for explaining mineral market behavior.[29] These doubts can be divided into (1) those concerning the implications of perfect competition, and (2) those concerning its underlying conditions. The implication that efficiency can only be attained in a competitive framework is questionable. Welfare maximization can be improved in certain cases, such as those dealing with income distribution by adopting a less efficient solution. And supranormal profits may be necessary to offset the risk of exploration as well as to obtain the financing required to expand rapidly.

Concerning the underlying conditions, all of them depend on the absence of externalities. But mineral supply is highly burdened with problems of externalities such as those related to environmental considerations. In addition, it is difficult for a firm to minimize average cost in some cases without displaying perceptible market power. In the steel industry, for example, a firm would have to supply up to 5 percent of the total U.S. market in order to achieve minimal economies of scale.

The impact of the above is that it is difficult to say how much competition is needed to achieve desirable economic performance. Indeed the production, processing, and trading of mineral commodities is characterized by firms and institutions which have varying degrees of market power and hence the capacity to influence market prices. The existence of this power among mineral suppliers can be verified by measuring industry concentration, normally computed as the percentage of total industry supply accounted for by the largest firms. An example of concentration on a world level is provided in table 2–4. Indeed, iron ore, copper, and aluminum are shown to be markets dominated by a handful of firms. To learn more about the causes of such concentration, we examine five determinants: economies of scale, absolute costs, control over technical knowledge, government policy, and control over the resource commodity.

Economies of Scale. Economic theory implies that firms will adjust their sizes and their numbers in order to maximize efficiency or minimize costs. Implied here are the existence of forces which induce efficiency as a goal and the stipulation that the degree of efficiency attained is influenced by the size of the firm. In analyzing this drive for economies of scale, Behrman notes the existence of real as well as pecuniary economies.[30] Real economies at the plant production level include: lower unit costs through specialization in the use of labor and capital, lower set up costs due to larger volume, the "two-thirds" rule in processing industries (within certain physical limits output is proportional to volume and capital cost is proportional to surface areas), fixed transaction costs, lower backup requirements per unit of capacity at higher volumes, and greater "learning by doing" due to a larger cumulative volume. To these can be added savings from bypassing the market system such as price shopping, centralizing management staff functions, and conducting centralized research

Table 2–4
Concentration in International Mineral Supply

	Number of Leading Firms	Percent Market Share	Observations and Date
Copper	4	34.0	Mining capacity, 1975
	8	50.4	
Tin	4	50.4	Smelting capacity, 1976
	8	72.1	
Bauxite	4	38.3	Mining capacity, 1973
	8	56.4	
Iron ore	4	34.3	Mine shipments, 1975
	8	56.6	

Source: Summarized from tables appearing later in the text.

and development. Pecuniary economies accruing to large firms relate to the lower prices paid by larger firms for inputs because of their superior bargaining power.

Most of the above economies are related to the size of the firm and are reflected in its output relative to that of the total industry, that is, its horizontal size. Another source of economies for a firm is its vertical growth or extension based on its integration of preceding or succeeding production stages, that is, its vertical integration.[31] One example of such economies in the mineral industry concerns the case where technologically complementary production processes at successive stages can be brought together in a single plant. For example, the making of pig iron, converting it into billets, and the rolling of the billets into semifinished products, while the metal retains its heat, results in considerable energy saving. Another example concerns the major capital requirements that the mining and minerals industries face. As capital requirements push production and processing costs to high levels, economies of scale force integration throughout the various stages of the industry. As an example most steel, copper, and aluminum firms own or control domestic mineral deposits or have substantial mineral investments abroad that provide them with most of their mineral requirements. Finally, costs of transactions and holding inventories at different stages are reduced, and pecuniary economies involving intrastage profits paid to other firms are gained.

It should be noted, however, that vertical integration is not economical in all cases. Some limiting factors are the actual characteristics of the production process at succeeding stages, the stability of demand of the end product, the ability of the production process at each stage to absorb the output of a potentially integrable component, and the coordination of economies of horizontal scale at successive stages.

Of importance in analyzing economies of scale from the view of ultimate impact on price formation are the magnitude and degree of the economies. Behrman poses the following related questions:[32] What size of plant or firm is needed to realize all scale economies? What cost and revenue disadvantages are associated with operation at the suboptimal scale? And how do these disadvantages compare to the additional managerial and coordinating costs which large-scale operations impose? There is little empirical work to draw on in answering these questions. On the supply side, we do know that efficient extraction of exhaustible resources requires large-scale investment in capital equipment and in most cases in transportation systems as well. On the demand side, there is some evidence that large firms are not an absolute necessity.[33]

Absolute Costs. A second important determinant of supply concentration is the presence of absolute cost barriers. A normal consideration for any resource market is that production costs for a new firm will be above that of an existing firm over the full range of output. In the case of copper, high-grade deposits occur in only a small number of locations throughout the world. Where those deposits are owned by existing processers, a new entrant to the industry meets entry costs so high as to constitute a barrier. This is particularly restrictive to small firms. In the case of aluminum, six of the largest U.S. producers had facilities valued over $700–800 million in Jamaica in 1973, and these are formidable amounts for new entrants to match.

Control over Technical Knowledge. The absolute cost barrier can also be considered in the form of existing patents or new technological innovations. This knowledge will give a firm certain market power, although this will eventually decline because of parallel or imitative developments by rivals. But substantial concentration can be expected in the interim period. The exploitation of such knowledge has been most evident on the supply side in mineral markets. In particular, by developing mining, extraction, and beneficiation processes, firms have come to achieve a real market advantage. There is also the consideration that only large firms can support research programs of minimum efficient size. This will promulgate the size and power of bigger firms.

Government Policies. The government may influence industry concentration in a number of ways. Government purchasing procedures have influenced concentration through encouraging research and development in firms, such that the latter acquire an advantage in future contract bidding. Alternatively, governments have fostered the development of plants which were later sold to the private sector. Furthermore, certain tax laws may favor large firms as well as those integrated vertically. Distinct from its involvement with firms and industries, the government can control the quantities of a resource being exported to or imported from the related international commodity market. It can also attempt to raise prices or to stabilize them. Such commodity control can typically be exerted through marketing boards, state trading agencies, production quotas, export and import regulations, and buffer stocks. The latter can be national or they can be international, involving participation in international commodity agreements. Where such agreements might be expanded in the form of cartels, the degree of control can even be tighter. Examples of such action can be found in the study of commodity cartels by Eckbo, as well as in the study of the impact of the restriction of resource supplies by Charles River Associates (CRA).[34]

Control over the Resource Commodity. A final factor underlying concentration is the drive in a particular industry to acquire exploratory and concession rights for deposits well in advance of the time when such deposits will be mined. Such has been the case in bauxite as well as in other resource markets. Of course, the degree of control attained will depend on the lack of competitive materials with relatively high substitutability. There is also the possibility that new discoveries, technological change, or reductions in transportation cost will result in new competitive materials. Although control over supply may be less effective in the long run, it still can enforce a concentration pattern for a substantial period.

Power in Supply

Competition. The market power and hence price influence which results from concentration varies among mineral markets. To some extent, forces are present which maintain a certain degree of competition: a division of interest among firms within a nation, the influence of secondary production on supply, desires to expand international trade, and the many small firms which often surround the dominant few.[35] Regarding the first of these, divisions of interest appear to stem from two conflicting emphases. One is custom processing operations which create a need for substantial production but not for price stabilization. The other is integrated processing which encourages price stabilization but neglects production expansion.

With respect to secondary production, the scrap base and recycling create a mineral supply that can compete with new or primary supply when the prices of the latter become relatively high. There is also a drive to compete on international markets, even though a national market may be less competitive. Finally, the small firms constituting the competitive fringe of an industry often are capable of exerting sufficient influence to prevent large firms from obtaining substantial control.

Monopoly. The conditions underlying perfect competition have several implications for long-run equilibrium: (1) the marginal cost of a unit of output is equal to the price paid by consumers for that unit; (2) price is equal to average total cost for the representative firm, avoiding supranormal profits; (3) each firm is producing its output at the minimum point on its average total cost curve; and (4) firms are price takers. Although this suggests that competitive firms basically face a horizontal demand curve for their output, the essential difference of a monopolistic firm is that it faces a downward sloping demand curve.

The above implications change with monopoly. The profit-maximizing firm with market power will increase its output as long as marginal revenue exceeds marginal cost. For the case of monopoly, output is expanded until marginal revenue equals marginal cost. Given that output is positive, marginal revenue is necessarily less than the monopoly price, the latter exceeding marginal cost. As long as the monopoly is operating on the inelastic portion of the declining demand curve, it could increase revenue by raising prices, because the percentage by which prices could be raised on all units would exceed the percentage by which output would fall. Concerning implications (2) and (3), firms with market power may deviate from the zero-profit and minimum-cost conditions associated with perfectly competitive equilibrium, but they need not do so.

The actual presence of monopoly power is probably best reflected in the pricing methods practiced, as will be shown later. Within mineral markets, monopoly in the strict sense is difficult to find. One example often referred to is the pre–World War II aluminum industry in the United States, where all bauxite sources and aluminum ingot production were controlled by the Aluminum Company of America (ALCOA).

Oligopoly. The structure of mineral markets with supply power more typically falls somewhere between perfect competition and monopoly. This range represents some degree of monopolistic competition. Firms are small relative to the market, with market entry being relatively free. The one structure most frequently identified is oligopoly, where sellers number more than one, but still are reasonably few enough in number to result in some awareness of interdependence regarding price and output decisions.

As compared to strict or one-firm monopoly, the competitive assumptions cannot be manipulated in the form of a theory that would define price behavior in terms of related output and cost conditions. To explain prices, we must turn to some of the underlying conditions that surround the oligopolistic coordination of pricing and output decisions. Among these, Sherer includes the perception that joint action will maximize collective profits, the free and rapid exchange of information, the similarity of output preferences due to similar cost structures and market shares, the acquired understanding that price cuts will be promptly countered, the maintaining of price discipline by letting inventories and order backlogs fluctuate, and increased reliance on order and inventory feedback signals in preference to marginal rules in output determination.[36]

Pricing institutions that facilitate coordination include overt and covert agreements, price leadership, rule-of-thumb pricing, and focal point and tacit pricing. However, coordination in pricing is not always possible; some limiting factors are low concentration relative to a large competitive fringe, product heterogeneity, high proportions of fixed to total costs, substantial dependence on large and frequent orders, and lags in retaliation for price cuts.

Mineral markets for the most part do display some degree of oligopolistic behavior and hence many of the above conditions. Coordination in pricing and output can be seen to be facilitated by a number of factors. Some minerals have well-defined grades or quality differentials and are traded under similar conditions, for example, copper, tin, lead, zinc, and silver. Some also have a high degree of concentration at the export level, for example, tin and iron ore.

Others possess a relatively small competitive fringe, for example, bauxite and alumina. And some have a history of price leadership and a willingness to accumulate inventories, for example, copper.

The consequences of these possibilities for cooperation among suppliers has been the growing perception that increased cooperation can lead to higher profits. In particular, governments of some developing countries that supply commodities see the formation of producers organizations and possible cartels as essential to the "new international economic order." A listing of some of the associations that have been formed in this regard are given in table 2–5. Whether these will lead to increased market cooperation, however, is questionable.

In reviewing fifty-one significant commodity cartel organizations, Eckbo found that only nineteen achieved price controls which raised price levels to consumers significantly above what they would have been in the absence of agreements. But these price cartels did not last long.[37] Some of the problems encountered which constrained cartel success included substitution induced by higher prices leading to a loss of markets, and the discovery that stockpiling of minerals within producing countries can be very costly. In addition, reducing production in alliance countries can stimulate production in other countries. Such a production increase can further complicate the problem of allocating market shares. Finally, fluctuations in demand can prevent the maintainance of artificial prices. A more elaborate analysis of the possibilities of cartel action appears in the recent CRA study involving bauxite/aluminum, chromium, manganese, cobalt, and copper.[38]

Market Conditions: Demand

Explaining the role of demand in mineral price formation also requires that we analyze its underlying determinants. Most important is the fact that a typical mineral is utilized in many different products, and that this diversity exists at several sequential demand stages. As shown in figure 2–5 these stages include primary or refiners demand, intermediate, fabricators, or manufacturers demand, and final or consumers demand. Also analyzed here are the underlying economic determinants, technology, substitution, and market organization.

Elements of Demand

End-Use Structure. An understanding of the structure of end uses is essential to demand analysis. Since the main consumer of a mineral often is the refiner or fabricator, it is difficult to determine which products are responsible for

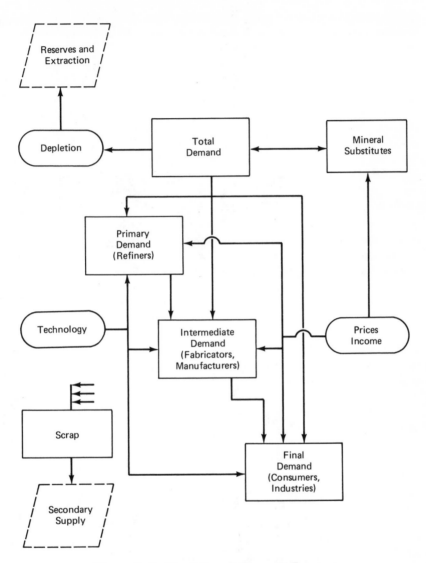

Figure 2–5. The Mineral Demand Process

most of the demand of a particular mineral. One possibility is to trace minerals through successive processes until they reach the product in which they are finally embodied. This can be accomplished by examining the input-output accounts common to interindustry analysis.[39] These accounts trace the origin and distribution of all shipments of a commodity for each sector of the

Table 2-5
Producer Associations and Multilateral Organizations for Mineral Commodities, 1975

Commodity	Value of (1970) World Trade (U.S. millions of dollars)	Producer Association		Consumer and Producers Multilateral Agreements or Association
		LDCs or "Group of 77" only	All Producer Countries	
Bauxite	2.730[a]		International Bauxite Association (IBA 1974[b])	
Copper	6.180[c]	Conseil Intergouvernemental des Pays Exportateurs du Cuivre (CIPEC, 1973)		
Iron ore	2.200[d]		Association of Iron Exporting Countries (AIEC, 1975)[e]	
Lead and zinc	1.170			International Lead and Zinc Study Group
Mercury	—		(Association of mercury producing countries, under preparation)[f]	
Petroleum	23.780	Organization of Petroleum Exporting Countries (OPEC, 1880)		

Phosphates	450	(Association of phosphate producing countries, under preparation)[g]
Tin	650[h]	International Tin Organization and Agreement (1972)
Tungsten		UNCTAD Committee on Tungsten

Source: H. Hveem, "The Political Economy of Raw Materials and the Conditions for their 'Opecization,'" Oslo: International Peace Research Institute, 1975.

[a]Refers to ore and first- and second-transformation mineral.

[b]Members are Australia, Jamaica, Guyana, Sierra Leone, Guinea, Surinam, and Yugoslavia.

[c]Copper mineral and first transformations.

[d]Only iron ore.

[e]Members are Algeria, Australia, Brazil, Chile, India, Mauretania, Peru, Sierra Leone, Sweden, Tunisia, and Venezuela. Canada, Liberia, and the Philippines have participated in the preparations of the association but did not sign the agreement.

[f]Member founders will be Algeria, Turkey, Mexico, Italy, Yugoslavia, and Spain. Canada has attended the four consultative meetings as an observer.

[g]Potential members are Morocco, Senegal, Togo Spain, and Tunisia.

[h]Refers to all fertilizer base materials, that is, even potash.

economy. As such, they identify the demand interdependency existing among the producing sectors who buy mineral products as inputs from each other and use them in producing other goods which are sold, in turn, as outputs to other producing sectors. As an example, table 2–6 illustrates the interindustry structural linkages between the iron ore mining industry and the other industries using its products. The implication of this demand structure is that the demands for mineral commodities are derived demands which are inter-mediately derived from the markets for intermediate goods. The demands for the latter in turn are derived from the markets for final goods. Some industries of final demand for iron ore are construction, transportation, electrical, producers' and consumers' durable goods, container manufacturers, and machinery manufacturers.

Each of these demand stages are related directly to the sequential processing stages that characterize a typical mineral industry. One normally associates the processing or refining stage with the mining stage such that demands for the primary product occur at the refining stage. Here this has been termed primary demand. The next stage of process normally is fabricating, and the associated industries thus create intermediate demands. The manufac-turing process also generates intermediate demands, but some of these demands will be met by the fabricating industry and others by the refining industry. Final demand refers to the demand in markets in which mostly manufactured but sometimes fabricated goods are sold to final consumers.

Also characteristic of end use is the actual rate of intensity with which demands are being made. Often mentioned is the intensity-of-use ratio. A low ratio means that a small amount of minerals are needed for a given output; a high ratio means that a large amount of minerals are needed for a given output. The actual tendency of this ratio depends on the stage of industrial develop-ment of the nation in which it is examined. For example, in the United States the ratio has been decreasing even though overall demand is increasing. As will be explained later, this is due to technological developments leading to a more efficient utilization of minerals, for example, the development of alloys, precision designing, and improvements in material strength. Nations in less advanced stages of industrialization have high intensity-of-use ratios during the takeoff or modernization stages. Once the nation reaches a certain level of industrialization, the ratios then decline slowly.

Economic Determinants. To explain the economic determinants underlying mineral demand, one begins with the assumption that the demand for any commodity depends ultimately on individual utility maximization, given preference functions and market prices for products and for factors of production owned by the household. Given that income determination can be handled separately from consumption decisions, utility is normally maximized subject to an appropriate budget constraint. Quantities of the commodity of

Table 2-6
Intermediate and Final Demand for Iron Ore[a]

Row	SIC Code	Consuming Industry	Direct Requirements[b]	Volume of Transactions[c]
5.00	1011	Iron and ferroalloy mining	.05270	91.9
6.01	102	Copper mining	.00276	2.0
6.02	103, 104, 105, 108	Nonferrous metals except copper mining	.00261	2.4
7.00	11, 12	Coal mining	.00009	.3
10.00	147	Chemical and fertilizer mineral mining	.00117	1.2
36.01	3241	Cement, hydraulic	.00150	1.9
36.03	3253	Ceramic wall and floor tile	.00164	.3
36.04	3255	Clay refractories	.00723	1.9
36.21	3297	Nonclay refractories	.01459	5.6
37.01	331	Blast furnaces and basic steel production	.05949	1496.5
38.03	3333	Primary zinc	.00417	2.0
38.06	3341	Secondary nonferrous metals	.00198	2.6
55.01	3641	Electric lamps	.00123	1.0
68.01	491, pt. 493	Electric utilities	.00002	.3
71.02	65, 66	Real estate	.00006	3.6
27.01	281 (excl. 28195)	Industrial inorganic and organic chemical	.00276	47.1
42.11	3499	Fabricated metal products	.00052	.7
88.00		Total intermediate demand		1661.5
99.02		Total final demand		82.2
99.03		Total output		1743.7

Source: *Input-Output Structure of the U.S. Economy 1967*, Supplement, *Survey of Current Business* (Washington, D.C.: U.S. Department of Commerce, 1972).
[a]SIC (1011).
[b]Per dollar of gross output.
[c]Millions of dollars at producers price.

interest as well as other commodities and services are then selected to maximize household utility, given the prices of those commodities and household income. The solution of the maximization process shows that demand for that commodity is a function of its price, the prices of substitutes, and income. Because the final consumers of such commodities are typically too numerous to affect price, the resulting demand relationship reflects the conditions of competition on which it is based.

Whether this approach can be used to derive the demand for minerals at the intermediate level is questionable. These consumers only purchase products in which minerals have been used as an input at earlier stages. Behrman, however, suggests that if the intermediate buyers are purely competitive in the international markets in which they purchase the un-processed commodity and in the final goods market where they sell the final product, their profit maximizing behavior is analogous to that of the mineral producer described in the previous section.[40] One can then substitute the market equilibrium condition for the finished product into the sum of the demand functions for the commodity at the intermediate level. This yields an intermediate demand relation. Demand depends on the price of the mineral commodity, the prices of other final demand goods, the prices of other material inputs, and income. Such a demand relation has both intermediate and final demand considerations collapsed into a single relationship.

The relationship between demand and own price is an inverse one. As price increases, the quantity demanded decreases; as price decreases, the quantity demanded increases. However, the short-run demand for minerals typically is highly price inelastic. This implies that demand is not reduced significantly when prices increase. In this case, the end products do not use sufficient enough amounts of the mineral to increase costs substantially. The cost of shifting to another mineral might be too costly, or the final consumers might consider the products as necessities. In addition, technology and substitution can enter in the long run to make demand more elastic. Some examples of this shift were given in table 2–2. Another important influence is that demand changes in proportion to changes in income, gross national product, or industrial activity.

Energy has been among the most important of the prices of other material inputs. Of all the energy consumed in the United States in 1972, for example, 19 percent was absorbed in the production and processing of minerals. These higher energy prices are obviously placing an upward pressure on mineral prices. Those minerals with a very high energy input may thus see a curtailment of demand.

Technology. The importance of technology in mineral demand should now be apparent. Since the demands for a mineral are derived from its use in the production of other goods, demand analysis requires a technical knowledge of the production processes of the user industry. For example, the short-run demand for iron as well as for its substitutes (iron and steel scrap) is derived directly from information about mineral user technology. This requires understanding the various combinations of iron and scrap possible, given the engineering design underlying the open hearth process as compared to the basic oxygen furnace process. Although the rates of substitution between two materials normally vary inversely with their respective price ratios, the materials can be substituted for each other only so far as the engineering design permits. Technology also affects demand in other ways. It can provide a means for producers to respond to consumers' preferences and requirements, it can affect changes in the intensity-of-use ratio, or it can affect end-use patterns over the long run by shaping the variety of goods we use.

Substitution. As suggested above, demand for a mineral is related positively to the prices of any other mineral with which it is a potential substitute. If that mineral can be replaced by the substitute or competitive mineral at a lower price, then its demand will decline. If the prices of the other mineral should increase relative to its own, then its demand will increase. Substitution is generally considered to be of two types: functional substitution and product substitution. An example of the former is the replacement of copper by aluminum in the production of electrical wire or cable. The latter could entail the replacement of copper wiring in transmitters by a wireless transmitter. Functional substitution is generally found more often.

In describing the rate and direction of such substitution, the following factors are normally considered: (1) pricing and costs, (2) technology, (3) taste or quality, (4) environmental effects, and (5) availability.[41] Substitution away from a mineral can occur if it has a high price, if it is not susceptible to technological innovations, if it is involved in products that have become obsolete, if its production causes environmental damage, or if it is not readily available. In interpreting these factors, it is important to realize that several of them can vary at the same time, making substitution a difficult phenomenon to explain. When relative prices change, one commodity will be used in place of another in intermediate production. Sometimes this change can take place fairly rapidly; at other times complications can arise. Changes in technology will be required and this depends on a price differential existing over a long time period. Substitution technology also implies changes required to improve efficiency in production, and this may lead to shifts among commodity inputs. Finally, some substitution will occur simply because consumer tastes or preferences demand it. An end product will employ a material because it imparts a quality preferred by consumers.

The minerals which undergo functional substitution the most are those which share properties such as conductivity, ductility, and strength. Examples of minerals sharing such properties are copper, aluminum, and iron as one group and tin, zinc, and lead as another. However, plastics are also playing an increasing role in functional substitution. They are now used more than aluminum, copper, lead, and zinc combined.

Demand Organization and Power

Market organization among consumers can also exert a perceptible influence on price. Because not much evidence has been gathered on this, concentration and power on the buyer's side is generally considered to be more modest than concentration on the seller's side. The structure of input-output accounts can be of help here also. In inspecting the accounts, Scherer suggests that most mineral refiners and fabricators sell their products to a large number of different industries and are dependent upon any single class of industrial buyers for only a small fraction of their sales.[42] However, the industry definitions used in the accounts are often too broad to reflect the true amount of seller dependence on specific buying sectors. Behrman does cite the case for market power among consumers in primary commodity markets.[43] In many cases, these buyers are using the commodity as an input in the production of a product that is then sold in a final product market where there is also some market power. He also mentions the theory of countervailing power, which suggests that power on the supply side of a market creates the need for power on the demand side.[44]

Monopsony. The most elementary case of the exercise of buyer power is that of a single buyer. Monopsony can occur because a mineral is much more productive in a particular end use than any other. It also can arise where the buyer in question is not a consumer but a further processor, and thus exercises the same conduct in buying as he would in selling. In either case, the buyer seeks a route to obtain his materials at the lowest possible cost. As a consequence, the monopsonist's output level will be chosen with regard to its consequences on the demand for inputs and the prices of these inputs. The demand curve reflecting this response will be a marginal curve that is downward sloping. Drawing upon price theory, the equilibration of the monopsonist's demand and marginal cost curves will result in a level of input purchases smaller than those of a competitive industry or a group of ordinary consumers.

Oligopsony. The other recognized case of buyer power is that of a concentrated group of buyers facing a large number of smaller sellers. In minerals markets, however, these buyers more typically face a concentrated group of sellers. The bargaining strategy most often employed by large buyers is that they can integrate vertically upstream, producing their own requirements of a mineral input, unless sellers hold prices near cost. Because there is an advantage to buying rather than making, the large buyers are likely to remain in this position rather than actually to expand.

They thus look to bargaining devices of a reinforcing nature such as long-term contracts; these are negotiated to cover transactions extending as long as thirty years. Sellers are attracted to these agreements, since they can be assured that their production capacity will be utilized at expected levels, and they can even pass on some cost savings. In addition, they are normally protected from severe risk by formulas that fix future prices to changes in appropriate cost and price indexes. Such contracting arrangements have been dominant in sales arrangements among mineral producers and consumers.

The underlying conditions determining the behavior of oligopsonists are parallel to those of oligopolists and need not be further explored. There is the additional difficulty of trying to explain what is rather complex behavior with analytical tools that are often found wanting.

Market Structure

Up to now mineral market organization and power have been considered as they relate either to mineral supply or mineral demand. In this section, we further develop the framework by integrating the supply and demand sides. An example of how this will take place is given in table 2–7; market structure as well as market power are shown in relation to price formation for the four prototype commodities.

Market Organization

The starting point for analyzing mineral market structure is with the degree of concentration, barriers to entry, and multinational presence. The degree of concentration in mineral markets has already been mentioned as one measure of market power, and possibilities for providing empirical measurements will be discussed later. Motives behind concentration have also been explored, including economies of scale, absolute costs, control over technical knowledge, government policies, and control over the mineral resource. The configuration that is used for examining market concentration is the number of firms appearing on each side of the market.

Number of Sellers	*Number of Buyers*
One—monopoly	One—monopsony
Few—oligopoly	Few—oligopsony
Many—competition	Many—competition

Table 2-7
Market Structure, Bargaining Power, and Price Formation

Resource Commodity	Supply		Demand		Process Stage of Price Determination[b]	Price Formation	Observations on Price Formation
	Market Power[a]	Multinational Presence/ Country Action	Market Power	Multinational Presence/ Country Action			
Copper	Homogeneous oligopoly with relatively large competitive fringe (50%)	Limited domination/ limited producer country action	Many fabricators but concentrated	Limited domination	Refined metal (LME) wirebars)	Flexible	Price competitively determined on LME but trade is marginal.
Bauxite/ aluminum	Tight oligopoly (56%)	Dominated by six firms/ limited producer country action	Tight oligopsony	Dominated by six firms	Ore (U.S. imports, CIF)	Tightly controlled	Trade primarily between producing firms. Ore prices reflect country/ company bargains.
Tin	Oligopoly (76%)	Partially dominated/joint producer country action	Oligopsony	Increasing national interest	Smelting/metal (Penang, grade A)	Flexible with limited buffer-stock control	Price control instigated by consumers as well as producers.
Iron ore	Weak oligopoly/competition; increasing coordination at the national level (57%)	Vertical integration/ limited producer country action	Oligopsony. National bargaining units typical, except in U.S.	Concentration among steel producers	Concentrates (Kiruna D or Brazil CIF North Sea)	No market as such. Prices relate to private transactions which consist of three major contractual forms.	

[a]Figures in brackets are concentration ratios for the largest eight firms.
[b]Major price quotation given in brackets.

Any number of sellers can face any number of buyers such as in the combination of oligopoly and competition or oligopoly and oligopsony.

A more precise evaluation of concentration can be made based on the proportions of industry output or industry purchases attributable to a fixed number of sellers and buyers. Bain recognizes oligopolies or oligopsonies as possessing high, medium, and low concentration where eight firms account for 80, 60, and 40 percent of the total quantity sold or bought, respectively.[45] Also to be considered is the number of small firms which operate as a fringe around the few large firms. This fringe could be considered small, medium, or large depending on whether they number in the region of 5, 20, or 50. Bain suggests that a highly concentrated oligopoly is one in which the largest eight firms supply 70 percent or more of the output with a small fringe, while a moderately concentrated one would supply from 70 percent down to roughly 30 percent with a medium fringe.[46]

A major reason for distinguishing among markets according to degree of concentration is that a tighter concentration pattern will affect market performance more significantly. A more concentrated oligopoly could result in expressed or tacit collusion, and thus performance of a more monopolistic character. Obviously, a less concentrated oligopoly could result in performance nearer to the competitive norm.

Other characteristics of market structure are the conditions of entry or the barriers to entry. This refers to the advantage in cost or price which firms well established in an industry have over firms which are potential entrants.[47] The degree to which established firms can persistently maintain their prices above minimal average or competitive costs before making it attractive for new firms to enter can also be stratified. Bain suggests three levels of condition: (1) easy—no barriers to entry; (2) moderately difficult—some barriers; or (3) blockaded.[48] There are two ways in which these entry conditions can influence market participants. First, a long-run limit on price can emerge, because established firms are not likely to exceed that limit in order to forestall entry. And second, even when entry is induced and competition exists, the firms taken together will not want price to rise beyond such a limit.

When considering mineral market structure at the international level, the presence of multinational mining corporations (MMCs) is important. Their presence implies a gradual evolution of exchange in many mineral markets away from competition toward large-scale distribution by firms with diversified or conglomerate commercial and financial interests. These firms often control access to a large proportion of a mineral's sales and relevant technology as well as management and investment financing. Though some of this influence is associated with vertical integration, the more typical property is conglomerateness.[49] Their power base is further enhanced, since such firms maintain favor with political groups in their home country as well as in the host country where they extract needed minerals. Thus, the multinational's presence embodies more than its market share; its influence on market structure is derived from its collateral political and economic capabilities. Although it is difficult to typify the influence of the dominance of MMC's on market structure, certainly the major market variables such as trade, investment, and prices are in some way affected.

Market Power

Market power is reflected in a number of different phenomena. For example, one can examine the share of raw material costs in final product prices or alternatively the difference between prices and marginal costs. Although the latter can usefully serve to detect distortions from competitive marginal cost pricing, marginal cost data are difficult to obtain. Long-run net profits also can reflect market power, but here also data problems exist. A slightly different measure might be the ability of trading parties to inflict losses on each other through negotiation. While such information cannot easily be incorporated into an index of power, one could alternatively examine the sensitivity of a firm's output to changes in prices of a competing firm. However, the problems of measuring such price elasticities are considerable.

As a consequence, we are relegated to measuring market power in terms of market share. The statistic normally employed for this purpose is the concentration ratio. In using this ratio, one must realize that counting the number of firms for a particular market suffers from the problem that any measure of power depends on the size distribution of the firms as well as the definition of industry bounds. Also, the actual domination of sales or purchases by a single firm does not necessarily imply the exercise of power or the control of a market.

There are four basic ratios which are frequently computed to measure the percentage of total industry output or purchases accounted for by the largest of producing or consuming units.[51] The simplest is the concentration ratio which reflects the percentage of total market output accounted for by the largest units. These can possibly be producing or exporting countries or firms within a country or a market. If y_i = market share of unit i, the concentration ratio (CR) for n principal units will be:

$$CR = \sum_{i=1}^{n} y_i$$

Some use has also been made of the Gini coefficient (GC). It is constructed first by ranking the market shares in increasing order:

$$y_1 < y_2 < y_3 < \ldots < y_n.$$

Sums are then made in increasing steps

$$B_1 = y_1$$
$$B_2 = y_1 + y_2$$
$$B_n = y_1 + y_2 + \ldots + y_n$$

Let

$$q_i = \frac{B_i}{B_n} \quad \text{and } P_i = \frac{i}{n}$$

Then

$$GC = \frac{\displaystyle\sum_{i=1}^{n-1} (P_i - q_i)}{\displaystyle\sum_{i=1}^{n-1} P_i}$$

which measures the unequal distribution of market shares or the departure from a distribution in which all units had equal market shares. This index has been noted to suffer from the problems of instability in deciding which additional firms to include. Where there are few units with equal shares, it implies the existence of little inequality but probably underestimates the attained market power.

The Herfindahl-Hirschman (HH) index, the one most often used, is defined as the sum of squares of the market shares of units

$$HH = \sum_{i=1}^{n} y_i^2$$

It has a value of one with only one unit, declines with increases in the number of units, and increases with rising inequality among any given number of units. A variant of this index found occasionally is the Herfindahl-Gini (HG) coefficient which is the square root of the above index.

$$HG = \sqrt{\sum_{i=1}^{n} y_i^2}$$

An example of estimated values of the above indices for the years 1972–1974 is provided in Tables 2–8 and 2–9. Based on the market shares of the major

Table 2–8
Principal Concentration Indexes: Exporting Countries, 1972–1974

Commodity	Year	Four Countries				Eight Countries			
		CR	HH	HG	GC	CR	HH	HG	GC
Copper	1974	48.2	0.062	0.248	0.174	74.2	0.080	0.282	0.248
	1973	48.2	0.060	0.245	0.137	74.5	0.078	0.280	0.228
	1972	47.0	0.057	0.240	0.148	72.9	0.075	0.274	0.234
Tin	1974	76.6	0.266	0.516	0.560	90.8	0.272	0.521	0.615
	1973	81.4	0.272	0.522	0.498	92.6	0.276	0.525	0.634
	1972	80.8	0.246	0.496	0.459	93.8	0.251	0.501	0.606
Aluminum	1974	46.8	0.056	0.236	0.078	72.8	0.074	0.271	0.214
	1973	47.6	0.057	0.238	0.022	73.8	0.075	0.274	0.203
	1972	48.3	0.061	0.247	0.159	73.5	0.078	0.279	0.254
Iron ore	1974	63.5	0.107	0.327	0.174	81.8	0.116	0.341	0.394
	1973	62.1	0.103	0.321	0.181	80.8	0.113	0.336	0.391
	1972	58.7	0.092	0.303	0.191	82.8	0.108	0.328	0.321

Source: *Yearbook of International Trade Statistics*, vol. II, 1974 (New York: United Nations, 1976).

Table 2-9
Principal Concentration Indexes: Importing Countries, 1972–1974

Commodity	Year	Four Countries				Eight Countries			
		CR	HH	HG	GC	CR	HH	HG	GC
Copper	1974	47.8	0.058	0.241	0.077	75.3	0.079	0.281	0.211
	1973	48.8	0.061	0.248	0.123	78.2	0.086	0.293	0.213
	1972	49.2	0.062	0.249	0.098	76.1	0.082	0.286	0.225
Tin	1974	63.0	0.115	0.339	0.293	82.6	0.125	0.354	0.414
	1973	66.5	0.135	0.367	0.333	84.3	0.143	0.378	0.458
	1972	69.7	0.161	0.402	0.410	85.9	0.168	0.410	0.507
Aluminum	1974	36.2	0.033	0.182	0.053	63.5	0.052	0.228	0.115
	1973	41.1	0.044	0.210	0.126	66.8	0.061	0.248	0.192
	1972	46.2	0.056	0.236	0.154	68.7	0.069	0.262	0.261
Iron ore	1974	76.3	0.200	0.448	0.429	93.9	0.209	0.457	0.527
	1973	78.7	0.211	0.460	0.410	94.4	0.218	0.467	0.548
	1972	78.1	0.214	0.463	0.421	95.1	0.222	0.471	0.534

Source: *Yearbook of International Trade Statistics*, Vol II, 1975 (New York: United Nations, 1976).

exporting and importing countries for the prototype commodities, market power appears to be sizable. Regarding the concentration ratios on the supply side, four countries account for at least one-half of world exports for the four commodities, with tin and iron ore representing an even larger portion. At the eight-country level, at least two-thirds of world exports are included. A ranking of the degree of concentration follows from values of the Herfindahl-Hirschman index. At both the four- and eight-country level, the highest is in tin, followed by iron ore, copper, and aluminum.

The amount of concentration on the demand side is only slightly less. Values at the four-country level suggest that at least one-half of world imports are accounted for, excepting aluminum. Again, at the eight-country level the ratios reach approximately two-thirds, excepting aluminum. The ranking of commodities according to degree of concentration based on the Herfindahl-Hirschman index results in a ranking different from the supply side. Iron ore becomes the first, followed by tin, copper, and aluminum.

Relative concentration of exporting countries as compared to importing countries based on this index is also significant. For tin, the exporters are more concentrated than the importers. Malaysia and Thailand account for approximately 60 percent of tin exports, while the United States, Japan, and the Federal Republic of Germany take 58 percent of the imports. For iron ore, the concentration balance is in favor of the importers. Australia, Canada and Brazil contribute 49 percent of the exports, while Japan, the Federal Republic of Germany, and the United States import 71 percent of the total.

Market Implications

The market implications to be examined here relate to the host governments in developing mineral exporting countries and the foreign mineral investing firms. The most essential characteristic of the governments is their dependence on mineral commodity exports for foreign exchange and income generation.[51] The fact that the primary export sector in these countries rarely has an internal demand base explains in part their inability to influence the price formation of their commodities in the international markets, even when in some commodities there are a few dominant producing countries. In most developing countries production for exports is concentrated in a few primary commodities (in many cases in only one or two commodities). The foreign exchange earnings from these exports are so critical for financing imports and government operations that this puts intense pressure on the developing countries to increase exports in order to secure larger foreign exchange receipts and government revenues.

We have also witnessed a period in which the prices of primary commodities have remained constant or fallen relative to the prices of industrial products. At the same time, increasing concentration on the buying side by mineral firms and industries in the developed countries, originating from their capacity to build stockpiles of commodities and to cooperate among themselves in market sharing and exchange of information, has given them a favorable advantage. However, such an advantage has not always been realized. A number of related problems have caused these firms and industries to lessen their investments in developing countries.[52] Among problems encountered, the desire among developing countries to coordinate their industries has produced fears of limitation in the availability of resources for use. In addition, the system of forming capital for mineral development appears to have broken down. Private investors have become disillusioned because of host government action, including taxation, nationalization, and increasing default on mineral contracts. These factors also have discouraged new exploration in developing countries. In fact, the preponderant share of new exploration since the early 1970s has been in the United States, Canada, Australia, and South Africa.[53]

Also of importance is the recent substantial increase in the capital cost of new capacity. With the costs of highly skilled labor and specialized equipment rising much higher than inflation, rising overall costs have created concern among those responsible for raising the necessary capital. The mentioned cost escalation has been further fueled by the costs of developing the infrastructure and of meeting environmental standards. Also to be added is the fear of political risks arising from the policies of governments and the uncertainties of their future actions. This problem becomes amplified in developing countries where political hostility to conventional sources of capital has been evident.

It is against the background of such problems that this attempt to evaluate market implications has arisen. While tradeoffs obviously exist in any final selection of the factors relevant to market implications, the following would seem to best serve the needs of the present framework.

Resource Export Dependence. Dependence implies that a country relies on one or at most several export commodities for the majority of its foreign exchange earnings and export income. Several criteria can be empirically judged for the host countries that reflect this dependence. Among these are: (1) the commodity concentration of a country's trade, (2) the growth in export earnings from primary commodities, (3) the change in the terms of trade taken on a single commodity basis, and (4) the instability in earnings resulting from price and quantity fluctuations at the export level.

Magnitude of Fixed Investment. The size of the fixed investment in resource mining and processing projects has grown immensely. In judging the magnitude of such investment relative to a country's ability to finance it, the investment value can be compared to the value of the country's gross domestic product, the mining sector's share in that product, and the gross domestic investment. Depending on whether the fixed investment is relatively large or small, the position of the foreign investor vis-à-vis the host government will be stronger or weaker.[54] For the case of an initial large investment, the foreign investor is in a strong position initially, but his position deteriorates as his investment places him in the situation of a hostage.

Nature of Technology. When the technology of mineral production is complex and changeable, it is less easy for a host country to develop its domestic cadre and to share in resource production and ownership. The foreign firm occupies a dominant position. For the case where the technology is simple and stable, the host country has a better possibility of expanding its share of rents. When technology is also simple at the processing stage, the country can attempt to integrate forward.

Control over Reserves and Production. The benefit that either party can derive from a mineral depends ultimately on its control over reserves and production. The patterns of ownership and control in a mineral market are fairly straightforward. The foreign firms may own the land they have explored and are exploiting or they may acquire mineral rights through leasing. A firm obviously has difficulties in mineral development where exploration rights are limited. This is increasingly the case in host countries where there is a determination to bring companies under control. These countries also have other devices for extending mineral control. They can expand their shareholding in a firm, they can organize state owned mining firms, or they can establish a state trading enterprise to coordinate domestic production and sales with external purchases.

Opportunities for Increased Processing. Processing offers the possibility for increased value-added as well as foreign exchange earnings. At present semiprocessed and fully processed mineral commodities account for only 10 percent of the exports being shipped from developing to developed countries.[55] Among the factors affecting the ability of a country to increase processing, a most important one is the complexity of the technology involved. Others include the tightness of industry integration, tariff and nontariff barriers, and restrictive business practices.

Of course, there are a number of possibilities for a host country to intervene in the investors' processing network.[56] (1) The parties can agree when signing a contract that processing facilities are to be built by a certain date. (2) The government may require the firm to undertake feasibility studies on processing facilities. (3) The government may offer tax or other fiscal incentives, such as refunding some or all of the taxes collected in the first years of a concession, if the firm will use the money to build processing facilities.

(4) The government can offer tax holidays to profit accrued from processing. (5) The host country may levy tariffs or quotas on raw materials leaving the country and erect protective tariffs on imports. (6) The government may require the investor to offer output to any local processor, at a price not higher than that sold to other buyers. Although there are other methods of encouraging processing, these are probably the most common.

Material Share in Product Prices. The mineral producer will be able to increase prices or demand more concessions when the raw material is a relatively unimportant cost item in relation to the final product sales price.[57] The share of the raw material cost in final product price depends on two factors. First, it will tend to be higher, the more processing is undertaken before the material is sold. Second, it will be negatively related to the value-added created by the buyer. The higher the value-added per unit of sales, the less important will be the raw material cost to the buyer. Buyers with far-reaching forward integration, therefore, will ordinarily be less affected by the price changes of raw materials bought and will find it easier to absorb such changes in their total costs.

Obsolescing Bargain. This factor as well as the two remaining ones concentrate on the evolution of bargaining power over time.[58] The presence of risk and uncertainty such as at the beginning of the investment process makes the foreign investor stronger. As this uncertainty declines, his position becomes weaker. Evidence would appear to support this evaluation in the mineral investment process. Before an initial investment is made, the foreign firm must develop a project with an uncertain outcome and can thus demand contractural terms in its favor. But once this investment is made, these concessions can become reduced as uncertainty and technological advantage lessen in importance. Vernon has termed this an "obsolescing bargain."[59] There is a regular and predictable effort made by host governments to readjust agreements with the foreign firm. The government scrutinizes the profitability of the resource extraction and export operation, and desires to share in these profits as a means of satisfying national goals.

The actual process by which this is carried out can include pressures for negotiations, surtaxes, recomputations, and adjustments. Usually there is an evolution from an increase in taxation to an increase in equity participation and finally to outright nationalization. Once nationalization is complete, the government has little power to demand further concessions or to transfer wealth.

Nature of Competition. The competitiveness of a market indicates the extent to which new entrants can appear and lessen any oligopolistic or monopolistic power that a major mineral firm may have had in a market. In such a case, the position of the host government relative to the investing firm becomes stronger. As will be shown later, most of the major mineral markets have experienced an increase in the number of competitors over the 1960s and 1970s. Japanese and European firms particularly have entered the market to assure supplies of minerals to meet their needs. The developing countries can now more easily enter the market as well; they can also more readily choose among alternatives in selecting sources of investment as well as buyers for their raw materials.

The nature of competition in the market where the raw material buyer sells his product is also important. It is likely that a buyer will negotiate more stubbornly against increases in his raw material costs where he has to absorb these himself, and that he will be more amenable to accept the seller's demands in situations where the cost increase can be passed on by way of higher prices on his sales. The rationality of this argument is obvious. In the former case his profits will be directly affected by the increase in costs. In the latter they will not. From this point of view, it would be an advantage to the sellers of the primary resource to trade with processors who have a strong monopoly or oligopoly in the market where they sell their products. A low price elasticity of demand in the final product market would add to the bargaining advantage of the mineral producers. For example, the petroleum companies know that they can pass on most of their cost increases to the final consumers. This probably contributes to their ready acceptance of the raised tax demands of the oil-producing countries.

Government Learning Process. Often a host country reaches its obsolescing bargain by attracting new investments and then tightening its terms; it slowly advances along a learning curve. The learning process includes improved understanding of the cost structure and operating techniques of the industry as well as increased negotiating skills. The historical case has been that of host countries first observing mineral industry operations with little understanding of them. Gradually the governments began to understand the operations, to demand hiring of nationals in supervisory positions and to require participation in expansion and marketing. Mutual accommodation on its part now becomes more demanding.

There can be two possible effects of the learning process. On the one hand, Erb finds that learning has led to tighter and more equitable contracts, replacing traditional concessions with more complex, modern ones.[60] Cited are an increase in government participation in the ownership of mining operations (equity sharing) and an expansion of the government's management role. On the other hand, Moran suggests that because of this learning, foreign investors now begin to face a tax rate ranging from 60 to 90 percent plus demands for local ownership, local control over marketing, and local regulation of profit remittances, irrespective of the original contract.[61] This seems to be particularly true for the "mature" minerals such as copper, tin, and bauxite.

Price Formation

The Choice of a Reference Price

The most basic commodity prices derive from exchanges, where buying and selling transactions occur almost continuously. These are referred to as *spot prices* and represent the prices of contracts which call for immediate delivery of the physical commodity on the spot. These same prices are designated *cash prices,* where cash payment is required. Because buying is often necessary prior to the use of a commodity in processing or intermediate production, forward transactions are also contracted. *Forward prices* thus relate to contracts which specify delivery at some time in the future. Because the forward arrangement involves sellers and there often is a need to cover the risks of sending a commodity to market or holding it for storage, forward sales can be accompanied by futures transactions. Speculators now enter the market to meet the need for hedging or risk coverage through futures contracts. *Futures prices* thus relate to contracts which specify forward delivery but which also permit easy transfer of liability. Among major futures markets in industrialized countries, Chicago, London, Hamburg, and New York are the most important. Among developing countries, Calcutta, Manila, and Buenos Aires are significant.

The above forms of price quotations are available for a number of minerals markets. In addition, there are *arms length prices* which refer to quotations for transactions between individuals, firms, and other private organizations, as obtained on the open market. *Producer prices* are the prices received by producers on domestic sales, and *consumer prices* are the prices paid by consumers for domestic purchases. Inherent to most of the above transactions are *contract prices.* The *basis price* for a contract normally refers to a stated degree of quality or purity, with a sliding scale added for deviations from this standard.

In contrast to these open market prices, mineral firms frequently compute *international prices.* These prices represent the values placed on primary commodities produced at one stage and subsequently embodied in production at another stage, such as in vertically integrated industries. Commodity valuations of this type are common to the internal transactions of multinational enterprises. *Transfer prices* refer to the process of pricing goods traded within such firms. Intrafirm trade is here defined as transactions involving shipments of commodities (including capital, intermediate and finished goods, but excluding technology or services) which can be domestic or can extend between countries.[62] An internal price less often referred to is the *accounting price,* which includes all internal costs but may or may not include tax elements. Another type of price quotation relates to prices or price ranges set by government arrangement. These transactions normally take place within multilateral contracts such as for wheat and possibly coffee or within bilateral contracts such as that of the Commonwealth Sugar Agreement.

Finally, the difficulty of establishing or obtaining open market prices in some circumstances requires that we work with imputed values on an FOB or CIF basis. These prices normally provide a good indicator of the value of commodities to countries at the level of international trade. *Export prices* (FOB) signify the value at which goods are sold by an exporter; they also include the cost of transportation and insurance necessary to move the goods to the frontier (international shipping point) of the exporting country. In contrast, *import prices* (CIF) represent the value at which goods are purchased by the importer, plus the cost of transportation and insurance to the frontier of the importing country.

Given such a wide range of prices, the price analyst has severe problems in determining the reference or equilibrium price for a particular market. Referring to the example of iron ore used by Bosson and Varon, one finds that in the late 1960s roughly 40 percent of world iron ore trade took place between importers (steel companies) and captive mines abroad.[63] Another 40 percent took the form of long-term contracts of up to twenty years, and 20 percent occurred on what they term the "free market." In addition to determining which modality might serve as the basis for a reference price, there is the further problem that the share of transactions among the modalities has been changing.

How then in such a situation does the analyst arrive at a set of reference prices which is useful for analyzing mineral price formation? Several possibilities exist. A first one is to compute a price index which involves weighting prices by the quantities traded within each modality or submarket. In this case, nonetheless, the long-term contract prices involved are difficult to incorporate. They depend on the complex provisions of each contract, including the terms of marketing, investment, and processing as well as the mutual concessions agreed upon. This leads to a more popular alternative which is to use the quotations obtained on the major commodity exchanges, such as the London Metal Exchange (LME). These provide good reference prices, even though the volume of transactions may be marginal because the market participants accept them as a basis for contracts. This is particularly true for copper and tin traded on the LME.

Where the mineral has neither a futures market nor a producer price, the practice is to use the quotations provided in reputable trade periodicals such as the *Metal Bulletin.*[64] However, caution is necessary with some minerals because of the variations in grade and degree of beneficiation, including the trend toward trading in concentrates. For certain commodities, attempts to establish a high degree of standardization reduce this difficulty. Finally, FOB and CIF prices can be obtained or imputed from the international trade statistics of one or more countries. Where no reference market price exists, such as for the case of iron ore, import values have been accepted as a standard. Both the Kiruna D (65 percent, CIF Rotterdam) and the Brazilian (65 percent, CIF North Sea ports) import prices have served this purpose.

Price Trends and Fluctuations

An examination of patterns in mineral price formation can provide further insight into the knowledge we hope to gain from a study of price formation. As an example, consider first the trends in extremely long-run or secular price movements shown in figures 2–6 to 2–9. Provided are the actual and deflated prices for copper, tin, iron ore, and bauxite from 1890 to 1977 (excepting bauxite where the data begins later). The general trends in prices have been more or less stationary. When integrated with the trends reported for the earlier period from 1870 by Herfindahl, the overall trends can be regarded as slightly downward sloping.[65]

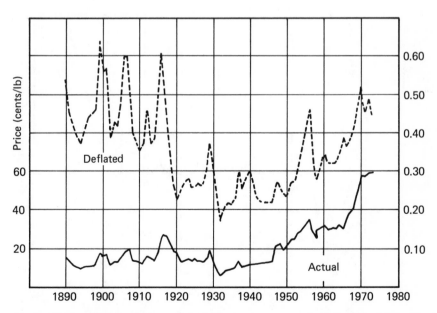

Figure 2–6. Annual Copper Prices (cents per pound) from the American Bureau of Metal Statistics.

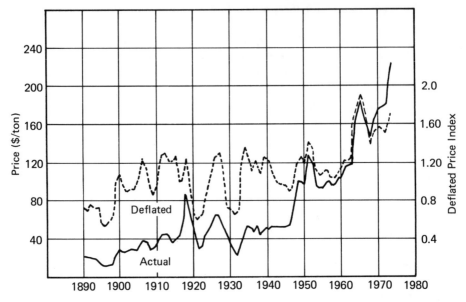

Figure 2–7. Annual Tin Prices (dollars per ton) from the NY Straights Tin.

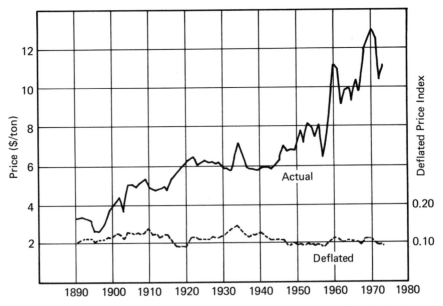

Figure 2–8. Annual Bauxite Prices (dollars per ton) from the RFF Price
Index.

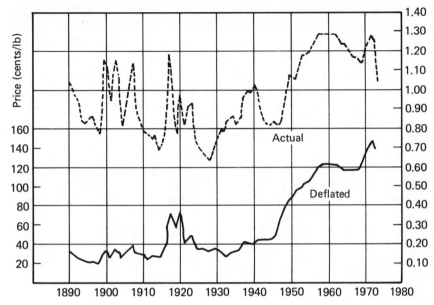

Figure 2-9. Annual Iron Ore Prices (cents per pound) from the RFF Price Index.

The major assumption underlying these long-run prices is that they are basically cost determined. The costs themselves can be said to be the net effect of two forces.[66] First, there is the tendency over time for mineral production to be based on resources of an increasingly diffuse nature. Although concentrated deposits will occasionally be discovered, the direction is toward lower-grade (or deeper) deposits as well as deposits occurring in more remote locations. Second, offsetting this upward cost pressure is the possibility of using improved technology. Improvements in technology normally require less energy in the extraction and concentration of the mineral, decrease the environmental impact of mine wastes, and offset rising labor costs by increasing productivity.

Barnett and Morse view price formation in this manner. For example, they conclude that resource scarcity has been avoided through technological changes which allow the substitution of low-grade resources for higher ones, thereby increasing effective supplies.[67] Smith has recently updated the price series they examined and has employed a more rigorous methodology in analyzing the trends.[68] He confirmed that the trend in relative prices had been negative for most of the full period, but cautioned that the rate of decline has recently tended to diminish in absolute magnitude.

Such a reversal in the price trend appears inevitable, since the absence of scarcity in the past does not necessarily imply future abundance at low prices. A number of reasons have been suggested to support this position.[69] Mechanization in the minerals industry is probably reaching certain limitations. Technological advancements also require a higher degree of employee training with the concomitant costs of education and higher pay scales. Furthermore, improvements in technology lead to the problem of acquiring the necessary capital to implement the improved technology. Because of these factors, therefore, production costs for resources have probably turned upward and are likely to continue in that direction.

Mineral price behavior has also been characterized as highly cyclical. Figures 2–10 through 2–13, which employ quarterly price observations, better illustrate the nature of this cyclicality. Taking copper as an example, prices reached record levels in 1970 because of earlier uncertainty over Zambian suppliers, the major strike of 1968 in the United States, and the war in Vietnam. They then declined and reached a peak again in 1973–1974, because of the coincidence of booming economic activity and hence inflation among major industrial nations during 1972 and 1973. While attempts to explain these fluctuations have typically been demand based, emphasizing the effects of cycles in the industrial activity of mineral users, Bosworth has recently drawn attention to the supply side by illustrating inadequacies in capacity adjustments.[70]

Basic Price-Making Forces

Given the diverse characteristics of mineral prices, how can the above explanations of price formation be expanded? As a first step, let us consider the basic market conditions. Conventional theory states that mineral supply and demand combine to determine an equilibrium price, that is, that price which is both the maximum that consumers will pay and the minimum necessary to induce producers to supply the commodities in the amount demanded at the price. Changes in price caused by changes in supply will, in turn, have a feedback effect on demand. Price increases act to decrease the quantity demanded and vice versa. For supply, the effect of these increases in price is the opposite.

The first complicating factor in applying this theory is the necessity of distinguishing between the short run and the long run. In the short run, mineral supply has been pointed out as being generally price inelastic. Resources are finite, limited by the time required to increase capacity. Mineral demand also exhibits this characteristic. Substitution of other minerals or materials in a production process also requires time, and an extreme price change would be required before production capital is adjusted away from the use of a particular mineral. Together supply and demand inelasticities are responsible for the

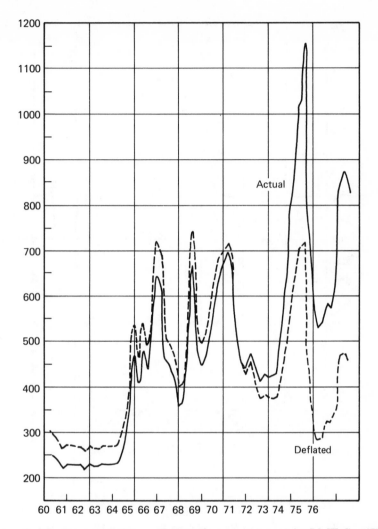

Figure 2–10. Quarterly Copper Prices (£ per metric ton) for LME Cash Wire Bars.

wide price swings that occur with shifts in quantity. However, since shifts in supply occur less frequently for mineral commodities, it is primarily demand shifts caused by changes in business cycles in the industrialized countries that tend to generate price fluctuations.

The major link between short-run and long-run price formation is inventories. Mineral inventories are held for a variety of reasons. Economic theory tells us that they satisfy precautionary, transactions, and speculative motives.

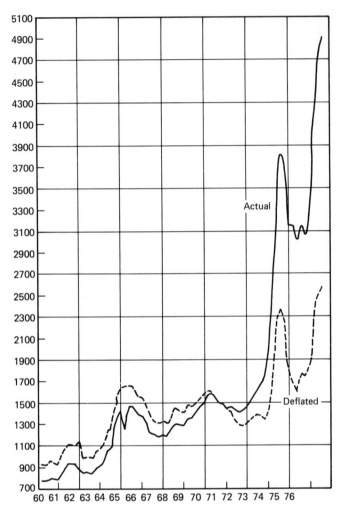

Figure 2–11. Quarterly Tin Prices (£ per metric ton) for LME Cash Wire
Bars.

The precautionary motive relates to the behavior of producers and consumers.
Producers might hold inventories to lessen swings in the downward direction
and release inventories to mitigate price swings in the upward direction, which
might otherwise lead to substitution. Since resource commodities are often of a
strategic nature, consumers also hold inventories for precautionary reasons,
such as the U.S. General Services Administration (GSA) stockpiles.

Transactions motives relate typically to inventory demand. Consumers

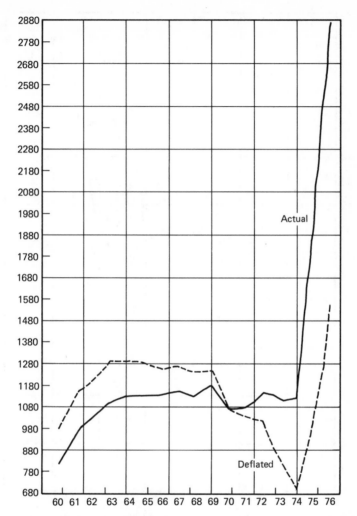

Figure 2–12. Quarterly Bauxite Prices (U.S. Import Value CIF Jamaica).

need to maintain inventory/consumption ratios at certain levels to facilitate concentrating, fabricating, and manufacturing activities. Speculative stock holding reflects the desire of market participants to take a long or short position in forward of futures trading in response to expected price movements.

Where a market possesses a highly concentrated structure, inventories are more likely to be used to support an orderly pricing structure. Among the explanations for orderly pricing, firms working under such a price structure

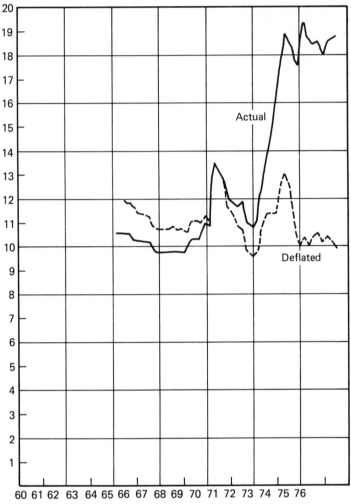

Figure 2–13. Quarterly Iron Ore Prices (dollars per metric ton) (Liberia Bong Range CIF North Sea Ports).

will reach their output decisions for the next period by the conventional method of bringing marginal revenue and marginal cost into equality. However, expected and actual production are scarcely equal and inventories will build up. Order backlogs will be reduced or inventories stored, but prices will not be cut.[71] The inventories not only serve as a buffer to prevent tampering with the price structure, they also will serve as feedback signals to improve planning in future production periods.

Another explanation is that oligopolists under certain conditions of collusion will establish prices which approximate some joint profit-maximizing level. This price will take into account costs and demand conditions anticipated for a period of several months. Although it may not be ideal for all firms, each firm recognizes the need for orderly pricing. Thus, output determination policy becomes a passive one; no one attempts to dispose of commodities at a lower price. Here, inventory adjustments can again serve to maintain a particular price structure.

As we move toward the long run, the role of inventories diminishes. Supply as well as demand are now more price elastic. Higher prices will lead to the development of resource deposits which were not viewed as profitable in the short run. If the price increase is substantial and is expected to prevail for some time, the rate of exploration may be increased, although new sources may not necessarily be developed. Conversely, on the demand side, higher prices will cause consumers at intermediate demand levels to shift to production functions in the long run which utilize less expensive resource inputs or which decrease the resource input per unit of finished products.

Just how much these adjustments will affect the direction of long-run price formation depends on the feedback of prices on quantities. Any growth in supply has depended on the response of producers to higher prices, given trends in supply costs. The growth in demand has depended only partially on prices. Increases in population and income in various countries have also been important. If the latter factors decline, however, demand growth will be maintained only if the increase in intensities of use in other parts of the world offsets the decrease in the more heavily industrialized countries. Substitution and technological advances may work to balance supply against rising demand, but the magnitude of such effects is uncertain.

Whether the costs of producing minerals will influence prices depends on the two offsetting factors mentioned above. Also to be considered is the continued inflationary tendencies of both the domestic and foreign economies. The recent substantial increase in mineral prices not only has contributed to but also has been affected by the inflationary situation. Mineral prices rose by only 50 percent between 1950 and 1970 but jumped by 100 percent during 1970 to 1973.[72] Energy and specialized labor costs have been the most important factors underlying these trends. The effect of petroleum price increases is well known. Labor costs have been influenced by increases in resource and finished product prices through contractual and effective indexation of wages and other incomes. Higher interest rates in adjusting to inflation have lead to higher capital costs. To compensate for decreases in their levels of real income, workers are bargaining for larger wage increases, including cost-of-living escalator clauses.

Including Market Structure and Bargaining Power

Market conditions can now be integrated with market structure and bargaining power to provide a more complete explanation of price formation. The approach adopted is to examine the application of price theory to the basic forms of market structure relevant to minerals markets. The discussion is organized according to the major configurations of market organization, that is, the relative numbers of sellers and buyers.

Competition-Competition. In a market with large numbers of producers and consumers, all market participants have an infinitesimal impact on prices. With no barriers to entry and price information freely available, price formation is simply a consequence of equilibrium between total supply and demand. However, for most minerals traded on international commodity markets, the entities involved would appear to have more than an imperceptible influence on market prices. Additionally, geologic uncertainty precludes the existence of perfect information concerning future prices.

Monopoly-Competition. The monopolist differs from the competitive supplier in that he faces a downward sloping rather than a horizontal demand curve for his output. While output is similarly increased until marginal revenue equals marginal cost, marginal revenue is necessarily less than monopoly price, the latter exceeding marginal cost. As long as the monopolist is operating on the inelastic portions of the declining demand curve, revenues can be increased by raising prices. For the specific case of monopoly ownership of mineral deposits, it has been suggested that limitations in exercising market power may cause monopoly prices and competitive prices to be equal. Although in some cases monopoly will require marginal revenue rather than prices to rise at the rate of interest.

Oligopoly-Competition. Attempting to explain price equilibrium in this configuration based on price theory is more difficult than the above. Oligopolistic producers recognize that their best pricing policy depends on the decisions made by rival sellers. The producers in fact are acutely aware of their interdependence. Since each decision depends on the assumptions that they make about rivals' decisions and reactions, oligopoly pricing theories which have emerged are varied and complex. Although it is difficult to link price equilibrium to cost and demand conditions, this does not imply that explanations of price formation are impossible.

As a start, we do have a number of past attempts to formulate a pure theory of oligopoly pricing. Among those mentioned as significant by Scherer are: Cournot's (1833) pure theory of oligopoly where each firm chooses to market that quantity of output which maximizes its profits, assuming the quantities marketed by rivals to be fixed; Chamberlin's (1933) monopolistic competition theory where firms recognize their interdependence and set prices to maximize joint profits; von Neumann and Morgenstern's (1944) game theory approach where price formation satisfies conditions of the minimax strategy; the Hall and Hitch (1939) and Sweezy (1939) theory of kinked demand where rivals hold prices constant when one firm raises its price but cuts prices when one firm lowers its price; and the Salant (1976) application of Nash-Cournot bargaining theory where firm payments are maximized according to the nature of the coalitions formed.[73]

To glean from such theories the most common factors contributing to mineral price formation is not easy. What they all seem to imply is a tendency toward the maximization of collective industry profits. Yet such joint profit maximization is not easy to trace. To help identify the resulting price equilibria, we follow the suggestion of Scherer in examining institutions which have facilitated oligopolistic coordination.[74] Cited are price leadership, rules of thumb pricing, and focal point pricing.

Price leadership implies a variety of industry practices or customs under which price changes are normally announced by a specific firm designated as a leader by others who follow the leader's initiatives. Three variations are examined here: dominant firm leadership, collusive leadership, and barometric leadership. Dominant firm leadership occurs when the industry consists of one firm controlling at least 50 percent of total industry output and of a competitive fringe of small firms. This case is a special one in as far as the dominant firm attempts to maximize its own profits, given that it knows its own effective demand curve together with the competitive fringe supply functions.

A price pattern more associated with mineral pricing is collusive leadership. This requires that firms recognize their common interest in cooperative pricing and can practice price discretion. One or several of the largest firms are dominant, and other firms follow as mentioned above. Peck cites Alcoa to be the customary ingot price leader because of its low costs as well as its large market share.[75] However, Scherer indicates that U.S. Steel has occupied this position in the United States without being the lowest cost producer.[76] Barometric price leadership is of a similar nature, but the prices reached are not quite as monopolistic. This form of pricing has been suggested as having occurred in the U.S. copper industry. It probably has not existed in the international copper market.

Also mentioned above, rule-of-thumb pricing can facilitate industry coordination. There are variants on this approach, but they normally follow full-cost or cost-plus pricing. A desired profit or percentage return on investment capital is simply added to estimated unit costs to yield the commodity price. An advantage of this approach is that it can be usefully employed to prevent price cutting where firms have similar costs.

Although price leadership has been found in various industries, there are conditions which limit possibilities for such coordination. Often cited are lower concentration, a large competitive fringe, high proportion of fixed costs in total costs, dependence on large and infrequent orders, and substantial possibilities of covert price shading. To these must be added the difficulties of extending the coordination possible in domestic pricing to international pricing; for example, concentration in world production is normally less than in world exports. Concerning the high proportion of overhead costs, firms operating under such conditions are susceptible to pricing breakdowns, when a cyclical or secular decline in demand and orders forces them to operate well below plant capacity. This is particularly true of mineral industries that need substantial investments to develop their deposits. Such industries have the possibility of organizing commodity agreements or stabilization cartels to minimize these problems, but as Eckbo has shown, they have not been successful.

Another weakness of the theories of price leadership offered above is that they are of a static, short-run nature. In the long run, a firm will have to reconsider its price and profit-maximization policies for several reasons. One is that as demand for a commodity becomes more elastic, a threat of competition from substitutes may occur. For example, the high prices of copper in 1966 forced the U.S. automobile industry to begin reducing its copper consumption per car. To some extent U.S. copper producers responded by limiting price increases so as to deter such reductions over the long term.

Another possibility is that a firm may practice dominant price leadership by setting the price so as to maximize profits (marginal cost equals marginal revenue) according to the residual demand curve that it faces. Such a pricing policy, however, may confer short-run profits on the competitive fringe, inducing the fringe to expand at the cost of the market share of the dominant producer.[77] As a consequence, the market structure will depend more on the nature of long-run costs. The greater the numbers in the competitive fringe, the smaller will be the scale at which decreasing returns begin. The major policy option open to the dominant producer is to reduce supranormal profits of the fringe by pricing to deter entry, that is, setting the price low enough so that none of these firms earns supranormal profits. However, this attempt at limit pricing probably involves a search to find a price slightly higher than this lower level, so that the dominant firm can exploit some of its power without encouraging expansion at the fringe.

The use of limit pricing to explain a variety of conduct in price formation has been extensive. Concerning the possibilities of small-scale entry, two alternative price explanations have been paramount: (1) prices are set at a level which maximizes short-run profits and permits entry, unless it is clearly blockaded; and (2) prices are held at a level which deters all entry.[78] Actual practice has followed somewhere between the two, setting prices so as to encourage only a modest amount of entry. Where possibilities exist for large-scale entry, the pricing strategy is not as clear-cut. No precise theoretical explanations concerning adjustments in output and prices by the existing firms vis-à-vis the new entrants have been offered.

Because of such pressures, limit pricing or any other form of cooperative pricing are possible only when concentration among producers is sufficiently high, barriers to entry are formidable, and demand is relatively price inelastic. Some of these conditions, however, are present for minerals and this approach will help explain price formation for several of the prototype commodities.

One final form of pricing related to oligopolistic industries which are highly integrated is transfer pricing. This refers to the use of internal prices which represent the values placed on commodities produced at one stage by a firm that are than embodied in production at another stage. Commodity valuations of this type are common to the pricing of intrafirm trade within multinational enterprises. Intrafirm trade is here defined as transactions involving shipments of commodities (including capital, intermediate, and finished goods, but excluding technology or services) which can be domestic or extend between countries.[79]

It is worth adding that demand power can and does lead to lower transfer prices, at least for the case of an oligopolistic market where sellers are weak enough to recognize their interdependence but too weak to confront strong buyers. But there remains the vagueness of what transfer prices mean.[80] Since firms can assign whatever prices they like to transactions within their domain, any of the traditional explanations of pricing cease to be valid. Although open market transactions involve sellers and buyers attempting to maximize profits at each other's expense, any intrafirm transaction reflects adjustments between two units to maximize joint profits. In effect, transfer prices are used to transmit profits, in the sense of maximizing them while minimizing risk and uncertainty.

The effects of certain transfer pricing practices on mineral producing developing countries can also be significant. Their presence usually in oligopolistic markets makes the application of international trade theory to resource allocation less relevant. One source implies that transfer pricing practices can violate the basic principles of the General Agreement on Trade and Tariffs (GATT).[81] That is, they can prevent trade from being conducted in a nondiscriminatory manner and can constitute a form of trade restriction as well. Transfer pricing may thus not only limit exchange earnings from trade but it may also prevent some countries from pursuing areas of industrial development suitable to their given factor endowments.

Monopoly–Monopsony. For the case of bilateral monopoly, only a price range rather than a single price can be determined from the underlying cost and demand conditions. The upper limit of this range coincides with the price set by a monopolist facing a purely competitive buying industry. The lower limit is the price a monopsonistic buyer would impose on a purely competitive buying industry. Within these limits, the bargaining power yielded and the tactics employed by the trading partners in resolving their conflicts determine the price achieved. The price can be higher or lower than the equilibrium price attained from bilateral competition involving identical cost and demand conditions. A more competitive price might be reached where the power on the demand side can countervail power upstream on the supply side.

Oligopoly-Oligopsony. Determining prices under bilateral oligopoly depends on the means available to a few strong buyers to restrain the pricing actions of oligopolistic sellers. Among those possible, Scherer suggests the following: (1) oligopolists are inclined to cut prices to gain large orders, particularly if they have excess capacity; (2) large buyers can play off one seller against others to obtain price concessions; and (3) large buyers can issue credible threats to integrate vertically, unless prices are held close to costs.[82] These advantages become greater as the buyers are more powerful relative to sellers. The pricing behavior is likely to be relatively competitive, as long as buyers are large and the sellers loosely organized. The buyers, nonetheless, cannot do better than they would from competitive sellers. The best bargain will be limited to the supply conditions of the competitive case. Unfortunately, the theory applicable within this configuration gives us no indication as to what prices will emerge. Since the market structure for many minerals tends to approximate oligopoly-oligopsony more closely than oligopoly-competition, this makes explanations of price formation indeed difficult.

Notes

1. M. Radetzki, "Market Structure and Bargaining Power: A Study of Three International Mineral Markets," Working Paper (Stockholm: Institute for International Economic Studies, 1976).

2. This interpretation of theory has provided the basis for investigations by J.S. Bain, *Industrial Organization* (New York: John Wiley & Sons, 1968), p. 20.

3. This framework owes its origins to the work of Scherer on industrial organization. Nonetheless, it differs from what has been considered the subject matter of industrial organization. Emphasis is placed on the primary production stage, and the industry considered is international. For reference to Scherer's work see F.M. Scherer, *Industrial Market Structure and Economic Performance* (Chicago: Rand McNally, 1971).

4. This appraisal of the importance of the mining industry to growth in global society is well surveyed in R. Bosson and B. Varon, *The Mining Industry and the Developing Countries* (New York: World Bank and Oxford University Press, 1977).

5. R. Vernon, "Foreign Enterprises and Developing Nations in the Raw Materials Industries," *American Economic Review,* Proceedings 60 (1970): 122–26.

6. Radetzki, "Market Structure and Bargaining Power."

7. T.H. Moran, *Multinational Corporations and the Politics of Dependence* (Princeton: Princeton University Press, 1974).

8. This distinction is due to O.C. Herfindahl, "The Process of Investment in Mineral Industries," in D.B. Brooks (ed.), *Resource Economics* (Baltiore: Johns Hopkins University Press, 1974).

9. T.J. Koopmans, "A Proof for the Case Where Discounting Advances the Domesday," *Review of Economic Studies,* Symposium, 42 (1974): 117–20.

10. D. Harris, "Geostatistics in the Appraisal of Metal Resources," in W. Vogely (ed.), *Minerals Material Modelling* (Washington, D.C.: Resources for the Future, 1975).

11. D.B. Brooks, "Mineral Supply as a Stock," in Vogely, *Economics of the Mineral Industries.*

12. Two recent studies which summarize current theory are F.M. Peterson and A.C. Fisher, "The Economics of Natural Resources," Working Paper (College Park, University of Maryland, 1976), and "Symposium on the Economics of Exhaustible Resources," *Review of Economic Studies* Symposium 42 (1974): 1–149.

13. O.C. Herfindahl and A.V. Kneese, *Economic Theory of Natural Resources* (Columbus, Ohio: Charles Merrill, 1974).

14. G. Heal, "The Influence of Interest Rates on Resource Prices," Working Paper (New Haven, Conn.: Yale University, Cowles Foundation, 1976).

15. Ibid.

16. J.E. Stiglitz, "Monopoly and the Rate of Extraction of Exhaustible Resources," *American Economics Review,* 66 (1976): 655–61.

17. D. Brodsky and G. Sampson, "Social Shadow Process, Externalities, and Depletion of Natural Resources Exploited by Developing Countries," Working Paper (Geneva: UNCTAD, 1976).

18. This particular definition of mineral lag structure is due to J. Burrows, *Tungsten: An Industry Analysis* (Lexington, Mass.: Lexington Books, D.C. Heath, 1971).

19. Price elasticity refers to the percentage change in quantity (supply or demand) caused by a relative percentage change in price. Values between 0 and 1 imply inelastic response, and values above 1 indicate elastic response.

20. This distinction derives from R. Adams, "Secondary Supply," in W.A. Vogely (ed.), *Economics of The Mineral Industries* (New York: American Institute of Mining Metallurgical and Petroleum Engineers, 1976).

21. See J. Burrows, "Econometric Models of Mineral Markets for Intermediate and Long Term Forecasting," Conference on Commodity Markets, Models, and Policies in Latin America, 1977.

22. H.J. Barnett and C. Morse, *1Scarcity and Growth: The Economics of Natural Resource Availability* (Baltimore: Johns Hopkins University Press, 1963).

23. See "Meeting America's Resource Needs: Problems and Policies," Report of the House Committee on Banking and Currency (Washington, D.C.: House of Representatives, 93rd Congress, 2nd Session, 1974).

24. A detailed description of the mineral investment cycle can be found in J. Tilton, *The Future of Nonfuel Minerals* (Washington, D.C.: The Brookings Institution, 1977).

25. Cameron recently examined a number of approaches explaining mineral investment, including economic theories, financial theories, and managerial theories. He found it most useful to concentrate on the role of government as well as on oligopoly pricing together with resource conditions of declining quality, but increasing uniformity and abundance. J.I. Cameron, "Investment Theory and Mineral Investment Practice," presented at the Meetings of the Council of Economics of the AIME, Washington, D.C., 1977.

26. Herfindahl and Kneese, *Economic Theory,* pp. 133–34.

27. Herfindahl determined that these would be equivalent in the long run and proceeded to use prices as an indicator of long-run costs in the copper industry. Bosworth has been able to make a distinction by removing Herfindahl's assumption regarding the difficulty of estimating capital costs. B. Bosworth, "Capacity Creation in Basic-Materials Industries," *Brookings Papers on Economic Activity,* 2 (1976): 297–341; and O.C. Herfindahl, *Copper Costs and Prices: 1870–1957* (Baltimore: Johns Hopkins University Press, 1959).

28. J.R. Behrman, "International Commodity Market Structures and the Theory Underlying International Commodity Models," in F. Adams and J. Behrman (eds.), *Econometric Modelling of World Commodity Policy* (Lexington, Mass.: Lexington Books, D.C. Heath, 1978).

29. Bain, *Industrial Organization;* Behrman, *Commodity Market Structures;* E.S. Mason, *Economy Concentration and the Monopoly Problem* (Cambridge: Harvard University Press, 1957); and F.M. Scherer, *Industrial Market Structure.*

30. Behrman, *Commodity Market Structures.*

31. Bain, *Industrial Organization,* p. 156.

32. Behrman, *Commodity Market Structures.*

33. See Scherer, *Industrial Market Structure.*

34. P.L. Eckbo, "OPEC and the Experience of Previous International Commodity Cartels," Working Paper No. 75-008WP (Cambridge: MIT Energy Laboratory, 1975); and Charles River Associates, "Impact of Supply Restrictions on the Nonferrous Metals Markets: Summary Volume" (Washington, D.C.: ETIP, National Bureau of Standards, 1976).

35. "Meeting America's Resource Needs," p. 89.

36. Scherer, *Industrial Market Structure.*

37. Eckbo, "OPEC."

38. Charles River Associates, *Impact of Supply Restrictions.*

39. See K.L. Wang, "Interindustry Analysis," in Vogely, *Economics of the Mineral Industries,* pp. 322–36.

40. Behrman, *Commodity Market Structures.*

41. "Meeting America's Resource Needs," p. 8.

42. Scherer, *Industrial Market Structure,* p. 240.

43. Behrman, *Commodity Market Structures,* p. 35.

44. J.K. Galbraith, *American Capitalism: The Concept of Countervailing Power* (Boston: Houghton Mifflin, 1956).

45. Bain, *Industrial Organization,* pp. 32–33.

46. Ibid.

47. This definition is due to Bain, *Industrial Organization,* p. 33.

48. Ibid.

49. One possible source describing the development of multinational influence is N. Girvan, "Multinational Economies," *Social and Economics Studies,* 19 (1970): 490–526.

50. The present purpose is only to estimate several indexes for comparative purposes and not to evaluate their relative qualities. The latter can be found in F. Pryor, "International Comparison of Concentration Ratios," *Review of Economics and Statistics* 54 (May 1972): 130–40.

51. This dependence is more completely outlined in "Social Valuation and Pricing of Natural Resources," Research Memorandum No. 58, Research Division (Geneva: UNCTAD, 1976).

52. See *Mineral Development in the Eighties: Prospects and Problems,* B.N.A.C. Report No. 19 (Washington, D.C.: British-North American Committee, 1976).

53. Ibid., p. 14.

54. Several of the criteria selected, including size of fixed investment, are those suggested by Moran as being most important in describing the bargaining relationship between multinational firms and host governments. T.H. Moran, "Multinational Corporations and the Changing Structure of Industries that Supply Industrial Commodities," Working Paper, Washington, D.C.: Institute for Advanced International Studies, 1977.

55. UNCTAD, "Processing of Primary Products in Developing Countries: Problems and Prospects" (Geneva: UNCTAD/MD/79, 1976).

56. D. Smith and L. Wells, *Negotiating Third World Mineral Agreements* (Cambridge, Mass.: Ballinger Publishing Co., 1976).

57. The suggestion of this criterion is due to Radetzki, "Market Structure and Bargaining Power." Supportive data can be found in UNCTAD, "Proportion between Export Prices of Selected Commodities Exported by Developing Countries" (Geneva: UNCTAD TD/184/Suppl. 3, 1976).

58. These criteria relate to the work of Moran, "Multinational Corporations."

59. R. Vernon, "Long Run Trends in Concession Contracts," *Proceedings of the American Society of International Law,* 1967, and *Sovereignty at Bay: The Multinational Spread of U.S. Enterprises* (New York: Basic Books, 1971).

60. G.F. Erb, "Hard Rocks, Hard Choices: Trade and Investment Policies for Non-fuel Minerals," Working Paper (Washington, D.C.: Overseas Development Council, 1975).

61. Moran, "Multinational Corporations," pp. 3–5.

62. See S. Lall, "Transfer-Pricing by Multinational Manufacturing Firms," *Oxford Bulletin of Economics and Statistics,* 35 (1973), 173–93.

63. Bosson and Varon, *Mining Industry,* p. 107.

64. For example, see the *Metal Bulletin Handbook, 1976* (London: Metal Bulletin, 1976).

65. O.C. Herfindahl, "The Long Run Cost of Minerals," in *Three Studies in Mineral Economics* (Washington, D.C.: Resources for the Future, 1961).

66. See also U.S. Congress, House Committee on Banking and Currency, *Meeting America's Resource Needs: Problems and Policies,* Report of the Ad Hoc Committee on the Domestic and International Monetary Effects of Energy and Other Natural Resource Pricing, 93rd Congress, 2d Session, November, 1974, chap. 3.

67. Barnett and Morse, *Scarcity and Growth.*

68. However, Smith cautions us in the use of price indexes to reflect trends in costs and scarcity without detailed analysis of the specific commodity markets. This advice stems from his findings that the trend relationships for the relative price series appear unstable. See V. Kerry Smith, "Natural Resource

Scarcity: A Statistical Analysis," Working Paper (Washington, D.C.: Resources for the Future, 1977).

69. U.S. Congress, *Meeting America's Resource Needs.*

70. Bosworth, "Basic Materials Industries."

71. This explanation has been suggested in F.M. Scherer, *Industrial Pricing* (Chicago: Rand McNally, 1970).

72. Analysis of the factors responsible for these increases can be found in R.N. Cooper and R.Z. Lawrence, "The 1972–75 Commodity Boom," *Brookings Papers on Economic Activity,* 1976; W.C. Labys and H.C. Thomas, "Speculation, Hedging and Commodity Price Behavior: An International Comparison," *Applied Economics* 7 (1975): 287–301; and J. Popkin, "Price Behavior in Primary Manufacturing Industries, 1958–74," paper presented at the Annual Meetings of the Eastern Economic Association, 1976.

73. To summarize alternative approaches for explaining resource price formation in brief is indeed difficult, and the interested reader should read the four chapters devoted to this in Scherer, *Industrial Pricing.*

74. Scherer, *Industrial Pricing.*

75. M.J. Peck, *Competition in the Aluminum Industry* (Cambridge: Harvard University Press, 1961), pp. 41–45.

76. Scherer, *Industrial Pricing,* p. 39.

77. See D.A. Worcester, "Why Dominant Firms Decline," *Journal of Political Economy* 65 (1957): 338–47.

78. These and a variety of other explanations are offered by Scherer, *Industrial Pricing,* chap. 4.

79. See S. Lall, "Transfer Pricing."

80. A good discussion of the meaning appears in H.C. Verlage, *Transfer Pricing for Multinational Enterprises* (Rotterdam: Rotterdam University Press, 1975).

81. "Transfer Pricing, The Multinational Enterprise and Economic Development," MR 153 (Ottawa: Canadian Department of Energy, Mines and Resources, 1976).

82. Scherer, *Industrial Pricing,* pp. 117–21.

3

Copper

Market Conditions

The copper industry is characterized by the sequential nature of its primary processing.[1] As reflected in figure 3–1, the very low metallic content (roughly 0.3–5.0 percent) of copper requires that it receive beneficiation before entering trade as concentrates (11–40 percent metal). These concentrates provide the main input into the copper smelting process, which produces blister (over 95 percent metal). The latter contains impurities which must be removed for most applications through a refining process which results in ingots or cathodes (over 99.9 percent metal).

As shown in table 3–1, most of the trade takes place at the refined stage. In 1975 concentrates accounted for 23 percent of all copper trade (Cu content), blister for 14 percent, and refined for 63 percent. A further stage of processing occurs at the semifabricating establishments which transform refined copper into shapes such as sheets, strips, rods, tubes, wires, rails, and so on. The parallel secondary or scrap industry accounts for about 14 percent of total refined copper production in the industrialized countries.

The structure of the market described in figure 3–1 indicates that the industry consists of independent as well as integrated mining firms, smelters, and refiners. Refined copper prices are shown to play a key role in the world market including semimanufactured goods. That is, ore prices in different countries are tightly linked to the refined metal quotation, the difference consisting of smelting and refining charges to convert concentrates or blister into refined copper metal. The prices of semimanufactured and some manufactured goods are shown to be linked to the input or refined copper price plus fabrication costs and a profit margin. Other important institutions making up the market are the dealers who operate through the two major terminal markets, the London Metal Exchange (LME) and the Commodity Exchange, New York (COMEX). Consumers of copper products shown on the right are the electrical, construction, machinery, transportation, and consumer goods industries.

Production

Copper is a much rarer material in the earth's crust than both aluminum and iron, accounting for the exploitation of much lower copper ore grades than for

75

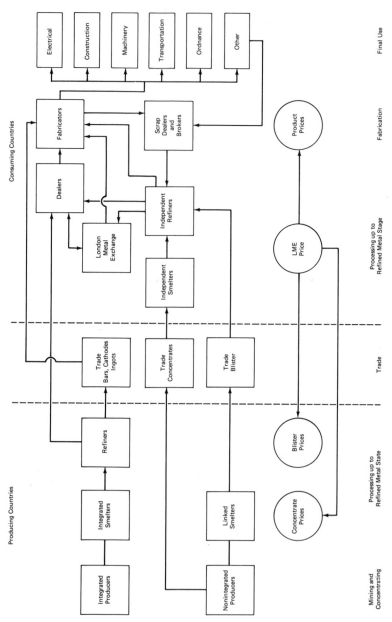

Figure 3–1. Market and Price Structure for Copper

Table 3–1
World Balance Sheet for Copper
(thousands of metric tons)

Commodity Flow	1955	1960	1965	1966	1967	1968	1969	1970	1971	1972	1973	1974	1975	1976
Mine production (Cu content)	3,109	4,239	5,060	5,314	5,080	5,482	5,942	6,386	6,462	7,041	7,509	7,653	7,296	7,880
Refined production	3,836	4,991	6,058	6,322	6,000	6,659	7,200	7,578	7,398	8,086	8,524	8,899	8,369	8,831
Ore imports (Cu content)	173	249	232	284	318	420	453	515	613	875	1,091	1,193	1,040	1,175
Blister imports (Cu content)	563	768	727	672	673	756	773	783	737	747	756	797	680	619
Refined imports	1,189	1,975	2,155	2,232	2,349	2,522	2,427	2,528	2,537	2,744	2,990	3,078	2,640	3,247
Ore exports (Cu content)	197	283	308	330	409	510	486	575	691	894	1,129	1,210	1,062	1,242
Blister exports (Cu content)	555	796	827	741	767	810	730	748	739	734	759	798	633	759
Refined exports	1,149	1,889	2,057	2,196	2,323	2,499	2,431	2,577	2,571	2,748	2,862	3,167	2,849	3,219
Refined consumption	3,777	4,769	6,190	6,438	6,189	6,519	7,142	7,310	7,320	7,952	8,766	8,316	7,471	8,509
LME refined price (U.S. cents per pound)	43.93	30.74	58.56	69.35	51.14	56.31	66.52	64.19	49.06	48.56	80.78	93.36	56.00	63.56

Source: UNCTAD, "Copper statistics" (Geneva: TD/B/IPC/Copper/AC/L.5, 1977).

either of these metals. Currently, they vary between a maximum of around 5 percent metal content in some of the African mines to as low as 0.4 percent in countries like Canada and Sweden. The spread between the highest and lowest (about 1:12) is far greater than in bauxite and iron ore and gives rise to substantial variations in production costs. An offsetting cost factor stems from the fact that copper processing is usually undertaken in the country of extraction, transport costs thus accounting for a much smaller share of total delivered copper costs. Therefore, the geologic quality of a deposit becomes more important, but its geographic location somewhat less consequential in the case of copper as compared with bauxite and iron ore.

World copper resources are widely based, located on land, in the seabed, or in the existing stock of products. Our principal concern is with the land reserves of which some 451.0 million tons (Cu content) were estimated as of 1976. Following a recent survey of copper reserves, this total can be divided as follows: 67 percent in producing mines, 13 percent in projects presently under construction, and 20 percent in reserves which appear to be exploitable under present economic and technological conditions.[2] The geographic distribution of these reserves is given in table 3–2. North and Central America are shown to contain the greater proportions of deposits, some 30.1 percent. Together with South America, total reserves amount to some 56.4 percent. Among country groups holding these reserves, the developing countries contain some 52.9 percent.

Table 3–2
Estimated World Copper Reserves, 1976

Country	Quantity (hundreds of metric tons)	Percent of World Total
United States	84,400	18.4
Chile	84,400	18.4
U.S.S.R.	36,300	7.9
Canada	31,200	6.8
Peru	29,800	6.5
Zambia	25,600	5.6
Zaire	25,600	5.6
Philippines	16,800	3.7
Poland	12,700	2.8
Papua New Guinea	8,900	1.9
Australia	7,600	1.7
South Africa	2,700	0.5
Rest of world	90,000	19.6
Total world	459,000	100.0

Source: *Commodity Data Summaries, 1977* (Washington, D.C.: U.S. Department of the Interior, 1977).

Concerning the adequacy of these reserves, if the 451 million tons are exhausted at the current annual production level, they will last some fifty-nine years from 1976. If production is permitted to grow at a rate of 4 percent per year, then this total would be exhausted in thirty-one years. Against such levels of exhaustion, one should compare the rates of exploration. During the last fifteen years, reserves have increased by almost 300 percent. Thus, the above static and dynamic measures of reserve life are higher than they were in 1960. The reserve position might be improved even further once more accurate estimates of seabed reserves and reserves of scrap in products become available.

The investment costs of bringing copper mines into production are relatively high. They vary with circumstances such as richness of the ore, size of the ore body, geographic location, and the amount of infrastructural investments required to get the operation going. Recent estimates provided by Takeuchi, Thiebach, and Hilmy give the capital cost per metric ton of capacity as follows in 1975 dollars.[3]

Copper mining	$3,000–$5,000 per ton
Copper smelting-refining	$2,000 per ton

Mikesell in updating these figures suggests a cost of $4,600 per ton for mining and concentrating facilities and $3,200 per ton for expanding existing mines in 1977 dollars.[4] Assuming the ratio of new mine development to mine expansion to be 3 to 2, the average investment costs for mining and smelting come to $4,040 per ton. To this could be added $2,000 per ton for smelting capacity and $460 per ton for refinery capacity. None of these figures, however, include such infrastructure items as transportation facilities, energy networks, or new community development.

In recent years there has been considerable variation in the size distribution of copper mines. At the lower end, there are a great number of copper ventures which were to begin production in 1974–1976 that have annual capacity levels between 20,000 and 50,000 tons of copper content per year.[5] The investment requirements in such ventures would vary from some $50 million at the lower capacity end for a unit producing concentrates, to some $200 million at the 50,000-ton capacity level for a plant supplying refined metal. At the higher end, there are considerable economies of scale which are beneficial in mining low-grade copper deposits. Ventures of this kind become most economical when operated at capacity rates of between 100,000 and 200,000 tons of copper content. Investments in such ventures easily reach and surpass the $500-million level. Examples are that of the Southern Peru Copper Company in Evajone with 150,000 tons of capacity and an investment cost of $725 million and the SMTF in Zaire with 130,000 tons of capacity and a cost of $800 million.[6] Over time, this kind of venture is becoming increasingly important in overall additions to world copper supply.

At present, the amounts of capital required to open up small or medium-sized copper mines are hardly large enough to constitute a serious deterrent to entry in the industry. But with the growing importance of new copper ventures of large size, the ability to generate the capital investments required will undoubtedly become increasingly restrictive to new entrants.

One important feature of copper investment costs appears to be the rapid rate at which they are increasing. For example, the costs of a new mining complex in the western United States has risen from $3,500 per annual ton of new capacity in 1970 to more than $6,500 in 1976.[7] Between 1973 and 1975, the rate of increase was particularly sharp. The increase in average annual capital investment required for U.S. copper mining and metals projects was about 15 percent for a facility of about 100,000 tons.[8] Investment cost behavior in other countries during this period would depend on their respective rates of inflation.

Concerning mining and processing technology, the sequential production process suggested above is based on the traditional primary copper process. Among possibilities for changes in this process, one is the extraction of copper from nodules in the seabed. Another possibility is a process which involves the leaching of oxide ores.[9] About 15 percent of all primary copper produced is based on this method. There are also two new variants of hydrometallurgical technology employing leaching, solvent extraction, and electromining which could be important. These include processes that permit copper cathodes to be produced by leaching concentrates from sulphide ores and in situ leaching or solution mining. Although either method could be cost saving, the first has the favorable quality of lower air pollution levels. However, none of these methods is likely to replace the traditional copper process; the latter still provides the basis for most copper production.

The location of the world's mining, smelting, and refining capacity for 1973 is given in table 3–3. North America is shown to be the region with the greatest capacity at all three stages of production, some 35.7 percent, 31.9 percent, and 37.2 percent respectively. Mine capacity in the other regions generally follows the given distribution of reserves. The production of concentrates at 7.3 million metric tons has expanded substantially from the 3.1 million tons reported for 1955 but not as greatly from the 6.4 million tons given for 1970.

Also evident from table 3–3 is that excess capacity exists in mining as well as in smelting and refining. Changes in smelting and refining capacity can be adjusted more quickly than that of mining because of the shorter construction period required. Recent estimates of capacity changes across these stages indicate some differences in geographic distribution.[10] It is unlikely in the near and mid term that much change will take place in the location of mining

Table 3-3
World Copper Capacity and Production, 1973
(thousand short tons)

Area	Mine		Smelter		Refinery[a]	
	Capacity	Production	Capacity	Production	Capacity	Production
North America						
Canada	1,000	899	640	546	610	548
United States	2,000	1,718	2,000[b]	1,744[c]	2,910	1,868
Other	100	97	100	81	80	58
Total	3,100	2,714	2,740	2,371	3,600	2,474
South America						
Chile	900	819	900	650	660	457
Peru	270	241	220	148	50	43
Other	30	18	10	5	40	32
Total	1,200	1,078	1,130	803	750	532
Europe						
U.S.S.R.	800	772	830	772	800	733
Other	640	611	1,070	991	1,800	1,748
Total	1,440	1,383	1,900	1,763	2,600	2,481
Africa						
Zaire	550	538	530	508	270	246
Zambia	870	779	840	759	770	704
Other	360	318	290	262	140	134
Total	1,780	1,635	1,660	1,529	1,180	1,084
Asia						
Total	680	604	1,300	1,287	1,340	1,244
Oceania						
Total	490	443	220	179	200	159

Source: *Mineral Facts and Problems, 1975* (Washington, D.C.: U.S. Department of the Interior, 1976).

[a]Capacity for many plants includes capacity for processing scrap; tabulated production, to the extent possible, is for primary material only.

[b]Includes equivalent capacity for direct-electrowinning plants bypassing smelting operations.

[c]Primary materials only.

capacity, the total estimated increase amounting to some 2.5 million tons between 1977 and 1990. However, some change in distribution is expected in smelter capacity, with the total estimated increase amounting to some 1.8 million tons between 1977 and 1981. About 20 percent of these additions will take place in North America, and 15–30 percent each will occur in Asia, Oceania, South America, Africa, and Europe. Regarding announced additions in world refining capacity, about 25 percent is forecast in North and Central America, 30 percent in Africa, and 20 percent in South America. It is expected that the major consuming countries will experience a reduction in their share of the world's refining capacity, with the exception of the United States.

Regarding production costs for copper, they have been shown to vary significantly among different areas and operating units. Radetzki has estimated the 1974 net operating cost for delivered refined copper in non-Socialist countries to be between $480 per ton and $1,000 per ton, with the median about $680.[11] The same study assumes that capital costs of about $880 per ton are needed to cover depreciation and to provide the return on capital required to induce new investments. On these assumptions, total production costs would be above $1,540 per ton in more than half the copper industry in the non-Socialist world.

As shown in table 3–4, differences in production costs between regions are not substantial. Of course there are some producers in each continent with extremely high or low operating costs. These costs, which do not take capital or financial changes into account, show the United States to be the highest cost producer. Like investment costs, production costs have risen sharply since 1970. Africa appears to have suffered the most, with its costs now as high as the United States. Latin America and Asia/Australasia still remain as the lowest cost producers, with the others in between.

Table 3–4
Average Net Operating Costs for Primary Copper Production[a]
(U.S. cents per pound)

Area	1970	1975
Latin America	29.8	37.5
United States	32.3	48.5
Canada	30.4	44.5
Africa	28.0	48.5
Asia/Australasia	30.2	34.0
Europe	30.3	39.0
Total nonsocialist world	30.3	44.5

Source: Commodity Research Unit, *Copper Studies* (London: Commodity Research Unit, August 5, 1977).

Copper production has two other characteristics of importance. First, copper is often mined jointly with other nonferrous metals, principally nickel, zinc, lead, and silver. To a lesser extent, copper production also yields gold, molybdenum, selenium, tellurium, and platinum. Thus, the determination of the costs of producing copper can involve consideration of joint production processes. Second, a considerable secondary industry exists involving new, or process, scrap and old, or obsolete, scrap. The supply of scrap forthcoming in any particular year depends on the structure of the copper processing industry, the degree of industrialization, scrap recovery costs, and the price of refined copper.

Consumption

The world's consumption of copper has not increased appreciably since 1970. As shown in table 3–5, total consumption reached 7.3 million metric tons in 1970, peaked at 8.7 million tons in 1973, and subsequently decreased. Consumption in most of the countries shown has stagnated at the 1970 level or has declined. Japan and the U.S.S.R. have been the exceptions. The United States still remains the largest consumer with a consumption share of 21 percent in 1976. The shares of Japan and the U.S.S.R. are 15 and 12 percent, respectively.

The demand for copper is a derived demand, based chiefly on its use in the electrical and the construction industries. Electrical applications derive from copper possessing the best electrical and thermal conductivities among metals, except for silver and gold. The only metal approaching it in this quality is aluminum, the latter now substituting for copper in many uses. Construction applications stem from its resistance to corrosion as well as its high thermal conductivity. Here, as in other nonelectrical applications, copper is used in alloyed form which contains at least 40 percent of the metal. Some major copper alloys include brasses (5–45 percent zinc), bronzes (2–20 percent tin), copper-aluminum (4–15 percent aluminum), and copper-nickel (5–30 percent nickel).[12] Copper not used for electrical wire is employed in brass mills which produce copper alloy sheet, copper alloy rod and mechanical wire, and plumbing and commercial tubing.

Although aluminum is the major substitute for copper, other materials also compete, namely stainless steel, polyvinyl chloride (PVC), titanium, sodium, lead, cadmium, and niobium. These materials have been substituted either because of their relatively more stable and lower prices or their superior physical properties. Concerning price stability, the supply elasticity for copper has been shown to be relatively low (0.06), whereas the demand elasticity is relatively high (−0.36 to −2.50). As a consequence, fluctuations in world economic activity have led to fluctuations in demand and subsequently to

Table 3-5
World Consumption of Refined Copper[a]
(thousand metric tons)

Country	1955	1960	1965	1970	1971	1972	1973	1974	1975	1976
United States	1,363	1,225	1,844	1,860	1,833	2,030	2,221	1,995	1,396	1,782
Federal Republic of Germany	354	516	536	698	630	672	727	731	635	744
United Kingdom	504	560	650	554	517	535	541	497	450	458
U.S.S.R.	395	652	783	950	985	1,030	1,100	1,100	1,200	1,250
Japan	105	304	428	821	806	451	1,201	881	821	1,050
France	194	237	287	331	344	390	408	414	364	367
Canada	126	107	209	229	220	223	248	270	196	206
Australia	52	72	102	114	116	112	133	122	125	112
Belgium, Luxembourg	69	92	121	145	147	153	164	178	174	228
Italy	114	185	192	274	270	283	295	308	290	322
Rest of world	496	819	1,041	1,346	1,464	1,586	1,744	1,837	1,843	1,918
World total	3,777	4,769	6,193	7,322	7,332	7,965	8,782	8,333	7,494	8,437

Source: Metal Statistics (Frankfurt: Metallgesellshaft AG, 1955–1976).

[a]Primary and secondary consumption.

fluctuations in copper prices. The aluminum industry, in contrast, has a much tighter vertical integration, and supply and demand conditions have not caused prices to fluctuate as frequently or widely. In addition, aluminum production costs are also lower. This is reflected in the copper to aluminum price ratio, which has varied from 1.23:1 in 1960 to 2.0:1 in 1970 and 1.60:1 in 1975. Concerning the physical properties of copper and aluminum, adjustments in substitution cannot take place easily, and longer-term technological adjustments are often necessary.

To obtain a better understanding of copper consumption, it is necessary to examine the pattern of end uses given in table 3–5. With the exception of the U.S.S.R., the electrical industry is shown to be the most important consumer. Here copper faces its major competition from aluminum in high- and medium-voltage distribution lines as well as in service-entry cables. Thicker insulation requirements make aluminum less advantageous for insulated cable use. Both materials, however, may be affected by the growing interest in optical fibers for transmission purposes.

The second major use for copper is in the construction industry, mainly in tubes, faucets, and building wire. Plastic tubing has made gains as a substitute, but rising petroleum costs may make it relatively more expensive. Concerning other uses, copper centenary cables are necessary for the electrification of railways. It is also used in industrial equipment manufacture such as heat exchangers, machine tools, and tubing.

Trade

World exports of primary copper constitute somewhat less than half of world production. The total value of refined exports has varied considerably from $2.6 billion in 1971 to $4.5 billion in 1973 and $3.6 billion in 1975. An overwhelming proportion of the global copper exports ends up in western Europe and Japan. In 1973 these two areas accounted for 61 percent and 9 percent of total exports. Japanese supplies originate primarily in Canada, the Philippines, Papua New Guinea, and Zambia. The western European market, on the other hand, takes its supplies from a diversified group of producing countries located on different continents. The major exporters to the United States are Canada and Peru.

In view of its own large copper production, the United States is only marginally dependent on copper imports. Eastern Europe is also highly self-sufficient in copper. Western Europe and Japan, in contrast, satisfy between 80 and 90 percent of their primary copper requirements through purchases abroad.[13]

International copper trade has been transacted according to traditional and well-established patterns, with relatively little change over the years. The ordinary form for copper exports is an annual contract, specifying delivery times, payment periods, and other conditions. Where the transaction relates to refined metal, the contract ordinarily stipulates that the CIF price should be equal to the cash London Metal Exchange (LME) quotation. In a majority of cases, the buyer is given the option of selecting LME prices for a few days within a two-month period, to determine the value of each shipment. Because of this pricing facility, buyers ordinarily succeed in obtaining their contracted copper at prices a few percentage points below the LME averages.

Trade in unrefined copper by and large is transacted following similar rules. However, two important differences should be mentioned. First, most contracts for concentrate and blister exports, at least until recently, were of a much longer duration, frequently stretching over periods of ten years or more. Second, though pricing is based on the LME, deductions are made for smelting and refining costs according to complicated formulas, with premiums for recoverable precious metal content. In addition, escalation clauses safeguard the buyer against inflation-induced cost increases in metal processing.

Market Structure

The structure of the world copper market can be characterized as follows:

1. Most exchange takes place at the refined copper stage of processing.
2. The concentration of refined copper producers is greater than that of consumers, but this concentration has been decreasing over time.
3. Although most exchange is in the form of contracts between refiners and semifabricators, transactions in the LME play a central role in price formation.
4. Governments have sought to increase their control over copper production. This is reflected to some extent through the organization of the Intergovernmental Council of Copper Exporting Countries (CIPEC) and the concerted action of governments within that body.

Organization and Concentration

Recent attempts to achieve an integrated production capability have resulted in the construction of smelting and refining facilities proximate to copper deposits. This locational aspect is reflected in the chagnes in geographic investment patterns discussed earlier. In table 3–1, refined copper exports are shown to be larger than concentrate or blister exports. As has been indicated, prices of concentrate, blister, and scrap are based on and closely related to prices of refined copper. Thus, this stage is the most important for examining the market structure for copper.

The production side of the refined copper market can be termed a homogeneous oligopoly with a large competitive fringe. Table 3–6 implies reasonably high concentration with the eight largest firms accounting for 50 percent of total mining capacity and for 44 percent of refining capacity.[14]

On the demand side, primary copper is absorbed mainly by the fabricating industry, which transforms the refined copper bars or cathodes into various shapes and in some cases processes them further. Since capacities in the fabricating industry are not as well documented as capacities of copper mines, only a rough estimate of concentration in demand is possible in table 3–6. Even though the large U.S. fabricators are missing, it does appear that concentration in the mining or producing sector is greater than in the fabricating sector. None of the fabricators possess a capacity approaching the largest units at the mining stage, even when the domestically oriented U.S.S.R. copper mining industry is excluded. The nine fabricating companies listed account for no more than 2.6 million tons of copper processing capacity. The nine leading mining concerns have a production capacity which is twice as large. Total world capacity for copper fabrication is only some 15 percent higher than that of copper mines. This increment is due primarily to the fact that fabricators have to accommodate recycled copper supplies.

This uneven concentration between producers and consumers is not a new phenomenon; it is now less than it once was. For example, the big three copper producers in the United States were able to hold their share of domestic mine production above 80 percent from 1947 through the Korean War.[15] This market condition was one of the factors which led to the Federal Trade Commission report on monopoly in the copper industry. Since then, the share of the big three has fallen, first to 69 percent in 1960 and then to 61 percent in 1970.

This trend is reflected in table 3–6 which features the seven largest international firms existing at the end of the Second World War: the Anglo-American and Roan-American metal groups in Northern Rhodesia (Zambia), the Union Miniere group in the Congo (Zaire), International Nickel of Canada, and Anaconda, Kennecott, and Phelps Dodge of the United States. Whereas their share of world production was 70 percent in 1948, it fell to 60 percent by 1960 and to 54 percent in 1969.[16] If more recent firms are added to this group such as American Smelting and Refining, the Newmont Mining majority holdings, and the various Japanese domestic producers, this trend is still not reversed.

Moran would attribute this trend toward a more diluted concentration to five factors in particular.[17] First, the continual discovery of substantial new sources of copper has reduced barriers to entry for new firms. Second,

Table 3-6
Concentration in the World Copper Industry, 1975

	Copper Mining Capacity			Smelting Capacity		
Firm	Shares (%)	Capacity (000 LT)		Firm	Shares (%)	Capacity (000 MT)
Largest four						
USSR (State Co.)	11.0	1,120.0		International Nickel Co. (Can.)	20.2	5,079.2
Zambia (Roan Con. Ltd.) and Nchanga	10.0	950.0		Kennecott Copper Co. (U.S.)	8.0	2,013.5
Chile (State Co.)	8.0	760.0		Asarco Inc. (U.S.)	7.7	1,937.4
Zaire (Gecamines)	5.0	510.0		Phelps Dodge Co. (U.S.)	6.7	1,677.9
Subtotal	34.0	3,340.0		Subtotal	42.6	10,708.0
Indexes (4)						
CR = 0.340				CR = 0.426		
HH = 0.031				HH = 0.058		
HG = 0.176				HG = 0.240		
GR = 0.196				GR = 0.319		
Lesser four						
RTZ (Can., S. Afri.)	4.4	430.0		Nchanga Con. (Zam.)	4.8	1,200.0
Asarco (U.S.)	4.3	420.0		Noranda Mines Ltd. (Can.)	4.3	1,088.4
Kennecott Copper (U.S.)	4.3	420.0		Magma Copper Co. (U.S.)	2.9	725.6
Newmont (Canada)	3.4	340.0		Corporacion del Cobre	2.8	715.0
Subtotal	50.4	4,950.0		Subtotal	57.4	14,437.0
Indexes (8)						
CR = 0.504				CR = 0.574		
HH = 0.038				HH = 0.063		
HG = 0.194				HG = 0.252		
GR = 0.265				GR = 0.397		
All other	49.6	4,850.0		All other	42.6	10,686.3
Total	100.0	9,800.0		Total	100.0	25,123.3

	Refinery Capacity			Copper Fabricating Capacity		
Firm	Shares (%)	Capacity (000 MT)	Firm	Firm	Shares (%)	Capacity (000 ton)
Largest four						
Asarco Inc. (U.S.)	7.8	674.0		BICC (Aus., Can., India, N.Z., Pak., Por.)	19.4	500.0
Metallurgie Hoboken Overalp (Neth.)	7.3	630.0		Anacondia (Braz., Can., Mex.)	14.6	380.0
Kennecott Copper Corporation (U.S.)	5.9	512.4		Drawn Metal Tube Co. (U.S.)	12.2	315.0
Phelps Dodge Ref. (U.S.)	5.6	487.0		Sumitomo (Japan)	11.6	295.0
Subtotal	26.6	2,303.5				
Indexes (4)						
CR = 0.266						
HH = 0.018						
HG = 0.134						
GR = 0.100						
Lesser four						
Canadian Copper Refinery (Can.)	5.0	435.4		Furukawa (Japan)	9.2	240.0
Nchanga Co. Ltd. (Zambia)	4.9	430.0		Societe Generale (Bel., France)	9.2	240.0
Corporacion del Cobre (Chuquicamata, Chile)	4.3	375.0		Delta Metal (U.K.)	8.4	220.0
Generale des Carreres (Zaire)	3.4	290.0		IMI (U.K.)	7.7	200.0
				Pirelli	7.7	200.0
	44.2	3,833.8		Total for 9 units	100.0	2,590.0
Indexes (8)						
CR = 0.442						
HH = 0.026						
HG = 0.161						
GR = 0.160						
All other	55.8	4,822.7				
Total	100.0	8,656.6				

Source: *Metal Bulletin*, 1974, edited by Ruby Packard, London. American Bureau of Metal Statistics, 1975, *Non Ferrous Metal Data*, New York.

government subsidies such as those found in the United States have helped to finance and launch new companies. Third, smaller existing companies have integrated backward and forward from mining through fabricating so as to grow in size. Fourth, fabricators and consumers of copper have been willing to finance new entrants to the market. Fifth, natural resource firms not previously associated with copper mining have formed or bought copper mining companies. Thus, the copper industry can be seen as becoming increasing competitive.

Another major characteristic of the market is the dual market system which accommodates refined copper exchange by contracts and on the spot. Most trade is in the form of contracts between refineries and semifabricators. This normally involves the use of one-year contracts which specify monthly delivery limits within which the buyer may choose a specific quantity each month.[18] Longer-term contracts also exist, but these are arrangements made to assure supplies of copper ores and concentrates as well as to facilitate the financing of copper mines.

A minor proportion of the trade, however, takes place on the two terminal markets, the London Metal Exchange and the Commodity Exchange of New York (COMEX). In addition to differences in technical contractural relations these markets vary in structure, the former being a principal's market and the latter more of a clearing house.[19] In terms of volume of trading, COMEX is the less important of the two. It is also directed more to domestic than international transactions. However, the opportunity for arbitrage between the two markets causes the prices to be highly related.

The most important feature of the LME is that it is a truly marginal market for refined copper. Physical turnover on that market is commonly no higher than 5–10 percent of world trade in copper. A major share of the physical transactions is for secondary refined copper from numerous smaller suppliers, but buyers and sellers of primary metal also use the exchange to dispose of surpluses or to satisfy marginal deficits. Although the small quantities traded on the market provides an equilibrating mechanism between world supply and demand, such trading appears to add to price instability, at least in the very short run. One or a few somewhat larger buy or sell orders will have a heavy impact on the market balance and will strongly influence short-run prices. Such gyrations increase the potential advantage that buyers of contracted copper can derive from the pricing facility.

Nationalization

In recent years some copper producers in developing countries have attempted to increase their control over copper production by integrating forward to the refining stage. The related governments also have moved to increase national participation in firms, if not outright nationalization. These efforts began to accelerate in the late 1960s. At that time, the four largest privately owned copper firms controlled about 50 percent of the mine production of the market economies.[20] By 1974, this control was reduced to less than 20 percent. At the same time, the share of mine capacity held by majority or wholly state-owned mining establishments increased from near zero to about 35 percent. This increase occurred almost exclusively in the producing developing countries.

In terms of a real control transfer, this process could proceed at a relatively fast pace in a country like Chile. In Zaire and Zambia, on the other hand, the process has been slower in view of the lack of national personnel qualified to handle complex administrative and technical tasks at the time of formal nationalization. The output controlled by companies like Anaconda, Kennecott, Union Miniere or Anglo-American has been correspondingly reduced. In addition, Poland has emerged recently as a substantial copper producer, thus increasing the government-controlled share of world copper capacity to over 35 percent. The capacity share effectively controlled by governments is likely to increase in future years, as the national administrations in producing countries like Peru and Papua New Guinea, or in potential producing nations like Iran, establish themselves more firmly in the copper sector.

Producer Coordination

The machinery for policy coordination by governments of certain copper-producing countries exists in the Intergovernmental Council of Copper Exporting Countries. The council was established in 1967 by Chile, Peru, Zaire, and Zambia. In 1975, Indonesia joined as a full member, and Australia and Papua New Guinea joined as associate members. Mauretania was added to the list in 1976. In late 1974, the membership of CIPEC undertook its first action to influence copper prices. This action took the form of a joint reduction of copper exports by 10 percent and subsequently by a further 5 percent. In as far as such action had not subsequent influence on price, one could argue that the sellers have failed to take advantage of their relatively strong market power by relegating price determination to an outside institution like the LME.

However, as indicated by Eckbo, there are a number of factors which have prevented the full realization of price control by international cartels.[21] For the case of copper-exporting developing countries, their dependence on copper is so strong that they would probably be forced to yield and accept inferior terms in a bargaining situation, where the alternative is a threat to stop or severely reduce earlier trade flows. These same countries, in addition, possessed such high basic quotas that the 15 percent reduction did not reduce exports in a number of cases. To this can be added the fact that the countries simply did not control a sufficiently high proportion of world production.

Market Implications

Export Dependence

The impact of market performance varies with the extent of the dependence of the major exporting developing countries on copper trade.[22] Three of the four major exporting countries shown in table 3–7 have a high degree of dependence. The share of copper in total exports for 1974 was 66 percent for Chile, 23 percent for Peru, 66 percent for Zaire, and 93 percent for Zambia. Two other copper-exporting countries exhibiting dependence are Papua New Guinea with 57 percent and the Philippines with 18 percent.

This dependence can be seen to be critical for these countries in view of the decreasing value of copper in real terms. Although this trend has been continuing for some twenty years, its severity can be readily witnessed in table 3–7. The deflated LME price declined some 47 percent between 1965 and 1975. The deflated export unit values have fallen almost as much for the countries shown, except for Zaire. For Chile the decline was 60 percent; for Peru, 84 percent; and for Zambia, 78 percent. In contrast to this decline is the recent period of rapidly rising investment and operating costs. This combination makes the situation for copper investment and development a difficult one.

The wide and frequent fluctuation in copper prices has been pointed out. The extent to which this has created instability in prices and export earnings is also demonstrated in table 3–7. The variability in real copper prices at 25 percent is higher than that for tin with 17 percent, iron ore with 6 percent, or aluminum with 12 percent. For Chile, Peru, Zaire, and Zambia, the variability in total export value is also higher than for most of the other developing mineral exporters.

Magnitude of Fixed Investment

Beginning with static factors affecting the division of gains, the substantial size of fixed investments in copper mining is important. It has been stated that requirements for an initial large investment tends to shift more bargaining power to the side of the firm relative to the host government, at least in the beginning of the investment. This implies that copper investing firms have an initial advantage in bargaining. Just how large the investments are relative to

Table 3-7
Trend and Variability of Copper Export Values and Unit Values
(millions of dollars and dollars per metric ton)

Year	Chile Export Value	Chile Unit Value	Chile Deflated	Peru Export Value	Peru Unit Value	Peru Deflated	Zaire Export Value	Zaire Unit Value	Zaire Deflated	Zambia Export Value	Zambia Unit Value	Zambia Deflated	Copper Price (LME) Price (¢/lb)	Copper Price (LME) Deflated
1965	179.7	820	932	26.4	690	784	89.2	584	664	379.4	715	813	58.50	66
1966	355.4	1160	1289	35.5	1130	1256	128.5	820	911	558.8	1090	1211	69.35	77
1967	449.3	1210	1330	37.4	1090	1198	160.5	1000	1099	533.2	1020	1121	51.14	56
1968	455.2	1190	1308	35.9	1060	1165	208.8	1250	1374	615.5	1120	1231	56.32	62
1969	574.0	1340	1426	43.4	1340	1426	236.5	1290	1372	864.4	1390	1479	66.52	71
1970	638.2	1450	1450	44.1	1350	1350	255.0	1420	1420	818.8	1420	1420	64.19	64
1971	466.5	1070	1019	24.6	980	933	176.2	890	848	533.0	1000	952	44.06	47
1972	353.7	870	770	35.1	1220	1080	223.8	1040	920	605.6	970	858	98.56	43
1973	649.3	1670	1256	43.3	1600	1203	368.0	1600	1203	1008.0	1610	1211	80.78	61
1974	1080.9	2220	1370	77.0	2000	1235	538.0	2130	1315	1232.9	1900	1173	90.36	56
1975	588.6	1010	555	44.21	1200	660	292.01	1230	676	751.31	1160	637	56.01	31
Price ratio (%)[b] 1976/1965	328	123	60	169	174	84	327	211	102	189	162	78	96	47
Variability (%)[c] 1970–1975	39	37	33	39	26	23	42	32	27	32	27	27	27	25

Source: U.N. *Yearbook of International Trade Statistics* (New York: United Nations, various issues); and UNCTAD, *Monthly Commodity Price Bulletin*, CD/CPB/92/Rev. 1 (Geneva: UNCTAD, 1977).

[a] Deflator is U.N. Index of Unit Value of Exported Manufactured Goods, 1970 = 100.

[b] Ratio between 1965 and 1976.

[c] Coefficient of variation in percent over 1970–1976.

national economic activity (GDP) can be judged by examining the size of the mining sector (MS) and gross domestic investment (GDI). These are given below as of 1973 in millions of dollars for the major exporting countries.[23]

	GDP	MS	GDI
Chile	6,878	1,136	395
Peru	6,705	1,002	401
Zaire	2,223	487	409
Zambia	1,576	276	400

The magnitudes of copper investment specified previously are in the vicinity of $500 million for mining and concentrating units with capacity rates between 100,000 and 200,000 tons of copper content. This is certainly larger than gross domestic investment of the four countries and exceeds recent annual income from the mining sector for Zaire and Zambia. Although smaller size units could be constructed, a recent survey indicates the size of most new projects to be larger than 130,000 tons of copper content.[24]

Nature of Technology

The basic technology required to mine and concentrate copper ore is relatively simple and stable. The sequence of processing for the treatment of sulphide ores, mining, beneficiation, smelting and refining, and the leaching of oxide ores followed by cementation of copper on scrap iron have long been established and have been developed to a high level of efficiency. More complexity can be seen as more advanced mining methods are employed in mining, particularly at the refining and concentrating stage. But it appears that the traditional pyrometallurgical process will continue to be employed in most copper production in the near future. As indicated by Moran, the technology and expertise required are not really sufficiently esoteric to exclude new entrants or government takeover.[25]

Control over Resources and Production

The organization of the copper industry has been more profoundly affected than the organization of the tin, bauxite, and iron ore industries by the efforts of the host governments to control resources and production. The multinational mining firms found are large, oligopolistic, and vertically integrated. As such, they have control over a combination of capital, technology, and funds that makes them highly effective in exploration, development, and processing. But this has not prevented host governments from gaining control, particularly in countries such as Chile, which moved from increased participation in the large mines in the late 1960s to full nationalization in 1971. In Peru, nationalization has not been so abrupt. Taxes and government levies were increased since 1967, and a number of ore bodies were returned. At the same time, the output of the state company, Mineral Peru, has been increasing relative to that of other firms. In Zaire, outright nationalization occurred between 1965 and 1967 after President Mobutu came to power. The Belgian-owned Union Miniere became Gecamines and in 1973 Sozacom was created to wrest marketing activities from Belgian control. Since then, however, new mining developments have been pursued by foreign-dominated firms. Nationalization also took place in Zambia in 1973 after several years of increased government participation.

Opportunities for Increased Processing

Possibilities for increased copper processing in developing countries appear to exist. The likelihood for expansion is reflected in a recent survey which suggests that of all refineries to be built in the early 1980s 25 percent will be located in North and Central America, 30 percent in Africa, and 20 percent in South America.[26] The developing countries share in refining will be about 50 percent above their contribution to past production levels. One of the limiting factors to such expansion is the scale of production required in refining. An efficient size for a copper refinery is 60,000 metric tons of annual capacity, and this is somewhat in excess of the annual mine output of some countries. The possibility of using the new hydrometallurgical process, however, may reduce the scale of operation for certain types of ores.

Opportunities of expanding at the semifabricating stage seem more uncertain, but they should increase as tariffs for fabricated goods decline. The incentive for moving to this stage can be seen in the differences in prices between wire bars, rods, and wires, which have been quoted at $1,208 per ton, $1,277 per ton, and $1,573 per ton, respectively.[27] To obtain rods, one has to build a casting plant together with a facility for drawing and producing wire and cable. Such capital expenditures, nonetheless, permit a company to move to the wire stage where value-added is much higher.

Material Share in Product Prices

The extent to which an increase in primary copper prices would affect fabricated product prices is substantial. Estimates indicate that the price of copper concentrates accounts for 52 to 55 percent of the wholesale price of copper wire in France and about 64 to 75 percent in the United States.[28] The ratio of the refined copper price to the wire price is 57 to 66 percent in France and between 77 and 90 percent in the United States. These figures represent averages for the period 1955–1973. While a 10 percent increase in refined copper prices could not easily be absorbed by fabricators, it could at least partially be passed on to final consumers. Fabricators typically do not gain nor lose on their copper deals. They could, therefore, be regarded as mere intermediaries who shape the copper metal on behalf of the electrical and construction industries. These industries bear the entire impact of the variations in copper prices, and it would not be unreasonable to view them, rather than fabricators, as the true buyers of copper. As such, a more correct assessment of the power of copper buyers in the final product markets would involve scrutinizing the conditions under which the electrical and construction industries sell their copper-containing products.

Obsolescing Bargain

Although the above variables have given some insight into a firm's initial bargaining position with a host government, they do not reflect the dynamics of the adjustment process. The first dynamic variable previously mentioned is that of risk and uncertainty. Initially if risk and uncertainty are high, then the firm occupies a strong position in relation to the host government. As the investment's life grows over time, there is an evolutionary pattern that has been described as an obsolescing bargain. That is, the government demands more of the gains, forcing renegotiation to take place. Moran finds that this evaluation has proceeded fairly completely for the copper industry, Chile being the best example.[29] Policy instruments related to the copper industry which help accomplish such shifts are taxation, increasing participation in equity, and outright nationalization.

Completing the description of the shift described in the previous section on control, the Chilean mines, up to the 1930s, were in the hands of the foreign firms, and their linkages to the rest of the economy were weak. Increasing national fervor resulted in the imposition of output taxes in the pre–World War II period. More recently, the country set up a sales monopoly in copper and also became a majority shareholder in the domestic firms. Nationalization followed in 1971.

When Peru became a major copper producer in 1960, it decided to gradually increase its taxes. From 1967 to 1970, taxes and levies as a share of pretax earnings in the mining and processing sector increased from 35 percent to 58 percent.[30] The government followed this action by expanding the production of Minero Peru on retained ore bodies and recently moved to transfer

equity from foreign-owned firms to Peruvians. In Zaire and Zambia nationalization took place as described above.

Although the bargaining process appears to culminate in a complete shift
in control, Radetzki suggests that there are limits to such shifts beyond which
necessary investment and capital funding are reduced.[31] For example, no
country can increase taxes to the point where national income declines or
where mineral firms begin moving to other producing nations. In some ways
the copper industry can be seen as a case where complete takeover by the host
governments had to be modified to maintain the high level of investment
required. Thus copper-producing countries vary considerably in the investment climate, willingness to attract foreign equity investment, and ability to
finance capacity expansion internally or externally. In this context, Mikesell
finds that several of the countries have made attempts to improve the investment climate.[32] He cites examples of new foreign investments in Chile, Peru,
Panama, and Argentina. Out of all the producing developing countries, only
the Philippines has been able to finance major expansion of capacity from
internal copper industry sources. Thus, the industry has evolved from foreign
ownership through partial or complete nationalization to one of shared control.

Nature of Competition

A number of factors relating to the nature of competition have been stressed.
On the one hand, the large copper multinationals, through their vertical integration, have had considerable power in formulating investment, pricing, and
marketing policy for the industry. Many of these policies reflect the behavior of
firms constituting a corporate system working under unstable conditions of
imperfect competition.[33] On the other hand, a system of domestic interest
groups attempting to stimulate development and national welfare has emerged
in Chile and in other copper-producing developing countries.

Substantial interaction between the two systems has been inevitable.
From the end of the Second World War through 1973, these interactions have
culminated in the previously described growth of host governments in controlling a greater market share of production and the accompanying dilution of the
copper oligopoly. The international copper industry as an oligopoly found
itself unable to hold its prices high enough to deter entry or to tighten control
further downstream from mining, smelting, and refining. Competing firms
were able to move backward through production stages to develop mines and
increase copper exploitation. And nationalization proceeded at the same time.

It has been pointed out, however, that nationalization has not led to tight
control of the industry by the host governments. The high costs of investment
and capital shortages have led the industry to a competitive position where

bargaining and the maintenance of a good investment climate are necessary for its survival.

Government Learning Process

At the end of the Second World War, linkages of the foreign copper industry to the host economies were weak. In Chile, for example, equity ownership was nil. The country played little role in supplying capital goods or managerial activities to the industry; most of the copper generated rents accrued to foreigners.[34] The country began to realize this weakness and responded by gradually building up cadres of qualified technicians and managers, establishing and fostering related institutional growth, and improving the understanding of the role of the industry within the nation. Thus, Chile was able to increase its control over production to the point of being able to nationalize the industry. Of course, the learning and transition process has been far from perfect. Like other producing countries, they are not able to expand capacity without foreign participation. Whether such managerial sophistication will be reached in other copper countries in the near future is doubtful.

Price Formation

Marketing and Pricing Methods

Most copper trade is in the form of refined metal, thus making the refined or wire bar price the most representative international price. Accordingly, unrefined copper prices, as well as prices of fabricated products, are closely linked to the refined prices. All three forms of copper—concentrate, blister, and refined—are sold mainly under bilateral sales contracts between a producer and a buyer. As indicated above, refined copper is also sold on the LME. Copper sales contracts are similar to other commodity contracts in their specifications of quantities, grades, dates, and so forth. However, they differ in that they do not specify the actual sales price. The pricing clause normally is of a very general type such as "the sellers price at the time of delivery."[35]

The marketing of concentrates is by long-term contracts, which may or may not be linked to provisions of finance by the buyer to develop the source of concentrates. Sales are usually made to smelters on the basis of the LME price less the cost of smelting and refining concentrates or of converting blister into refined copper metal. The main features of custom contracts are summarized below.

1. The price set by the smelter is based on the formula: LME (or U.S. producer) price times percent copper content, less conversion fee, less

unwanted byproduct removal charge, plus precious metal sale credit, plus other byproduct sale credit, minus transport cost if paid by smelter. The actual price received by a mine will depend on price participation, cost escalation, currency adjustment and byproduct clauses, and the payment terms specified in the contract.

2. Custom smelters normally make a percentage deduction in assaying the copper content of smelter feed received from a mine. Commonly this is about 1–1.2 percent. Smelters in the United States also usually pay for 97–97.5 percent of contained copper, after making the unit deduction; non-U.S. smelters normally pay 100 percent of the assay after unit deduction.

3. A conversion fee is added which comprises a charge for smelting (dollars per dry ton of material) and a refining charge (cents per pound of refined).

At the next stage, the marketing of blister is mostly to refiners or merchants through similar contracts, some of which may be "toll," that is, contracts where ownership remains with the producer. At the refined stage, copper is marketed primarily to fabricators who convert it to semimanufactures, the latter either being sold or further processed. Most of the sales of refined copper outside of the United States are based on annual contracts (calendar year) linked to the LME wire bar price. Within the United States, sales contracts are normally of a longer-run nature linked to the U.S. producer price. As indicated above, marginal amounts of refined copper are sold on the LME in Europe and on COMEX in the United States.

In determining which contracts specify use of producer prices as compared to market prices, producer prices are used for refined copper which is traded mostly within national boundaries. Although such reference prices

Table 3–8
Major Copper Price Quotations

London Metal Exchange
   Electrolytic wire bars, cash for delivery in warehouse.
   3-month, forward, electrolytic wire bars.
   Cash, electrolytic copper in the form of cathodes.
   3-month, forward, electrolytic copper in the form of cathodes.

New York Producers Price
   Domestic refinery price (*E&MJ*), electrolytic wire bars.
   From January 1967, FOB domestic net Atlantic seaboard refinery.[a]
   Same price delivered which includes shipping cost.
   Same price based on cathodes.

New York Commodity Exchange (COMEX) spot settlement price and futures price.

Federal Republic of Germany, electrolytic copper wire bars.

[a]*E&MJ* refers to the *Engineering and Mining Journal* price.

exist for countries such as Australia, Japan, South Africa, France, and Canada, the price in the United States is employed most frequently. As shown in table 3–8, this price is quoted New York and is an estimated weighted average based on U.S. mine production and the current selling price of U.S. producers. It can also be quoted refinery (less shipping costs) or in terms of either wire bars or cathodes. Today most U.S. producers follow a cathode basis. The producer price tends to be in line with LME and COMEX prices, though not always, as will be shown below.

Price-Making Forces

The price-making forces at work in the copper market have not always resulted in a simultaneous link between the U.S. producer price and the LME price. In fact the two prices have at times differed notably. This phenomenon has come to be known as "two-tier" pricing.[36] Periods in which it has been most evident are 1954–1957, 1963–1966, and 1966–1970. A number of reasons have been offered as to why the U.S. producer price has been lower than the LME price during these periods.[37] A first one has been the fear that higher prices may drive certain customers out of the market, perhaps seeking lower price offers from the competitive fringe. In addition, lower prices can be seen as an attempt to forestall substitution of aluminum and other materials in the various end uses. To this end, rationing, particularly of wire mills occurred during the latter two periods. Rationing also possibly permitted a portion of total profits to derive from price discrimination.

Regarding forces behind copper price fluctuations, the more important ones are those associated with medium-term price fluctuations rather than the very short-term fluctuations. The former tend to vary with fluctuations in demand caused by business cycles in the industrialized countries. During industrial booms, copper demand and, accordingly, copper prices on the LME tend to be high. Conversely, during industrial recessions, demand and prices tend to be low. To some extent these upward and downward swings are exaggerated by the presence of excessive speculation, which occurs when prices are expected to advance further before they turn.[38] The annual average prices of copper have varied by as much as 50–60 percent between adjacent years. This is considerably more than the corresponding variations in the prices of aluminum or iron ore.

These price fluctuations are also linked to the relative inelasticity of supply response compared to demand response. Any rise in demand will only result in small increases in supply, because copper production capacities are fixed in the short and medium term. Concerning any fall in demand, production will not decrease as much because such action is disadvantageous to individual producers who have a high burden of fixed costs. If producers are unable to sell all their copper on contract, part of that surplus will flow into the LME. Similarly, consumers unable to absorb the entire contracted quantity will unload some of their surplus on the LME.

The result is normally an adjustment in metal exchange stocks held not only in LME warehouses but also in those of COMEX. In this way there is a link between the overall surplus situation, metal exchange stocks, and LME prices.[39] That is, adjustments in metal exchange stocks help ameliorate the wide swings in prices often attributed to the marginal nature of the LME. These swings could equally well be caused by other features of copper production, consumption or trade, and be quite independent of the prevailing market structure.

Also important are the consequences of the LME pricing method on international trade. The fact that exporters and importers state their FOB or CIF contract prices in term of the cash LME quotation for wire bars would seem to have certain advantages. This arrangement simplifies negotiations, since there is ready agreement from the outset on an acceptable price. In addition, the acceptance of LME prices has the advantage of providing a uniform price level for all sellers and buyers. The prices emerging from bilateral negotiations may well show significant differences from one trade deal to another, but the problems of irritations from having reached the wrong price are likely to be avoided.

Let us now advance from these medium-run price influences to the long-run determinants of price formation. The analysis of market structure and its implications has suggested a more diluted concentration among copper producers. This, together with a more even balance in bargaining power between producers and consumers, implies a loose oligopoly further tempered by increased competition. Nationalization also has reached a degree, where producing countries are becoming more open to foreign investment. The precariousness of their position is further witnessed by their failure to attain a form of quantity control within CIPEC.

This means that more traditional economic forces will be shaping long-run price formation. On the supply side, the increases in mining capacity induced by high copper prices in 1975 have been mostly completed. After 1979, very few additions to capacity are foreseen. One forecast places additions over the 1980–1987 period at a mere 2 percent per year.[40] Refinery capacity will keep in line with this figure, although it is now relatively in excess. On the demand side, expected expansion of the utility industry together with less pressure on substitution should cause consumption to grow at a rate of 3–4 per cent per year over the 1980s.[41] Although there is some question as to the present size of copper inventories, this influence is more of a medium-run nature. Present possibilities for increasing capacity depends on the industry's target price, that price necessary to maintain long-run equilibrium in the market. Currently estimated at 119.8¢ per pound, prices which rise significantly above this figure for a substantial period will provide incentive for further capacity investment.[42] Until that investment begins and facilities completed, the long-run pressure on price formation is likely to be upward.

Notes

1. A more complete description of market conditions appears in R. Prain, *Copper, The Anatomy of An Industry* (London: Mining Journal Books, 1976). An updating of some aspects appears in UNESC, *Future Demand and the Development of the Raw Materials Base for the Copper Industry,* E/C.7/65, Geneva: UN Economic and Social Council, 1977.

2. UNESC, *Future Demand,* p. 25.

3. K. Takeuchi, G. Thiebach, and J. Hilmy, "Investment Requirements in the Non-Fuel Mineral Sector in Developing Countries," *Natural Resources Forum,* 1 (1977): 263–75.

4. R.F. Mikesell, "Financial Requirements and Sources of Financing for Expanded Free World Mining Capacity through 1990," paper presented at the Financial Conference of the American Mining Congress, Phoenix, 1978.

5. *Survey of Planned Increases in World Copper Mine, Smelter and Refinery Capacities 1974–1980* (London: International Wrought Copper Council, 1975).

6. "Capital Requirements and Probable Costs of Future Copper Operations" (Paris: Intergovernmental Council of Copper Exporting Countries, 1977).

7. British-North American Committee, *Mineral Development in the Eighties: Prospects and Problems* (New York: British-North American Committee, November 1976), p. 16.

8. Ibid.

9. UNESC, *Future Demand,* p. 9.

10. Ibid., pp. 32–35.

11. M. Radetzki, "Market Structure and Bargaining Power: A Study of Three International Mineral Markets" (Stockholm: Institute of International Economic Studies, 1976).

12. UNCTAD, "Substitution including the Relative Stability of Supplies and Prices of Copper and Competing Metals," TD/B/IPC/COPPER/AC/L.25 (Geneva: UNCTAD, 1977).

13. Figures derived from *Metal Statistics,* Metallgesellshaft A.G., Frankfort, 1955–1976.

14. Table 3–7 provides only a rough measure of concentration. Particularly on the demand or fabricating side, end-use production is so diffuse that concentration figures could not easily be obtained.

15. The principal source regarding the dilution of concentration is T.H. Moran, *Multinational Corporations and the Politics of Dependence: The Case of Copper* (Princeton: Princeton University Press, 1974).

16. Ibid., p. 30.

17. Ibid., pp. 32–37.

18. UNESC, *Future Demand*, p. 14.

19. These and other differences have been well specified in UNCTAD, "Marketing and Pricing Methods for Copper," TD/B/IPC/COPPER/AC/L.15 (Geneva: UNCTAD, 1977).

20. UNESC, *Future Demand*, p. 15.

21. R. Eckbo, "OPEC and the Experience of Previous Commodity Cartels," Working Paper (Cambridge, Mass.: MIT Energy Laboratory, 1975).

22. A more complete description of market performance and copper dependence can be found in M. Radetzki, "Copper Dependent Development," Working Paper UNCTAD-UNEP Project 005 (Geneva: UNCTAD, 1977).

23. Given at average 1967–1969 market prices. World Bank, *World Tables, 1976* (Washington, D.C.: World Bank, 1976).

24. UNCTAD, "Long-Term Trends in the Demand and Supply of Copper," TD/B/IPC/COPPER/AC/L.23 (Geneva: UNCTAD, 1977).

25. Moran, *Multinational Corporations*, p. 40.

26. UNESC, *Future Demand*, p. 34.

27. Prices quoted United Kingdom in 1975, *Metal Bulletin*, 1975.

28. Averages for the period 1955–1973. UNCTAD, "Proportions between Export Prices and Consumer Prices of Selected Commodities Exported by Developing Countries," TD/184/Suppl. 3 (Geneva: UNCTAD, 1976), p. 7.

29. T.H. Moran, "Multinational Corporations and the Changing Structure of Industries that Supply Industrial Commodities," Working Paper (Washington, D.C.: Johns Hopkins Institute for International Studies, 1977).

30. Radetzki, "Market Structure and Bargaining Power," p. 13.

31. Ibid., pp. 18–19.

32. Mikesell, "Financial Requirements and Sources of Financing," p. 18.

33. This view of the transition of power in the copper market is basically that of Moran, *Multinational Corporations*, pp. 45–98.

34. Radetzki, "Market Structure and Bargaining Power," p. 11.

35. Source of detail on marketing and pricing arrangements is CIPEC, "The Marketing and Pricing of Copper" (Paris: Intergovernmental Council of Copper Exporting Countries, 1977).

36. See D. McNicol, "The Two-Price System in the Copper Industry," *Bell Journal of Economics and Management*, 6 (1975): 50–73.

37. Ibid.

38. See W.C. Labys and H. Thomas, "Speculation Hedging and Commodity Price Behavior: An International Comparison," *Applied Economics,* 7 (1975): 287–301.

39. See CIPEC, "The Role of Copper Stocks and their Effect on Prices" (Paris: International Council of Copper Exporting Countries, 1977).

40. R.H. Lesemann, "Copper: The Next Ten Years," *Mining Congress Journal* (December 1978): 33–35.

41. R. Adams, "Why Copper Prices are Going to Triple over the Next Decade," paper presented at the AIME Annual Meeting, New Orleans, 1979.

42. Ibid.

4   Tin

Market Conditions

The world tin market as depicted in figure 4–1 involves producers or mining firms which can be classified as independent, foreign owned, or nationalized (including state owned). Mining which takes place mostly in tropical areas normally involves dealing with surface deposits by open pit methods. The tin oxide thus obtained goes through several stages of processing before it is smelted into refined metal. Implied in figure 4–1 is a commodity flow from producers to smelters, fabricators, and consumers. This representation, of course, is highly generalized. In both Bolivia and Indonesia, for example, mining is nationalized, but a significant proportion of the tin continues to be smelted in foreign-owned smelters. In other countries such as Malaysia, tin concentrates are smelted by a domestically owned rather than a foreign-owned firm.

Pure or primary tin metal obtained by smelting concentrates is termed unwrought tin (not including scrap) and is mostly in the form of ingots, blocks, bars, and slabs. Quality specifications are determined principally by grade designations. Most well known is commercially pure tin designated as "Straits" or "Grade A" with a minimum tin content of 99.8 percent. Electrolytic grades can be higher with a minimum tin content of 99.95 percent or even 99.98 percent. Hard tin contains 99.6 percent, and common tin 99 percent minimum. The tin metal then moves to the fabrication stage which takes place mostly in consuming countries. Tin is used principally in combination with other metals such as in tin plating and the manufacturing of white metal alloys, bronze, and solder.

The relative magnitudes of the production and consumption of different forms of tin on a world basis are reflected in table 4–1. Ore trade is shown to be much less than ore production, whereas trade in tin and tin alloys is only slightly less than production. Since 1965 the production and consumption of ore as well as primary metal has grown slightly, but trade in both forms has declined. Recycled or secondary tin metal is shown to be relatively unimportant compared to primary tin.

Production

The primary tin deposits of the world (from which in many instances placer deposits have formed) contain cassiterite as the principal tin mineral. A few

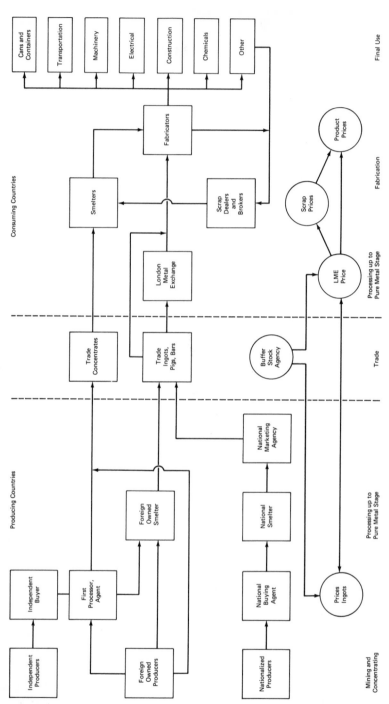

Figure 4-1. Market and Price Structure for Tin

Table 4–1
World Balance Sheet for Tin
(thousand metric tons)

Commodity Flow	1955	1960	1965	1966	1967	1968	1969	1970	1971	1972	1973	1974	1975	1976
Ore production	94.8	77.9	191.1	202.1	207.0	215.2	211.3	217.2	221.8	230.5	219.0	218.1	207.7	211.8
Primary metal production	196.6	199.1	185.6	195.2	213.6	223.6	216.5	220.3	224.3	232.6	225.5	222.2	219.9	221.9
Secondary metal production	5.5	12.0	8.3	7.5	9.2	9.0	10.4	9.8	9.3	15.8	8.9	10.0	11.3	12.4
Ore imports	95.8	77.9	54.2	47.2	52.6	57.9	55.9	58.8	47.9	48.8	48.3	52.4	53.2	53.0
Imports (tin and alloys)	143.9	147.1	135.2	139.8	148.5	163.7	173.1	164.3	159.2	174.5	172.7	166.0	119.6	120.1
Ore exports	96.0	76.8	56.1	46.4	55.0	52.6	53.6	54.8	46.6	47.7	41.7	48.8	49.0	49.5
Exports (tin and alloys)	140.5	138.0	135.0	138.6	148.7	164.5	167.8	167.1	171.3	173.8	172.7	175.5	135.2	136.3
Primary metal consumption	196.1	199.1	185.6	214.6	209.1	215.7	223.1	225.5	225.9	232.3	254.0	244.3	217.4	240.6
LME price (per metric ton)	—	784	1,390	1,276	1,204	1,303	1,428	1,531	1,438	1,506	1,967	3,495	3,090	4,242

Source: *Metal Statistics* (Frankfurt: Metallgesellschaft A.G., 1976), and earlier editions.

other tin-bearing minerals, of which stannite is the most important, are of some economic importance, but only in a few lode deposits. Cassiterite is tin dioxide (S_nO_2) in which ferril iron may substitute for tin up to perhaps one part in ten. The ordinary variety of cassiterite is known as tinstone and is found either massive or in crystals. Stream tin is cassiterite found in pebbles or in sand in alluvial deposits.

Like copper, the production of tin involves a primary as well as a secondary industry. The primary industry requires the following stages of production: (1) exploring for tin deposits, (2) developing mines, beneficiation, smelting, refining, and other facilities for conversion, and (3) processing tin in concentrates to metallic tin and then refining to remove impurities. Beginning with exploration, estimates of world tin resources available as of 1975 are reported in table 4–2. China is shown to have the greatest portion of the world's reserves, amounting to some 24 percent. The greatest concentration of reserves regionally can be found in Southeast Asia. Thailand has 15 percent; Malaysia, 12 percent; and Indonesia, 9 percent. The only other country with similar reserves is Bolivia in Latin America with 10 percent.

The mine development stage need not take as long as for other minerals, depending on the mining techniques employed. These include (1) dredging, (2) gravel pump mining, (3) hydraulic mining, (4) open-cut mining, (5) under-

Table 4–2
Estimated World Tin Resources[a]
(thousand long tons)

Country	Reserves	Other	Total
People's Republic of China	2,360	1,080	3,440
Malaysia	1,217	4,360	5,577
Indonesia	830	3,500	4,330
Brazil	600	3,748	4,348
Thailand	1,500	4,000	5,500
Bolivia	985	1,750	2,735
U.S.S.R.	620	1,900	2,520
United Kingdom	257	1,025	1,282
Zaire	195	2,000	2,195
Burma	500	500	1,000
Nigeria	276	600	876
Portugal and Spain	30	900	930
United States	42	153	195
Canada	20	228	248
Other	546	1,311	1,857
World total	9,978	27,055	37,033

Source: *Mineral Facts and Problems, 1975* (Washington, D.C.: U.S. Department of the Interior, 1975), p. 1131.

[a]Includes identified and undiscovered resources.

ground mining, and (6) dulang washing and panning. Of these the first two are open pit methods, and their application does not require substantial time lags. Dredging is the more capital intensive and is used mostly for the mining of alluvial deposits. Of a less capital-intensive nature, gravel pump mining is a method of surface mining of placer deposits that is widely used in small-scale operations in Southeast Asia. Mining by hydraulicking involves directing water under a natural head of pressure against the gravel bank to be mined. Dulang washing or panning is essentially a method of recovery rather than of digging or dredging.

Investment costs will, of course, vary depending on the scale of production and method employed. In general, the scale of production is small, except for dredging where the average dredge may produce up to 400 tons annually of tin in concentrates. Recent estimates of investment costs place the capital cost per metric ton of annual production capacity at $15,000 for dredging and $10,000 for gravel pumping in 1975 dollars.[1] Of course, these costs can vary considerably from country to country or from project to project. A more recent estimate of development costs presents an example of a new gravel pump mine covering 50 acres with 30 feet of overburden.[2] The mine is considered to take one year for prospecting, an additional year for installation and development, and overall from three to seven years for mining to actually begin. Costs for its development have been estimated as follows in 1977 dollars:

Prospecting costs	101,000
Capital expenditures	328,000
Development costs	137,000
Total	566,000

With annual capacity of 152 tons, the unit capital cost would be $3,723 per ton.

Another important aspect of tin production is variation in the size of tin mining operations. In Malaysia and Thailand, a dredge of average size produces about 400 tons per year; in Indonesia it yields about 250 tons per year. Far more tin is mined by methods which are typically of a smaller scale. Gravel pumping and hydraulic mining, which account for 50 percent of tin output in Southeast Asia and 40 percent of world output, produce on average 30 to 40 tons annually. Underground mines are of larger size but account for only a small proportion of world output. In Bolivia typical mine sizes range from 240 to nearly 6,000 tons on an annual basis.

After the tin ore has been mined, it must go through the process of beneficiation, smelting, and refining. The problem of the beneficiation of tin ores is essentially one of concentrating cassiterite. There are three methods employed for the concentration and recovery of cassiterite. In order of importance, they are gravity concentration, floatation, and electrical concentration. Smelting is the process by which the tin oxide is converted to metallic tin. There are three types of furnaces used for the process of smelting tin. They are the blast furnace, the reverbatory furnace, which is the most popular, and the electric furnace. The first two are fuel fired, whereas the electric furnace utilizes electric power. Tin smelting consists of the following three stages:

1. Primary smelting, in furnaces
2. Retreatment of slags produced by primary smelting
3. Refining of the reduced metallic tin to remove the metal impurities reduced by the smelting

The distribution of the world's tin mining and smelting capacity as of 1973 is given in table 4–3. Production of tin in concentrate is found mostly in the area of greatest reserves, Southeast Asia accounting for 63 percent. There is some variation in production levels among countries. Malaysia accounts for 31 percent; Bolivia, 13 percent; the U.S.S.R., 12 percent; and Indonesia, 10 percent. The number of firms involved in this production are numerous, most of them small. The two largest state-owned international mining companies are P.N. Timah in Indonesia with about 10 percent of world output and Corporacion Minera de Bolivia (COMIBOL) with about 9 percent.[3]

The largest international privately founded tin mining group until 1976 had been the London Tin Group, Ltd. In 1977, pressure by the Malaysian government to shift the firm domicile to Kuala Lumpur culminated in the government's takeover of the group by a new company, New Tradewinds. The latter is 71 percent owned by Pernas Securities and 28 percent by Charter Consolidated, both Malaysian companies.[4] The new company will soon be named Malaysia Tin Berhad. The result is the largest tin mining group in the world with interest in 18 tin mining companies mostly in Malaysia but also in Thailand and Nigeria. Its production amounts to 27,332 tons of 70–75 percent tin concentrate as of 1976, representing approximately 11.5 percent of world production.

Companies owning tin smelters generally are separate from the mining companies. Some exceptions are, for example, the financing of smelting firms by Patino mining interests of Bolivia through Consolidated Tin Smelters Ltd. The latter firm has interests in three smelters (one each in Australia, Malaysia, and Nigeria) accounting for some 40 percent of world smelting capacity. Smelters have made no attempts to integrate forward to the consuming stage.

Since smelting takes place with few exceptions in the same country as mining, concentration of smelting production also rests in Southeast Asia. Of a world total of 227 million tons smelted in 1973, Malaysia accounted for 36 percent, Thailand for 10 percent, and Indonesia for 6 percent. Considerable capacity also exists in the U.S.S.R. and China, with 11 percent of production accounted for by the former and 9 percent by the latter. Regarding smelting in consuming countries, about 7 percent of production took place in the United

Table 4–3
World Tin Mining and Smelting Capacities, 1973
(long tons)

Area	Mine		Smelter	
	Capacity	*Production*	*Capacity*	*Production*
North America				
United States	300	W[a]	20,000	4,535[b]
Canada	500	138	—	—
Mexico	1,000	287	2,200	287
Total	1,800[c]	425	22,200	4,822
South America				
Bolivia	33,000	29,825	10,000	7,700
Brazil	4,000	3,158	10,000	3,660
Other	2,000	768	1,500	—
Total	39,000	33,751	21,500	11,360
Europe				
Belgium	—	—	18,000	3,611
East Germany	1,100	1,100	1,500	1,100
West Germany	—	—	3,600	1,024
Portugal	900	525	1,000	516
Spain	500	323	7,000	4,191
U.S.S.R.	40,000	29,000	39,000	29,000
United Kingdom	5,000	3,604	17,000	16,764
Other	700	472	—	—
Total	48,200	35,024	87,100	56,206
Africa				
Nigeria	10,000	5,726	12,000	5,889
Southern Rhodesia	1,000	600	1,100	600
Republic of South Africa	3,000	2,634	2,500	860
Zaire	8,000	5,453	4,000	1,400
Other	4,000	2,466	100	12
Total	26,000	16,889	19,700	8,761
Asia				
People's Republic of China	30,000	20,000	35,000	20,000
Indonesia	25,000	22,135	15,000	14,401
Japan	1,000	796	3,500	1,329
Malaysia	80,000	71,119	95,000	81,166
Thailand	25,000	20,232	40,000	21,626
Other	2,000	1,664	1,000	820
Total	163,000	135,946	189,500	139,342
Oceania				
Australia	12,000	10,369	9,000	6,795
World total	290,000	232,404	349,000	227,286

Source: *Mineral Facts and Problems, 1975* (Washington, D.C.: U.S. Department of the Interior, 1975).

[a]W = withheld to avoid disclosing company confidential data.
[b]Estimate.
[c]Excluding U.S. mine production.

Kingdom. Tin mining or smelting capacity is adequate in the market economy countries. Although the world excess of available capacity over production has been 25 percent in mining and 54 percent in smelting, some firms were in various stages of increasing capacity, and some older firms probably fell short of the stated levels.

Regarding investment costs in smelting, very few estimates are available.[5] In 1965, a smelter of 40,000 tin capacity was installed in Thailand at a cost of $5 million, which amounts to $125 per ton annual capacity. This cost would be roughly doubled in 1975 dollars. One smelter installed in the early 1970s in Bolivia probably cost much more, but here there was a need to utilize technology capable of dealing with poorer-grade concentrates. An estimate made later in 1975 indicates that the cost of adding 3,000 to 4,000 tons per year to a smelter in South Africa during 1978–1979 would be $4.5 million. This implies a capacity cost of $1,125 per ton.

Given the heterogeneity of mining methods and mine sizes, one would expect considerable variations in tin production costs. This is confirmed in table 4–4 which traces the evolution of tin production costs from 1971 for the principal tin-producing countries. The cost index shows a marked increase in costs since the petroleum crisis of 1974. In 1977 Bolivia is shown to be the highest cost producer at 403¢/pound; Australia is the lowest cost producer at 303¢/pound, with Malaysia in the middle at 364¢/pound. The LME spot cash price for the year was 490¢/pound.[6]

Consumption

The recent changes in the world consumption of primary tin metal are shown in table 4–5. Consumption appears to have reached a peak in 1973 with a small decline since then. The United States is shown to be the major consumer, its share being approximately 28 percent in 1976. Japan has the second largest share of 18 percent, with the Federal Republic of Germany, United Kingdom, and France taking 8 percent, 7 percent, and 5 percent, respectively. To understand these patterns, one must consider the derived nature of its demand.

Of the major uses, table 4–5 shows that more than twice the amount of tin goes to tinplate than to solder. Tinplate, which consists of a tin coating applied to thin steel plates, is used mostly to make tin cans. A major factor in the demand for tinplate is that technology has permitted the minimum thickness of tin to be reduced gradually as new tinplate plants come on stream. In 1960 the average composition of tin in tinplate was about 0.8 percent; today it is below 0.6 percent.[7] This represents a change in yield of 125 tons of tinplate from 1 ton of tin to 167 tons from the same.

Among substitutes for tin plate are electrolytic, lacquered, enamelized, or plastic-coated bonderized plates. Also important for making cans is the substi-

Table 4-4
Tin Production Costs[a]

(weighted average unit costs, cents per pound equivalent)

Country	R[b]	1971	1972	1973	1974 Jan.–June	1974 July–Dec.	1975 Jan.–June	1975 July–Dec.	1976 Jan.–June	1976 July–Dec.	1977
Australia	+R	128	151	191	235	242	266	306	282	274	363
	−R	128	150	190	232	241	265	303	278	268	246
Bolivia	+R	176	190	235	295	310	324	343	360	386	403
	−R	160	160	176	219	235	256	274	297	300	319
Indonesia	+R	146	133	171	239	281	234	270	289	281	360
									247		
	−R	132	128	154	207	295	212	241	257	317	280
Malaysia	+R	128	137	161	248	270	248	256	279	281	364
	−R	97	103	122	165	188	182	189	199	186	218
Thailand	+R	120	122	138	219		233	247	283	283	312
	−R	86	87	98	145		165	176	207	193	208
United Kingdom	+R	177	180	164	224	278	294	380	261	286	374
	−R	173	178	160	221	275	291	376	257	288	363
Average[c]	+R	140	148	176	251	273	265	283	297	308	366
	−R	114	120	138	184	206	210	227	235	230	268
Index	+R	100	99	105	145	158	158	169	178	184	211
	−R	100	97	101	130	145	153	165	171	167	188
LME price		159	171	218	372		312		344		490

Source: International Tin Council Survey summarized in C. Rogers, "Commodity Case Study: Tin," Working Paper (Geneva: Commodities Division, UNCTAD, 1978).

[a] Weighted by the tonnage produced as stated in the replies to the survey conducted by the International Tin Council; figures for individual countries have been appropriately weighted according to the relative importance of different methods of mining in each country for each period.

[b] +R, including royalties, export duty, and tributes; −R, excluding royalties, export duty, and tributes.

[c] Weighted according to total production in each country.

Table 4-5
Consumption of Primary Tin Metal
(thousand long tons)

Country	1967	1968	1969	1970	1971	1972	1973	1974	1975	1976
Australia	4.5	3.9	3.7	3.8	3.9	3.5	4.3	4.3	3.3	3.6
Belgium	2.5	2.7	3.0	3.0	2.9	3.3	3.5	4.2	4.4	3.0
Canada	4.9	4.3	4.3	4.6	4.8	5.1	5.2	5.4	4.2	4.7
Czechoslovakia	2.2	4.0	3.0	3.4	3.4	3.5	3.5	3.8	3.4	3.5
France	10.8	9.7	10.7	10.5	10.4	10.9	11.7	11.3	10.3	10.2
Federal Republic of Germany	10.8	11.3	13.4	14.1	14.2	14.4	15.8	14.5	12.0	10.2
India	4.0	4.3	4.5	4.8	4.0	3.0	4.6	3.0	2.8	3.0
Italy	5.7	6.3	6.8	7.2	7.2	7.5	8.4	9.3	6.3	5.9
Japan	20.6	22.7	25.9	24.7	29.3	32.3	38.7	33.8	28.1	34.7
Netherlands	4.5	4.2	4.9	5.5	5.0	4.9	4.8	4.4	3.6	3.8
Poland	3.2	3.3	4.0	3.5	4.7	4.2	4.8	4.4	3.6	3.8
Romania	2.3	2.4	2.3	2.6	2.4	2.9	3.3	3.1	3.0	3.1
Spain	1.5	2.0	1.7	3.0	3.9	3.2	4.5	4.5	4.7	4.6
United Kingdom	17.6	17.4	18.1	17.0	16.4	14.6	16.6	14.5	12.2	13.4
United States	58.8	59.8	58.7	53.9	52.8	54.4	59.1	52.4	43.6	51.8
Others[a]	20.6	21.6	21.8	23.6	23.7	23.7	24.8	26.8	27.0	26.8
World total	174.5	179.9	186.8	185.2	189.0	191.4	213.6	199.7	173.2	192.0
Use in tinplate	80.4	79.6	83.3	79.4	80.8	76.8	81.4	86.1	72.0	79.4
Use in solder	26.6	28.3	27.8	30.2	30.3	35.2	39.4	29.3	27.6	32.8
Other uses	67.5	72.0	75.7	75.6	77.9	79.4	92.8	84.3	73.6	79.8

Source: International Tin Council, *Monthly Statistical Bulletin* (London: International Tin Council, various issues).

[a]Excludes Albania, the People's Republic of China, the Democratic Republic of Germany, Mongolia, North Korea, Vietnam (North Vietnam up to April 1975), and U.S.S.R.

tution of sheet steel coated with aluminum. In this regard the Weirton Steel Company has developed a "differential-coated" electro tinplate for the American Can Company. This consists of a different coating weight applied to each side of the steel sheet, as opposed to a uniform weight. Nonmetallic materials, copper, aluminum, and zinc-coated products have replaced tinplate in packaging as well as in roofing and construction. As a consequence, the relative importance of tin and tinplate has declined in most countries. Consumption of tin in solder has been maintained mostly by the continued development of the electronics industry. There has been no recent discoveries of substitutes for tin in solder, although the portion of the lead included has increased. The remaining industrial uses of tin vary considerably.[8]

This derived character of demand makes it particularly susceptible to fluctuations in the final demand for a number of products. The short-run price elasticity of demand given earlier is notably inelastic at −0.5 to −0.6. Consumers are generally not persuaded by substantial price reductions to use more and are not dissuaded by substantial price increases to use less. Over the historical period 1900–1970, the price of tin has risen more than the prices of other nonferrous metals. Consumption in the first half of the period rose also, but in the second half the increase slowed considerably. This may tend to confirm that even though the price of tin may be inelastic in the short run, the elasticity will increase after a certain point. Although relative tin prices are high, tin typically represents only a small fraction of the unit costs of goods incorporating the metal.[9]

Trade

Table 4–1 indicates that most of the tin produced is traded either in concentrates or metal, the former being the smaller of the two. In 1973 Bolivia was clearly the largest exporter of concentrates, shipping some 21,589 metric tons. The next largest exporters are Australia (4,495 tons), Zaire (4,384 tons), Indonesia (3,400 tons), and South Africa (1,748 tons). Of the countries which import concentrates, the United Kingdom is the largest with 15,156 tons, followed by Malaysia (9,267 tons), United States (4,552 tons), Belgium-Luxembourg (4,071 tons), and lesser amounts by Spain, U.S.S.R., Brazil, and Federal Republic of Germany.

Concerning metal trade, west Africa ships mainly to western Europe. Most of Bolivia's trade is with eastern Europe, but some of it goes to Argentina, the Netherlands and the United States. Australia ships mainly to North America and the United Kingdom. The trade patterns of Southeast Asian countries are more diverse, with shipments to most areas. Concerning the relative importance of the exporting countries, Malaysia, Thailand, and Indonesia export the most with, respectively, 48.5 percent, 13.1 percent and

8.6 percent of the world's total in 1973. Although the United Kingdom is not a producer, its ore imports are sufficient to maintain its position as a major country in smelting, and it thus accounts for some 11.2 percent. Among importers of refined tin metals, the United States is the largest, with a 1973 share of 26.3 percent. Japan is next with 22.1 percent, followed by West Germany with 9.9 percent and France with 8.2 percent.

Market Structure

The structure of the world tin market can be characterized as follows:

1. Most transactions in the market take place at the smelting stage. At this stage the market can be typified as a bilateral oligopoly.
2. The general scale of production has remained small and is not likely to expand.
3. Foreign and multinational participation has been more at the level of horizontal than vertical integration.
4. Foreign ownership and control of mining and smelting activities appears to have declined relatively more sharply over time than it has for the other minerals examined here.
5. There have been explicit attempts at international intervention in pricing, principally through the International Tin Council.

Organization and Concentration

The organization of the tin market is normally viewed as a bilateral oligopoly. Although there are many small firms on the supply side, the multinationals still retain a limited role. This is particularly true in the dredging sector which accounts for about 30 percent of output of tin in concentrates but only about 10 percent of employment in tin mining. Although the role of these firms once was more dominant, today there is countervailing power represented by the joint action of some of the developing producing countries. There also has been increasing nationalization. For example, "Bumaputra" policy in Malaysia has meant that the tin mining sector which was formerly owned and controlled from London now has its ownership and control vested in Malaysia.[10]

As shown in table 4–6 the concentration of smelting capacity is relatively high. The largest four firms account for 53 percent of capacity and the largest eight firms for 76 percent. More recently, the Bolivian state enterprise COMIBOL might replace Capper Pass and Son, Ltd. The role of the multinationals is believed to be strongest at the smelting stage, although some smelting companies do have ownership ties with mining companies. This

Table 4–6
Concentration in the World Tin Industry, 1976

Firm	Smelting Capacity	
	Shares (%)	Capacity (metric tons)
Largest four		
Datuk Keramat Smelting Bhd. (Malaysia)	18	70,000
Straits Trading Co. (Malaysia)	10	39,000
U.S.S.R. state-owned plants	16	60,000
China state-owned plants	9	35,000
Subtotal	53	204,000
Indexes (4)		
CR = 0.529; HH = 0.071; HG = 0.266; GR = 0.155		
Lesser four		
Thaisarco (Thailand)	7	25,000
Indonesia state-owned plant, Perusahaan Negara Tambang Timah	6	22,000
Capper Pass and Son, Ltd. (UK)	5	20,000
Gulf Chemical & Metallurgical Corp. (U.S.)	5	20,000
Subtotal	23	87,000
Indexes (8)		
CR = 0.764; HH = 0.087; HG = 0.295; GR = 0.269		
All other	24	43,100
Total	100.0	334,100

Source: G.S. Barry, *Tin*, Minerals Report No. 51 (Ottawa: Canadian Department of Energy, Mines and Resources, 1976).

linkage, nonetheless, is not considered to be an important factor in market arrangements between mines and smelters.

Table 4–6 also shows that two of the largest smelters are located in Malaysia, the Datuk Keramat Smelting Berhad with an 18.0 percent market share and the Straits Trading Company with a 10.0 percent share. The former, located on the Penang island, is partially owned by Patino N.V. The Straits Trading Company also has smelting works located in Penang. Its activities other than smelting involve finance and investment and the buying of ores and concentrates. It also has mining interests in Malaysia. The world's largest tin smelting organization is believed to be the Amalgamated Metal Corporation. It has substantial holdings in the major Nigerian smelter, Makeri Smelting Company.[11] Some other major AMC holdings are Australia's Associated Tin Smelters and Williams, Harvey and Company in the United

Kingdom. Although an equivalent number of firms exist on the demand or fabricating side, no information has been readily available regarding the extent of their concentration.

Industry organization at the mining stage involves three firms possessing an output substantially above all others.[12] As previously indicated, the largest is New Tradewinds (Malaysia Tin Berhad) in Malaysia, Nigeria, and Thailand providing about 8 percent of world production. Also important are the state-owned P.N. Timah in Indonesia and Corporation Minera de Bolivia (COMIBOL). P.N. Timah's production accounts for 10 percent of the world output and COMIBOL's for 9 percent. Before the forming of New Tradewinds, the London Tin Corporation was the major tin mining group and, together with two other groups, Anglo-Oriented and Patino, dominated the industry for years. At their height in the 1930s, the three accounted to about 25 percent of world tin mining production and over 33 percent of world metal production.[13]

Nationalization

From the nineteenth century tin was accepted in Indonesia as government owned, with the right to operate being farmed out to private persons with entirely Dutch capital. The system of farming out ceased in 1958, and the industry is now fully nationalized, both in ownership and management. Under the name of Perusahaan Negara Tambang Timah, it represents an executive agency of the Indonesian government and controls all phases of the tin mining industry, which includes exploration, mining processing and smelting, and marketing.

In the case of Bolivia, nationalization was applied in 1952 to three main groups—Patino, Hochschild, and Aramayo—which had become associated in Bolivian thinking with exploitation and external ownership. The Bolivian state mining enterprise, COMIBOL, owns, operates, and manages a large group of mines in addition to tin. These include tungsten, copper, bismuth, lead, silver, and zinc mines. About 50 percent of the Bolivian industry has remained in private hands.

In contrast to such nationalization, multinational or foreign expansion has been more at the level of horizontal or foreign participation than vertical integration. With regard to forward integration, this has been minimal, because the use of tinplate is dominated by steel firms and the use of solder is limited to firms associated with the electrical and electronics industry. Only in isolated instances such as in pewter production has there been a natural extension by stage of process. Backward integration also has been limited; smelters may have wished not to expand their traditional sales. Ley, however, believes that to a limited extent certain barriers to entry at the mining stage have prevailed.[14] Because a few smelters purchase concentrate from a large number of mines, it is unlikely that the ore could be obtained at a lower price. Mines, because of their size, would not have sufficient output or financial leverage to operate a smelting operation efficiently. The actual cost of smelting is also very large. For example, the cost of smelting in Bolivia in the late 1960s was around $1,000 per ton of capacity, with the necessary size to obtain economies of scale being at least 1,000 tons of capacity. Another barrier to entry is excess capacity. Since excess capacity does exist in the smelting of tin, there is less incentive to invest in new facilities. Institutional factors also act as barriers to entry. Various legal requirements, existing claims on ore reserves, and licensing have inhibited further expansion into tin mining.

As indicated, nationalization together with joint producer country action are becoming more prevalent in the industry. Indonesia was one of the first to nationalize in taking over Dutch capital invested in the industry. It is also the only producer developing country in which vertical integration extends to international marketing. Though it provides sales information for its agents from its world offices, its principal function is setting terms for long-run contracts. Government control in Bolivia has been more of a limited nature. There, as in parts of Africa, the multinationals still play a strong role, for example, in investments in exploration and joint ventures.

Producer Coordination

Although there has been a history of attempts by producers to influence prices through stocking arrangements, these attempts were never highly successful, basically because of the presence of a large number of small and medium-sized independent firms. The formation of an organization capable of accomplishing this took place in 1954. The International Tin Council (ITC) was spawned by the first International Tin Agreement (ITA) in 1954 and was continued in later agreements.[15] The purpose of the Agreement has been mainly to influence and to lessen wide price swings through the use of export controls and buffer stocks.[16] The principal producing country members of the latest agreement are Australia, Bolivia, Indonesia, Malaysia, Nigeria, Thailand, and Zaire.[17] In 1971, these countries included 91 percent of world mine production (outside the U.S.S.R. and China). Brazil has remained a nonmember because the opening up of a new tin field in Rondonia has brought the Brazilian tin production to some 4,000 tons in 1970, with hopes for a very much higher increase in the near future. Another problem with the effectiveness of the ITA has been the lack of participation by consumers. Among these, the United States did not become a member of the council until the fifth agreement in 1976.

Market Implications

Export Dependence

The extent of the dependence of the producing developing countries varies with the share of their export earnings from tin relative to total export earnings.

These shares have been low for the main exporting countries, particularly when compared to that of the other minerals in this study. In 1973, tin exports accounted for 12.2 percent of total exports for Malaysia, 6.5 percent for Thailand, 2.0 percent for Indonesia, 9.6 percent for Bolivia, and 0.7 percent for Nigeria.

The growth in export value of these commodities since 1955 has been consistent, except for Nigeria. Table 4–7 provides a measure of the growth in trend. Although trade in the world tin market takes place principally in the form of ingots, only Malaysia's earnings have been derived totally from ingot trade over the period. Thailand exported tin in concentrates until 1965, then ingots from that year. Bolivia has seen growth in the exports of both tin in concentrates and ingots. Indonesia also exports both, but export growth has been only in ingots. Nigeria has exported only ingots since 1965.

The level of tin export earnings has risen for these four countries with the exception of Nigeria, as shown in table 4–7. The deflated unit values, however, have fallen for all countries except Bolivia, principally because of the later base year of that country. Surprisingly fluctuations in the deflated unit values of tin are roughly the same as for bauxite if not lower. This does not reflect the substantial price variability that was found for copper.

Magnitude of Fixed Investment

Tin production units have been characterized as small scale. Investment costs cited for a 152-ton-per-year gravel pumping facility in Malaysia are in the vicinity of $500,000. That these are the lowest investment costs of the minerals considered here can be seen by comparing the costs with the following measures of national economic activity. Gross domestic product (GDP), gross domestic investment (GDI) and the mining component of domestic product (MS) are given in 1973 dollars (million) for the major tin-producing countries.

	GDP	MS	GDI
Malaysia	4,644	204	842
Thailand	7,828	130	1,884
Bolivia	976	177	65
Indonesia	8,722	728	1,565
Nigeria	8,387	2,175	1,712

Under these conditions, the financing of tin projects cannot be seen as a major factor affecting the bargaining relationship between governments and the tin companies.

Table 4–7
Trend and Variability of Tin Export Values and Unit Values, FOB
(millions of dollars and dollars per metric ton)

Year	Malaysia Export Value	Malaysia Unit Value	Malaysia De-flated[a]	Thailand Export Value	Thailand Unit Value	Thailand De-flated	Bolivia Export Value	Bolivia Unit Value	Bolivia De-flated	Indonesia Export Value	Indonesia Unit Value	Indonesia De-flated	Nigeria Export Value	Nigeria Unit Value	Nigeria De-flated	Tin Price LME (¢/lb)	Tin Price De-flated
1955	141.4[b]	1956	—	20.6[b]	—	—	57.1[c]	—	—	59.4[d]	—	—	16.4[d]	—	—	—	—
1960	165.3	2130	2536	25.4[c]	—	—	39.7[c]	—	—	55.4	2111	2513	16.9[c]	—	—	99.6	119
1965	282.5	3787	4303	56.0[d]	3840	4364	78.4[c]	—	—	39.9	4000	4545	41.7[b]	3897	4428	176.5	201
1970	528.5	3574	3574	77.8[d]	3569	3569	102.4[d]	—	—	55.7	4465	4465	46.8	4266	4266	166.7	167
1971	294.3	3394	3232	74.5	3456	3291	105.9	3515	3319	62.2	3576	3406	34.7	4131	3934	158.4	151
1972	302.7	3666	3244	80.8	3692	3267	113.5	3727	3298	69.4	3696	3271	29.1	4217	3732	170.8	151
1973	269.8	4521	3399	99.8	4541	3414	129.9	4696	3531	84.4	4500	3383	23.5	4509	3390	218.3	164
1974	629.3	7387	4560	152.7	7538	4653	228.4	7736	4306	162.5	7550	4660	42.0	5453	3366	371.5	229
1975	465.9	6470	3555	106.2	6173	3392	189.1	6800	3736	133.7	6521	3435	31.5	5620	3088	311.6	171
Trend (%)[e] 1975/1965	165	171	83	190	161	78	241	193	113	335	163	76	76	144	70	177	85
Variability (%)[f] 1970–1975	37	35	14	30	35	15	36	36	17	46	32	16	25	14	12	38	17

Source: U.N. *Yearbook of International Trade Statistics* (New York: United Nations, various issues); UNCTAD, *Commodity Price Bulletin*, CD/CPB/92/Rev. 1 (Geneva: UNCTAD, 1977).

[a] Deflator is U.N. Index of Unit Value of Exported Manufactured Goods (1970 = 100).

[b] Metal.

[c] Concentrates.

[d] Concentrates + metal.

[e] Ratio between 1965 and 1975.

[f] Coefficient of variation in percent over 1970–1976.

Nature of Technology

The nature of technology in tin mining varies with the several different methods that can be employed. Since this technology is stable as well as simple in most cases, the host government would appear to have the advantage in industry control. Variations in mining technology provide different forms of industry structure. For example, gravel pump mining is not only simple but also labor intensive. It has been more popular among domestic mining operators in Malaysia.

Dredging, which is only slightly more complex but much more capital intensive, is preferred by foreign firms (such firms have had a strong if not majority Malaysian interest since 1960). Thoburn has shown that the host government may have to accept the latter technique because it is more viable at a wide range of prices and hence less risky.[18] The adoption of dredging would thus be to the advantage of the foreign firms rather than the host government. For the case of investment in smelting, the technology is more complex but sufficiently stable that the foreign firm has no advantage.

The technology of the mining process is also of importance in Bolivia. Since the country possesses only low-grade ore deposits, problems exist not only in concentration but also in the resultant production of some tin in concentrates which are not acceptable to many smelters. This situation does not appear to have influenced any shifts in power between the government and the tin companies.

Control over Resources and Production

The tin industry is characterized by strong private ownership patterns as well as by state-owned mining firms. Private domestic and foreign firms are still prevalent in the tin industries of Malaysia and Thailand. In Indonesia, mention has already been made of the industry being completely under control of the state-owned enterprise, P.T. Nimah. In Bolivia, COMIBOL is responsible for most of the tin production, some 67 percent in 1973–1974.[19]

There are indications, however, of increased government control in Malaysia. For example, discoveries have been made of tin dredging potential in the deep waters off of west Malaysia's continental shelf. As of 1975, the Malaysian government granted offshore exploration rights only to a subsidiary of the state-owned company, Pernas.[20] There is also a recent movement to bring more companies under domestic ownership, as is reflected in the Outline Perspective Plan (1973–1990). The intent of the government is to restructure the economy such that employment as well as the ownership of assets will more accurately represent the shares of population of different ethnic groups. The projections are for assets held by foreigners to be only 30 percent, Malays 30 percent, and other Malaysians 40 percent.[21] Although implementation may never be complete, at present all new foreign investments in tin mining require 70 percent Malaysian ownership. This has meant pressure toward entering into joint ventures with either the state-owned Pernas or with the Economic Development Corporation of each state. There also has been pressure on foreign companies to shift their domicile to Kuala Lumpur. Mentioned earlier has been the takeover of the London Tin Corporation by New Tradewinds.

Control of new investment in Malaysian mining is also being extended through the powers of individual states to grant leases on lands, including the right to transfer previous nonmineral lands to mining. The exercise of this power has been reflected in delays in granting as well as in renewing leases. Furthermore, property permits only are being issued which give the bearer no prior claim in obtaining a mining lease. According to Thoburn, this wielding of bargaining power on the part of the Malaysian government is significantly stifling the investment climate.[22]

Opportunities for Increased Processing

The first possibility for increased processing is at the smelting stage. Here two problems would appear to exist. First, tin has been one of the slowest growing commodities in the past decade. Between 1955 and 1972–1974, total demand for primary tin grew at only 1.7 percent annually.[23] The prospect for the period between 1972–1974 and 1985 is growth at only 1.5 percent annually. As previously indicated, this sluggishness has been mainly due to the use of thinner coats in tinplating and the substitution of tin-free steel and aluminum for tinplate.

A second problem is that current world primary tin smelting capacity exceeds world mine capacity and that this situation is not likely to change over the next fifteen years.[24] Recent additions have been made and planned additions to capacity are taking place in Indonesia, Bolivia, and South Africa. Nominal world capacity will soon rise to 250,000 tons per year which far exceeds current production levels, somewhat less than 200,000 tons per year.[25] Estimates of investment costs also suggest that new smelters will have to charge a fee higher than that of existing smelters in Malaysia to make treatment profitable.

Possibilities for further processing downstream seem limited. To begin with, the technical demands of users of most tin products tend to favor either manufacture in the industrialized countries or manufacture near the area of use. The considerable technical complexity of tin applications in production also inhibits smelters from entering this phase. In addition, smelters lose a degree of flexibility in adapting to markets in which they sell, particularly as the products become more complex. Finally, industrial products utilizing tin face a complex range of tariff and nontariff barriers.

Material Share in Product Prices

The proportions of tin metal in tin industrial products is indeed small. For example, the average composition of tin in tinplate, its major use, has been estimated at only 0.6 percent.[26] Because of the difficulty of obtaining prices on tin products, it has been difficult to estimate the proportion of material costs in product prices. Although it would appear that this small share constitutes an advantage for host governments to raise prices or increase taxes, the price of tin metal is already high relative to substitutes such as aluminum, glass, paper, plastics, and tin-free steel. Thus there seems little possibility for raising prices, given present patterns of end use.

Obsolescing Bargain

Foreign tin firms did at one time occupy a strong position in relation to host governments, but today governments are demanding more of the gains from industry. In the case of Indonesia and Bolivia, the transfer of gains has been for the most part completed through the process of nationalization. In Malaysia, the attempts to increase domestic participation in foreign companies together with pressure on their relocation in Kuala Lumpur suggests that the evolution of the obsolescing bargain is considerably advanced.

Although this normally implies considerable bargaining strength on the part of the host governments, excessive taxation appears to be hampering industry development. In fact, a major uncertainty faced by firms attempting to invest in the tin industry is the variability in tax rates and tax structures imposed by host governments. Thoburn has shown the effect of this on industry stagnation in Malaysia.[27] Gillis et al. elaborate on this problem as it exists in Bolivia as well as in other major tin-producing countries.[28]

Examples of the variety of taxes imposed on tin production are as follows: Malaysia has export taxes on tin in concentrates and metal, export duty surcharge on metals, and income taxes; Thailand has production royalties on tin in concentrates, business tax, income tax, and municipal taxes; Indonesia has land rents, royalties on tin in concentrates and metal, and corporation taxes (some proportion of these taxes also fall on state enterprises); and Bolivia has land rents, royalties on exports, and export taxes (some taxes apply to COMIBOL). In the case of Bolivia, Gillis et al. indicate a number of unfavorable effects.[29] These include less than optimal investment both in tin exploration and development as well as an improper choice of technology at the exploitation and beneficiation stages. The resulting industry distortions produced thus include underinvestment, excess production, and an over-reliance of government tax revenues on the tin sector.

Nature of Competition

The degree of concentration found for the tin industry in 1974 was high. The largest four firms account for 51.7 percent of total smelting capacity and the largest eight firms for 76.5 percent. On a country basis, Malaysia, Bolivia, Thailand, and Indonesia account for about 75 percent of world exports of smelted tin, developing countries as a whole accounting for some 90 percent. Such a level of concentration, however, does not imply a lack of competition in pricing. Not only are tin prices determined on auction, they are also highly interrelated with competitive buying and selling on the LME. In addition, Malaysia exports to a number of buyers throughout the world, and any of these buyers have some leeway to shift their purchases elsewhere. The declining role of the multinationals in the tin market also suggests increased competition. But with most production resting in the hands of the developing countries, this could create a force working against free-market trading.

Government Learning Process

There is no doubt that the governments of tin-producing countries are well advanced along the learning curve of industry contract negotiation and control. Compared to the other prototype minerals examined, governments own a considerable portion of the world's tin resources and tin capacity. However, in the process of obtaining control, it appears that distortions in policy instruments such as taxation have prevented the learning process from developing in a direction which would favor investment and increase resource exploitation.

Price Formation

Tin possesses no single marketing structure. Purchases of tin can be made directly by the consuming firms from smelters in the producing countries or from tin merchants who buy tin in the producing areas and sell it through brokers to the consumers. Merchants usually have their own brokerage firm, permitting them to deal directly on the LME with other brokers representing the consumer. Although different producer-consumer arrangements can be found, most often the consumer will deal directly with a smelter or have a contract with a merchant. The role of the latter normally is to buy tin ore or metal, to ship it, and to finance the entire transaction until it is delivered to the consumer.

The foundation of world tin prices stems from the physical market at Penang. Prices on this market are also closely coordinated with those of the LME and other world markets; the most important prices are listed in table

4–8. Most trade on the Penang market is between producers and the two major smelters who represent the Malaysian mines; however, a smaller amount of ore does come from Africa, Burma, Indonesia, and Thailand. Penang not being a true spot market in the sense of the LME, it still does guide the world tin price. The LME price for large volume transactions is basically the Penang price plus costs of shipping, insurance, and finance together with a markup.

The Straits Trading Company and Sharikat Eastern Smelting Bhol provide the basis for the Penang marketing system. Each day the approximate 1,000 mines in Malaysia offer a proportion of their output for sale. Weighing, sampling, and assaying of the concentrates arriving at the smelters takes place early in the morning so that the smelters know the quality of metal that is to be offered that day. The smelters then exchange the information they have received with each other, giving the total quantity of ore they have for inclusion in the day's pricing as well as the details of the bids they have received. Bidders can be dealers such as members of the LME or other agents acting on behalf of buyers.

By selling the quantity offered at the highest single price that it can be cleared, the market price is reached. This takes place by drawing a line at the price which will take care of all the day's offerings. Bids at a higher price gain the advantage of being met in full, while bids at a price lower than the day's price are subject to rationing. Producers thus have sold their offerings through the smelters, who then pay the export tax and convert the ore. The price reached, however, is neither a spot nor strictly a forward one, since the smelters have the option to deliver the metal on any day within the sixty days from the date of contract. Conversion then takes place as quickly as possible, and efficiency in transportation also reduces the costs of obtaining the metal.

Some other marketing points of interest in the world are Indonesia, Bolivia, Thailand, and the United Kingdom. Indonesia is unique in that its tin industry is vertically integrated into the marketing of its products and the entire process is under government control. Despite government control of its industry, Bolivia does not carry out its marketing and instead has contracts with various merchants. In Thailand, the Billiton Company has in the past handled both mining and smelting. The only marketing point of interest in an

Table 4–8
Major Tin Price Quotations

London Metal Exchange
    Standard tin, minimum 99.75%, cash for delivery in warehouse excluding duty.
    Forward for same.

U.S. import price, CIF New York, Straits tin.

Federal Republic of Germany, purity 99.9%, Loco Duisburg.

Penang market, Ex-works, Straits Grade A, minimum 99.8%.

industrialized country is that of the LME, which deals in transactions between various dealers regarding the buying and selling of refined metal. Since uncertainty exists between the time the ore is purchased from the smelter until it is delivered to the consumer (approximately eight weeks), merchants often use the forward contract facility of the LME to hedge their purchases.

Like other metals, tin prices fluctuate because of cyclical changes in demand induced by economic activity and a relatively fixed supply in the short run. The International Tin Council (ITC) has attempted to lessen these fluctuations through buffer stock operations. As designated by the ITC in its first agreement, the buffer stock manager directs stock purchases and sales so as to contain prices as observed on the LME within some specified band. When the market price falls below a specified level, then the manager can begin buying tin for the buffer stock on any of the tin markets. When the price reaches the ceiling, then an attempt to lower price is made by selling out of the stock. Export controls can assist in floor price operations.

Control of the tin price in this manner, however, has not proved highly effective. In particular, the buffer stock operation has run short of either capital or stocks. In 1957 the U.S. government through the General Services Administration stopped tin purchases for its strategic stockpile. At the same time the Soviet Union, having refused to join the Tin Agreement, increased its tin exports to the West, even though in 1958 the British and Dutch governments tried to shelter the ITC from the effects of these sales by restricting imports of Russian tin. By 1958, world economic activity had taken a downturn and prices were falling, and this time Bolivia had to request a U.S. loan of $26 million to help it through the resulting crisis. In September 1958, after spending $20 million on tin for the buffer stock, the manager's funds ran out and prices fell below the floor price, reaching a level of £640 a ton on the LME. Thereafter, recovery was rapid, and in June 1961 the entire tin stock was exhausted and prices rose. As this happened, it was suggested that releases from the U.S. stockpile could also be used to check price rises, but this time the president of COMIBOL, troubled by Bolivia's high production costs, remarked that such a move would constitute economic aggression against the developing country tin producers.

During the second International Tin Agreement, releases from the U.S. stockpile occurred, but prices still increased. The third agreement ran from 1966 to 1971, but near the end of that period, prices in the free market were so strong that the ITC again was incapable of checking them for long. In April of 1971, the buffer stock ran out again and was followed by a rise in price to a record £1,630 a ton. Prices fell slightly in 1970, and the buffer stock manager started to buy again. In January 1971, a fourth international agreement was reached. It differed in two major respects from its predecessors. Buffer stock operations were more flexible, and the Soviet Union joined the club, followed by the United States in 1976.

Obviously the success of the ITC in controlling prices is questionable. Smith and Schink, who analyzed its effectiveness, offer the following conclusions.[30] First, the tin agreement has only marginally reduced the instability of prices and producer income. A greater influence in supporting the ceiling price has been U.S. government stockpile transactions of tin made outside the tin agreement. Second, the agreement has endured while other agreements have failed, in part because it has lacked effective power in the face of the United States strategic stockpile to make critical price decisions which otherwise would have intensified producer-consumer conflicts. Finally, if the agreement had been designed from the beginning as an effective market stabilizer along the lines currently envisaged for other products, there is a good chance it would have been more successful. Some other important views on the successfulness of the ITC can be found in Brown.[31]

To summarize, our analysis of market conditions and structure has revealed a weak bilateral oligopoly, in fact leaning toward ingot pricing of a highly competitive nature. Competition in the industry has been increasing at the same time as increasing nationalization. Because of the active participation of consumers in the ITC, price control is directed more toward stabilization than changing the price trend. Since the tin buffer stock operation is likely to begin again, this time with increased capitalization, this form of control is likely to persist. For the immediate future, tin production capability appears to be fixed. Given an unexpected growth in demand in excess of 2 percent, this suggests an upward pressure on prices until capacity adjusts.[32] The major factor that could change this trend in price formation is presently unlikely—the future substitution away from tin in tinplate.

Notes

1. K. Takeuchi, G. Thiebach, and J. Hilmy, "Investment Requirements in the Non-Fuel Mineral Sector in Developing Countries," *Natural Resources Forum,* 1 (1977): 263–75.

2. K.K. Lim, "The Economics of Gravel Pump Mining in Malaysia," paper presented at the International Tin Symposium, LaPaz, November 1977.

3. Production and smelting figures from K.L. Harris, "Tin," in *Mineral Facts and Problems, 1975* (Washington, D.C.: U.S. Department of the Interior, 1975).

4. *Tin International,* July 1977, p. 251.

5. See UNCTAD, "Study on the Degree and Scope for Increased Processing of Primary Commodities in Developing Countries," vol. II (London: Commodities Research Unit, 1975), p. 151.

6. A major problem in adopting tin mining methods is not only relative cost differences but also differences between labor and capital intensities. An evaluation of the appropriateness of different methods and their relative profitabilities in a developing country context can be found in J. Thoburn, "Commodity Prices and Appropriate Technology: Some Lessons from Tin Mining," *Journal of Development Studies,* 14 (1977): 35–52.

7. D.A. Robbins, *Technological Developments in Tin Consumption Combat Substitution* (London: Tin Research Institute, 1977).

8. Tin and tin alloy coatings come in the form of pure tin, tin-lead, bronze, tin-nickel, and tin-zinc. Tin alloys, in addition to solder, include bronze, which has marine and electrical uses; tin base, which is used in pewter and jewelry; and fusible alloys, which are used in alarm systems. Inorganic tin compounds are employed as catalysts and reductants as well as in toothpaste and soap. Organic tin compounds appear in fungicides, insecticides, an stabilizers. In these latter areas, however, possibilities for replacement by chemicals are increasing. See B.T.K. Barry, *In Every Sphere* (London: Tin Research Institute, 1977).

9. R. Ley, "Bolivian Tin and Bolivian Development," unpublished Ph.D. Thesis, Washington State University, 1977.

10. C. Rogers, "Commodity Case Study—Tin," Working Paper (Geneva: Commodities Division, UNCTAD, 1978).

11. *Tin International,* June 1978, p. 216.

12. Figures from Harris, "Tin."

13. W. Fox, *Tin: The Working of a Commodity Agreement* (London: Mining Journal Books, 1974).

14. Ley, "Bolivian Tin."

15. The first agreement ran from July 1956 to June 1961, the second from July 1961 to June 1966, the third from July 1966 to June 1971, the fourth from July 1971 to June 1976, and the fifth from July 1976.

16. A complete description of the ITC, the history of the tin agreements to 1972, and buffer stock controls appears in W. Fox, *Tin.*

17. The consuming country members are: Austria, Belgium/Luxembourg, Bulgaria, Canada, Czechoslovakia, Denmark, France, F.R. Germany, Hungary, India, Ireland, Rep. of Italy, Japan, Rep. of Korea, Netherlands, Poland, Romania, Spain, Turkey, U.S.S.R., United Kingdom, and Yugoslavia.

18. Thoburn, "Commodity Prices."

19. See M. Gillis et al., *Taxation and Mining* (Cambridge, Mass.: Ballinger Publishing Co., 1978), p. 32.

20. Ibid., p. 130.

21. See J. Thoburn, "Malaysia's Tin Supply Problems," *Resources Policy* 4 (1978): 31–34.

22. Ibid.

23. World Bank, *Price Prospects for Primary Commodities,* Annex III, p. 14.

24. See UNCTAD, "Study on the Degree and Scope for Increased Processing of Primary Commodities in Developing Countries," TD/184/ Suppl. 3 (Geneva: UNCTAD, 1975), pp. 150–54.

25. Ibid.

26. Robbins, *Technological Developments.*

27. Thoburn, "Commodity Prices."

28. Gillis, *Taxation and Mining.*

29. Ibid., pp. 237–49.

30. See G.W. Smith and G.R. Schink, "The International Tin Agreement: A Reassessment," *Economic Journal,* 86 (1976): 715–28.

31. See chapter 5 in C. Brown, *The Political and Social Economy of Commodity Control* (London: Macmillan, 1979).

32. G.S. Barry, "Tin," Preprint No. 51 from the *Canadian Minerals Yearbook, 1976* (Ottawa: Department of Energy, Mines and Resources, 1976), pp. 17–18.

5 Bauxite

Market Conditions

Analysis of the bauxite market cannot be conducted independently of alumina and aluminum. The stages of production and of intermediate demand for these raw materials are closely linked as depicted in figure 5–1. That figure also shows the market to be dominated by major multinationals, which are vertically integrated from bauxite mining through smelting and even fabrication of aluminum end products. Three of the six major multinationals are domiciled in the United States, and one each are managed from Canada, France, and Switzerland. Together they control more than 50 percent of non-Socialist world capacity of bauxite, alumina, and aluminum. Their dominant position and the wide scope of their operations make it difficult to conceive of major new projects of international significance which do not require the participation of one or more of these firms.

The market also contains a small number of independent companies. The transformation of bauxite requires first conversion to alumina, and then smelting into refined aluminum. Figure 5–1 suggests that the major multinationals produced less bauxite than they needed at the alumina production stage, depending on the independents for the remainder. The former, however, have abundant alumina production, some of which is absorbed by the independents. The relative importance of bauxite, alumina, and aluminum production and trade are given in table 5–1 on a world basis from 1955. Since that time production and trade have grown immensely, some four or five times.

Production

Roughly 15 percent of the earth's crust is composed of aluminum compounds, and the availability of aluminum ores is ample and widespread.[1] Bauxite is a generic term given to any material containing at least 32 percent aluminum oxides (alumina). Most bauxite mined is of metallurgical grade, although it can also be of chemical, refactory, and abrasive grades. This basis grade contains at least 50 percent alumina (Al_2O_3), which corresponds to an aluminum content of about 25 percent in the ores.

Similar to other metals, the production of aluminum can be described in terms of a primary industry and a secondary industry. The former involves the

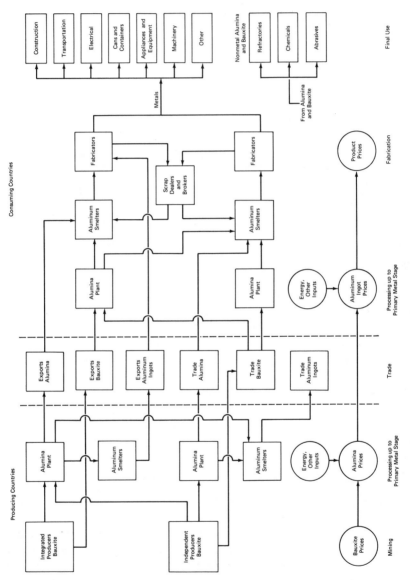

Figure 5-1. Market and Price Structure for Bauxite and Aluminum.

Table 5-1
World Balance Sheet for Bauxite
(metric tons)

Commodity Flow	1955	1960	1965	1966	1967	1968	1969	1970	1971	1972	1973	1974	1975	1976
Ore production (metal content)	3,800	5,922	7,979	8,776	9,654	9,954	11,706	12,971	14,261	15,082	15,990	17,995	16,527	17,272
Alumina production (metal content)	3,188	4,566	6,695	7,404	8,317	8,737	9,873	10,548	11,338	11,751	13,315	14,327	13,282	13,768
Aluminum production (primary)	3,105	4,543	7,209	7,208	7,933	8,515	9,459	10,257	10,936	11,649	12,707	13,824	12,705	13,083
Ore exports (metal content)	2,490	3,654	4,772	5,060	5,261	5,244	5,932	6,475	6,693	6,619	6,983	8,301	7,775	7,682
Alumina exports[a] (metal content)	328	704	1,230	1,613	1,778	2,147	2,480	3,806	4,373	4,862	5,370	6,288	6,031	6,262
Aluminum exports	—	1,418	2,240	2,563	2,600	3,107	3,635	3,729	3,625	4,118	4,704	5,170	—	—
Aluminum consumption (primary and secondary)	3,718	5,157	8,379	9,485	9,706	11,126	12,366	12,484	13,429	14,593	16,805	17,944	14,587	17,601

Source: UNCTAD, "The World Market for Bauxite: Characteristics and Trends," TD/B/IPC/BAUXITE/2/Add. 1 (Geneva: UNCTAD, 1978); and World Bank, "Market Structure of Bauxite/Alumina/Aluminum: And Prospects for Developing Countries," Commodity Paper No. 24 (3/77) (Washington, D.C.: United Nations, 1977).
[a]Estimates only.

necessary stages of aluminum production: (1) exploring for bauxite deposits, (2) developing mines, refineries, smelters, and other facilities for conversion, and (3) processing the bauxite into alumina and then to aluminum. The secondary industry involves the collection and subsequent recycling of scrap into the smelting stage.

Beginning at the exploration stage, some recent estimates of ore reserve levels are given in table 5–2. The figures relate to known reserves which are profitable to exploit at today's prices and technology. Guinea has the largest reserves at 33.9 percent followed by Australia (18.6 percent), Brazil (10.3 percent), Jamaica (6.2 percent), and India (5.8 percent). The developing countries shown account for a substantial portion of the total. If we take the 1976 world production of bauxite at 83 million tons gross weight, then the reserves could last as long as 296 years. Variations in the figure depend on growth in the rate of consumption relative to the rate of discovery as well as on new technological developments.

To advance from the exploration to the production stage is a lengthy and expensive process. Project development requires opening bauxite mines together with processing facilities before the ore can be converted into alumina and aluminum. The length of time for opening new facilities is about three years to five years. While the capacity of open-pit bauxite mines can be

Table 5–2
World Estimated Bauxite Reserves, 1976

Country	Reserve Grade (% Al_2O_3)	Quantity (million metric tons)	Percent of World Total
Guinea	54	8,330	33.9
Australia	50	4,570	18.6
Brazil	—	2,540	10.3
Jamaica	50	1,520	6.2
India	—	1,420	5.8
Guyana	58	1,020	4.1
U.R. Cameroon	—	1,020	4.1
Greece	50	760	3.1
Indonesia	—	710	2.9
Ghana	—	580	2.4
Surinam	58	500	2.0
Yugoslavia	—	410	1.7
Hungary	50	200	0.8
U.S.S.R.	50	150	0.6
United States	50	40	0.2
Rest of world		830	3.3
Total		24,600	100.0

Source: United States Bureau of Mines, United States Geological Survey, and International Bauxite Association.

increased fairly rapidly, expansions of alumina and aluminum facilities may take two years or more.

The investment costs of development have risen very quickly. Some recent estimates derived from industry sources give the capital cost per ton of capacity in 1975 U.S. dollars as follows:[2]

Bauxite mining	85
Alumina refining (integrated)	510
Alumina refining (nonintegrated)	750
Aluminum smelting (integrated)	1,900
Aluminum smelting (nonintegrated)	2,800

The total costs of an integrated facility would come to $2,495 per ton of capacity which breaks down to 3.4 percent at the bauxite stage, 20.4 percent at the alumina stage, and 76.2 percent at the aluminum ingot stage. To add a thermal power station for the smelting facility would add capital costs of roughly 24 to 44 percent to the above estimates. The cost of expanding existing integrated facilities has been estimated at about 60 percent of total facility cost.

Aggregating the capital cost per ton estimates to reach project totals reveals the amounts of investment capital required. Development of a bauxite mine for the Trombetas deposit in Brazil has been estimated to cost $280 million, and expansion of the mine and refinery at the Boke deposit in Guinea is estimated at $400 million.[3] Given these dollar magnitudes, such projects require participation by consortia of firms rather than individual firms to spread risks and costs.

Concerning mining and processing technology, over 90 percent of the world's bauxite is mined by open pit methods. Although there are environmental drawbacks to this method, it has the advantage that mining capacity may be expanded rather cheaply and fairly fast. However, underground mining is common in Hungary, the U.S.S.R., and other parts of Europe. Sometimes blasting of the ore is required as in Guyana and Surinam, or none is required as in Jamaica. Presently, the only commercial process for converting bauxite to alumina is the Bayer process.[4] The importance of this is that, while the American Bayer process is adapted to Caribbean bauxite and the European Bayer process is used for the processing of boehmite, the traditional Bayer process is designed for bauxite with less than 10 percent silicon content. It may be of some significance to note that in Europe a method that directly reduces bauxite to aluminum is in operation.

The location of the world's bauxite and aluminum capacity together with production for 1973 is given in table 5–3. Although bauxite can be refined into alumina at the point where it is mined, it has historically been shipped abroad for processing. Thus there is a discrepancy between the major countries producing bauxite and those producing aluminum. It is easy to note that many

Table 5–3
World Aluminum Capacity and Production, 1973
(thousand short tons of aluminum or aluminum equivalent)

Country	Bauxite		Alumina		Aluminum	
	Capacity	Production	Capacity	Production	Capacity	Production
North America						
United States (includes Virgin Islands)	650	442	4,044	3,825	4,893	4,529
Canada	—	—	722	664	1,210	1,030
Jamaica	3,700	3,120	1,724	1,239	—	—
Other	500	432	—	—	44	43
Total	4,850	3,994	6,490	5,728	6,147	5,602
South America						
Brazil	200	160	148	115	122	125
Guyana	1,200	870	201	136	—	—
Surinam	2,200	2,160	760	792	73	57
Other	—	—	—	—	25	26
Total	3,600	3,190	1,109	1,043	220	208
Europe						
France	800	691	747	728	457	397
West Germany	—	—	1,005	520	817	587
Greece	750	580	276	276	160	157
Italy	50	10	465	277	312	203
Norway	—	—	—	—	761	684
U.S.S.R.	1,000	940	1,823	1,354	1,578	1,500
Other	1,300	1,130	1,002	778	1,839	1,621
Total	3,900	3,351	5,318	3,933	5,924	5,149
Africa						
Ghana	100	68	—	—	162	168
Guinea	2,000	780	402	353	—	—
Other	200	147	—	—	118	107
Total	2,300	995	402	353	280	275
Asia						
India	450	280	362	180	254	170
Japan	—	—	1,368	1,141	1,356	1,215
Other	900	725	330	199	484	391
Total	1,350	1,005	2,060	1,520	2,094	1,776
Oceania						
Australia	4,600	4,175	2,828	2,311	253	228
New Zealand	—	—	—	—	123	121
Total	4,600	4,175	2,828	2,311	376	349
World Total	20,600	16,710	18,207	14,888	15,041	13,359

Source: *Mineral Facts and Problems, 1975* (Washington, D.C.: U.S. Department of the Interior, 1975).

of the major bauxite producers are negligible aluminum producers, let alone exporters. Further, the major aluminum capacity in the world today is located in the United States, Canada, the U.S.S.R., and Japan. There is some production in Europe and Australia, but in developing countries such as Jamaica and

Guyana it is negligible. One of the principal reasons why aluminum smelters have been located in developed countries is due to their high initial investment costs. The large multinationals have felt more secure about making large investments in countries such as the United States which has had abundant cheap energy in the past and a major need for aluminum smelters.

World bauxite production in 1975 was 16.5 million tons in metal equivalent. Corresponding to this was 13.3 million tons of alumina and 12.7 million tons of aluminum. From table 5–3 one finds that bauxite production originates in six countries: Australia, 25 percent; Jamaica, 19 percent; Surinam, 13 percent; U.S.S.R., 6 percent; Guyana, 5 percent; and Guinea, 5 percent. The growth in bauxite production over time has proven very rapid. Given a production of 8.0 million tons in 1965 and an annual cumulative growth rate over the decade amounting to 9 percent, production reached the 16.5 illion tons cited above. With one or two exceptions, the major producing countries in 1973 were also important suppliers ten years earlier. In Australia, however, large-scale bauxite production started only in 1963, and accounted in that year for no more than 1 percent of world output. By 1971 the country became the world's leading producer, with an output marginally surpassing that of Jamaica.[5]

The competitiveness of a bauxite mine depends only partially on the richness of its ores. Other factors of importance in the determination of total costs include the thickness of overburden which requires removal, the size of the ore body, the consequent scale of operations, and perhaps most importantly, the cost of transporting the bauxite to its final destination. In the late 1960s, typical mining costs in the Caribbean and Australia amounted to between $1.75 and $4.50 per ton.[6] Transport costs varied from as little as $1.65 per ton for mines close to harbor facilities with short sea routes to a high of $9 in extreme cases.[7] Caribbean and Australian bauxites have considerable competitive advantages in terms of total CIF costs in North America and Japan, accounting for the heavy concentration of production in these areas.

Some more recent estimates of costs of bauxite production in 1974 dollars are given below. They comprise average total costs of production, including wages, electricity, fuel, depreciation of machinery and interest costs.[8] Also averaged are regional cost differences within countries, so that each country could be represented by an average cost.

Country	Cost in dollars per metric ton
Australia	9.22
Brazil	6.57
Guyana	7.04
Jamaica	7.63
Surinam	7.18
Guinea	7.91
Greece	6.74
Hungary	8.06

Economies of scale may or may not be important in bauxite mining, depending on the need for infrastructure and the amount of overburden. Nonetheless, new mining ventures frequently exceed the 1-million-ton level. It is at the alumina and aluminum ingot stage that economies of scale become more important, and the size of the total facility is adjusted until the optimum size of plant is reached.

Consumption

The demand for bauxite and alumina is derived from the demand for primary aluminum and ultimately from the final demands for aluminum-based manufactures. It takes approximately 2.5 tons of bauxite to equal 1 ton of alumina, and 2 tons of alumina are required in the production of 1 ton of aluminum. This varies slightly with the bauxite type. Thus, an increase of 1 ton in the demand for aluminum dictates an increase in the demand for bauxite of 5 tons. In fact, bauxite is of several different types and demand is for one of three types of bauxite: (1) trihydrate and monohydrate (associated with Jamaica), (2) trihydrate gibbsite (associated with Surinam), and (3) monohydrate diaspore (associated with Europe). The degree of variations in alumina content among ores is given in table 5–2.

Although aluminum could be produced from other ores, bauxite is still favored. Because of the possibility that the International Bauxite Association (IBA) could evolve into a tighter cartel including price fixing and supply control, estimates have been made of the point at which nonbauxite ores would become economic. Assuming an energy cost of $1 per million Btu in 1974, aluminum could be economically extracted from clays at 1974 bauxite prices of $28 per ton and from anorthosite at bauxite prices of $35 per ton.[9] With improved technology, it is likely that those costs could be reduced further.

It is worth noting that the demand for aluminum is not greatly influenced by changes in the price of bauxite. The value content of the latter in the production of aluminum ingot rarely exceeds 20 percent, even when transportation and other changes are included. It was shown in chapter 2 that the price elasticity of demand for bauxite is low in the short run and is not likely to increase much in the long run. Because the demand for bauxite and alumina depend substantially on the demand for aluminum, the former are also highly elastic with respect to income. One final note on elasticities is that the cross-elasticity between aluminum and its substitutes such as copper and steel is known to be rather high, for example, the cross-elasticity with steel has been estimated to be 2.0.

The intermediate and final demands for aluminum are concentrated in the industrial sectors.[10] Some typical uses in the building and construction sector are doors, windows, gutters, and mobile homes. In the transportation sector, aluminum appears in all types of vehicles from aircraft and boats to containers. Also important are consumer durables which include aluminum in furniture, refrigerators and cooking utensils. Its particular physical properties are of most importance in the remaining sectors: Its conductivity makes it competitive with copper in wire and cable in electrical transmission; its resistance to corrosion makes it competitive with steel in machinery and storage tanks; and this same property provides application in packaging and containers. Given such a variety of uses, aluminum must compete with a number of substitutes besides steel and copper such as plastics, glass, and tinplate.

As shown in table 5–4, the world consumption of primary and secondary aluminum has expanded from 8,379.0 to 14,586.6 thousand tons over the decade 1965–1975. This represents an annual rate of growth of demand of 5.7 percent. Consumption is concentrated in the United States, United Kingdom, Japan, Federal Republic of Germany, and France. In 1975 they consumed 54 percent of the world's primary and secondary aluminum.

Trade

Bauxite trade involved some 7.5 million tons (metal content) of shipments in 1975, 50 percent of which came from countries around the Caribbean, and another 25 percent from Australia. The deficit areas have been the United States, Canada, and Japan, which between them absorbed 75 percent of the total. Europe appears to be almost self-sufficient in bauxite, with the import requirements of Germany, Italy, United Kingdom, and other countries about equal to the exports of Yugoslavia, Greece, and Hungary. Of the significant aluminum-producing countries, only France and the U.S.S.R. satisfy a major proportion of their bauxite requirements from internal sources.

The increase in world bauxite trade has been offset by an expansion of alumina trade, a result of increased processing in some producing countries. Between 1966 and 1974 the share of Jamaican bauxite output used for alumina production at home increased from 21 percent to 45 percent. The corresponding percentage shares rose from 14 percent to 44 percent in Surinam and from 42 percent to 61 percent in Australia.[11]

Some estimates have been prepared by the UNCTAD Secretariat of changes in bauxite export values over time (FOB).[12] These values have grown from $69.5 million in 1955 to $203.4 million in 1965 and to $528.5 million in 1975. These figures must be taken as rough approximations both in view of the incomplete data on export volumes, and still more so because of the lack of bauxite prices.

Market Structure

The structure of the bauxite, alumina, and aluminum market can be characterized as follows:

Table 5–4
World Consumption of Primary and Secondary Aluminum[a]
(thousand metric tons)

Countries	1955	1960	1965	1970	1971	1972	1973	1974	1975	1976
United States	1887	1943	3627	4425	4931	5320	6197	6291	4389	5747
United Kingdom	388	481	529	603	513	608	688	681	565	618
Federal Republic of Germany	271	429	558	881	918	970	1141	1146	957	1264
France	140	240	310	492	475	510	585	597	513	628
Canada	90	110	203	252	293	311	337	388	312	398
Italy	85	143	195	420	402	458	532	579	445	590
Japan	59	200	404	1178	1254	1515	1975	1638	1480	1922
Spain	13	25	76	156	179	204	223	263	252	267
Brazil	8	36	55	90	114	151	176	208	230	246
Eastern Europe	500	1100	1650	2500	2780	2890	3020	3550	3500	3720
Rest of world	275	451	718	1488	1569	1656	1932	2005	1924	2211
Total	3718	5157	8325	12485	13428	14593	16806	17444	14587	17601

Source: *Metal Statistics* (Frankfurt: Metallgesellschaft A.G., various years).
[a]Secondary consumption, includes the direct use of scrap by manufacturers, if available.

1. The six major aluminum firms hold a substantial amount of production capacity at each stage of processing.
2. The cost of production capacity at different stages varies substantially, helping to explain why smelters are usually located in developed countries.
3. Vertical integration of these major aluminum firms is significant, since little transactions take place outside the firm at the bauxite mining stage. The firms also have a strong multinational character.
4. Foreign ownership and control of ore and of productive activities in the producing, exporting countries is high, although declining.
5. The concentration of bauxite production is in developing countries and of aluminum production in developed countries.
6. The possibilities for the producing developing countries to exert leverage over prices has lead to a harmonization of interests in the form of the International Bauxite Association.

Organization and Concentration

As indicated, the world bauxite-aluminum industry is dominated by the six major multinationals which are vertically integrated from the production of bauxite to the manufacture of aluminum. From the concentration ratios provided in table 5–5, the following firms can be identified as belonging to this group: the Aluminum Company of America (Alcoa), Reynolds Metals Company (Reynolds), Kaiser Aluminum and Chemical Corporation (Kaiser), Alcan Aluminum Ltd. (Alcan), Pechiney Ugine Kuhlmann (Pechiney), and Swiss Aluminum Ltd. (Alusuisse). The market share attributable to the largest eight firms in each processing category shown is 54 percent of mine capacity, 67 percent of alumina capacity, and 53 percent of aluminum capacity. These shares, however, have been declining as a result of the acquisition of capacity by various governments and the growth of independent firms.

The multinational character of production and ownership is reflected in the fact that most firms have affiliates in several countries. The affiliates also have a special relationship to the parent firm's home country, reflected in the high correlation between ownership of deposits and destination of exports. The United States, France, Canada, and Switzerland are the home countries of the six major firms and to some extent dominate bauxite trade. For example, the United States imports 100 percent of the Dominican Republic's bauxite exports, 99 percent of Jamaica's and 80 percent of Surinam's. This comes as no surprise, since Dorr has found ownership to be the most significant factor in determining the flow of exports.[13] However, it is difficult to interpret these statistics, since many firms have processing facilities in different countries,

Table 5-5
Concentration in the World Bauxite-Aluminum Industry, 1973

	Bauxite Mine Production Capacity			Alumina Conversion Capacity			Aluminum Refining Capacity		
Firm	Firm	Shares (%)	Capacity (000 LT)	Firm	Shares (%)	Capacity (000 ST)	Firm	Shares (%)	Capacity (000 ST)
Largest four									
	Alcoa	14.7	11,530	Alcoa	18.3	5,766	Alcoa	12.1	1,816
	Kaiser	10.9	8,516	Kaiser	10.8	3,420	Alcan	10.1	1,519
	Reynolds	6.7	5,267	Alcan	9.4	2,981	Reynolds	9.1	1,362
	Rio-Tinto (Con. Zinc)	6.0	4,725	Pechiney	9.3	2,937	Kaiser	6.9	1,035
Subtotal		38.3	30,038		47.8	15,104		38.1	5,732
Indexes (4)	CR = 0.383; HH = 0.042; HG = 0.204; GR = 0.264			CR = 0.478; HH = 0.063; HG = 0.250; GR = 0.198			CR = 0.382; HH = 0.038; HG = 0.195; GR = 0.145		
Lesser four									
	Pechiney (France)	5.5	4,300	Reynolds	8.9	2,796	Pechiney	5.1	768
	Alcan	5.1	4,034	Rio-Tinto (Con. Zinc)	4.2	1,324	Alusuisse	4.1	617
	Alusuisse (Switzerland)	3.8	2,952	Alusuisse	3.7	1,177	Sumitomo Chemical	3.3	493
	Royal Dutch/Shell (UK)	3.6	2,800	Sumitomo Chemical	2.1	675	Showa Denko	2.1	309
Subtotal		56.4	44,124		66.7	21,076		52.6	7,919
Indexes (8)	CR = 0.563; HH = 0.050; HG = 0.223; GR = 0.301			CR = 0.667; HH = 0.074; HG = 0.272; GR = 0.353			CR = 0.528; HH = 0.044; HG = 0.209; GR = 0.327		
All other		44.6	34,219		33.3	10,468		47.4	7,122
Total		100.0	78,343		100.0	31,544		100.0	15,041

Sources: *Metal Statistics, 1975,* published by the American Metal Market, New York; *Minerals Yearbook,* U.S. Bureau of Mines, vols. I and III, Washington, D.C.: U.S. Department of the Interior, 1972; *Mining International Yearbook, 1973–74,* London, 1973; *Engineering and Mining Journal, 1973–74,* New York, 1974; *Industrial Minerals,* No. 75, December 1973; *Aluminum Industry Report,* New York, 1974.

such as Alcan. Bauxite may be exported to a subsidiary in another country, and then shipped to the home country.

At the international trade level, the structure of the market can be loosely termed an oligopoly-oligopsony, a deviating factor being the strong vertical integration of the six major firms. On the supply side there are five countries producing almost 70 percent of the world's bauxite, and on the demand side six aluminum firms own almost 60 percent of the world's bauxite deposits.[14] There thus exists concentration on both sides. Naturally, economies of scale are present at every stage, but more so at the refining stage. It has been estimated that for an alumina plant to be competitive it must be able to refine at least 330,000 tons of bauxite per year; other estimates are as high as 600,000 tons per year.[15] It appears that refineries are in need of the largest productive capacities, whereas smelters require lesser capacities but have higher absolute costs. This would suggest a barrier preventing developing countries from entering stages of production with higher value-added.

Nationalization

Also essential to market structure is the relation between firms and host governments and the dependence of the latter on bauxite for a substantial portion of their earnings. The multinational character of these firms causes them to be more involved with the worldwide interests of the parent corporation rather than with the particular interests of the host countries. This situation is further reinforced, since the firms have a strong vertical integration. Market control is a normal feature of the industry, such that it is difficult to help establish independent bauxite and alumina enterprises. The reaction of the host governments in the producing countries has been to attempt to increase their influence over bauxite reserves and production.

A first step has been to change the nature of the tax basis and to increase the level of taxes imposed on the bauxite industry. Jamaica was the leader in making two major changes in 1974.[16] The first was a standard royalty of U.S. ¢55 per long dry ton (LDT) of all bauxite mined. The second was a production levy of 7.5 percent of the averaged realized price of primary aluminum divided by 4.3 per LDT. Each firm also was required to produce at an annual tonnage level based on 90 percent of 1974 output. The immediate effect of this action was, first, an increase in taxes from about $2 to about $14 per LDT and, second, an increase in tax revenues and royalties for Jamaica of about 600 percent. New tax agreements were also enacted by Surinam, Haiti, the Dominican Republic, Guinea, Sierra Leone, Guyana, and Indonesia.

A second step has been for the host governments to increase their equity participation in domestic operations.[17] Jamaica in 1976 acquired a controlling interest in domestic bauxite operations and a significant interest in domestic alumina facilities. Guyana obtained total equity in the Demerara (Guyanese) bauxite company, a subsidiary of Alcan, in 1971 and Berbice Mines, a subsidiary of Reynolds, in 1974. Guinea acquired between 49 to 100 percent of interest of all of its domestic mining operations. And Brazil will have full control of the new Trombates project under its state-owned company, Companhia Vale do Rio Doce.

Producer Coordination

The major producing countries including Australia, Guinea, Guyana, Jamaica, Sierra Leone, Surinam, and Yugoslavia met in 1974 to establish the International Bauxite Association. Since then, the Dominican Republic, Haiti, Ghana, and Indonesia have joined to increase the proportion of world bauxite production contained within these countries to roughly 80 percent. The two major goals of the IBA have been to encourage development of the bauxite and aluminum industry and to secure greater and more reasonable returns. The association also has the potential of raising bauxite prices, since these increases would not have a dramatic effect on import bills or the exchange rates of developing countries. Although there is not sufficient unity within the association to control prices in the present, it has recently attempted to establish a floor price for metallurgical grade bauxite.

Market Implications

Export Dependence

Considerable export dependence can be seen for the major bauxite-producing countries. Bauxite at 26.9 percent and alumina at 45.6 percent make up 72.5 percent of Surinam's exports. For Jamaica the respective figures are 22.7 percent and 41.2 percent for a total of 63.9 percent. Guyana at 38.4 percent and 10.2 percent has the lowest share of the group.

The ramifications of this dependence vary with a number of factors, a most important one being trends and variability of bauxite and aluminum prices. Concerning bauxite, the average price has risen from $8.11 per ton in 1960 to $11.30 per ton by 1965. The price remained roughly constant until 1974, reaching $11.21 and then rose quickly to $28.74 by 1976. This sudden change reflects the wave of tax increases by Jamaica and other countries. When the deflated prices are examined, one finds a consistent increase from $9.65 in 1960 to $12.94 in 1963 which was then checked in 1964. Real prices then fell and did not return to that level until 1976.

Because of the difficulty of interpreting these prices at the country level, the unit export values FOB for separate countries are given in table 5–6. They have been deflated by the UN index of unit values of exported manufactured goods so that they might reflect single commodity terms of trade. For Surinam, Guyana and Guinea there has been an increase in the deflated value since 1965 of 128, 227, and 132 over a base of 100. Only for Jamaica was there a slight decline to 89.

The impact of the variability of bauxite prices is difficult to determine, since in some ways variability in export value is more significant. There is also the problem of variability relative to what standard. Based on the coefficient of variation, fluctuations of bauxite-deflated unit values amount to 12 percent for Surinam, 10 percent for Jamaica, 27 percent for Guyana, and 34 percent for Guinea. When compared to the variation found for copper and tin unit values, these levels cannot be seen as excessive.

Magnitude of Fixed Investment

The magnitude of the initial fixed investment in bauxite is large. Some idea of its size can be obtained by looking at the relative magnitude of the mining sector (MS) as well as of gross domestic product (GDP). The only readily available figures are given below in millions of dollars for 1972:

	GDP	MS	GDI
Jamaica	1,497	175	3
Guinea	334	26	8
Guyana	264	43	88

Recall from the discussion of investment costs that expansion costs for the Boke deposit in Guinea are $400 million. When comparing such costs which are typical for the industry to total gross domestic investment (GDI) of $8 million and $88 million in Guinea and Guyana, respectively, it is clear that these countries cannot finance such projects. Thus, the large investment outlays involved initially favor the bargaining position of the firm.

Nature of Technology

The technology involved in bauxite mining (open pit) alone is simple and stable. It is also stable for refining and smelting, although of a much more complex nature. This may be seen from the fact that the same refining and smelting processes have been used for quite a number of years. Also, Guyana more or less proved that the technology involved in mining and refining could

Table 5-6
Trend and Variability of Bauxite Export Values and Unit Values

Year	Surinam			Jamaica			Guyana			Guinea			Aluminum Price	
	Export Value	Unit Value	Deflated[a]	Export Value	Unit Value	Deflated	Export Value	Unit Value	Deflated	Export Value	Unit Value	Deflated	U.S. ¢/lb	Deflated
1955	20.9	6.83	13.66	12.1	5.48	10.96	14.5	6.58	13.16	2.7	6.01	12.03	20.9	41.8
1960	35.2	9.69	18.28	34.0	8.07	15.22	17.2	8.08	15.24	4.6	6.53	12.31	23.3	44.0
1965	42.7	9.77	17.45	83.8	12.16	21.71	21.8	12.21	21.80	1.7	6.97	12.44	29.5	43.8
1970	40.3	11.78	19.01	82.9	10.73	17.31	46.1	15.10	24.36	3.8	4.69	7.56	27.9	45.0
1971	44.1	12.26	18.86	91.8	11.89	18.30	48.0	17.29	26.52	4.6	4.75	7.31	28.4	43.7
1972	45.9	12.13	17.33	86.2	12.04	17.19	50.2	21.84	31.19	2.4	5.10	7.28	26.8	38.3
1973	47.6	13.06	15.93	87.4	11.83	14.42	51.5	21.79	26.58	4.3	8.31	10.13	27.2	33.2
1974	71.7	16.78	16.78	143.7	17.95	17.95	68.5	32.02	32.02	36.3	9.16	9.16	34.7	34.7
1975	49.9	22.18	19.81	117.5	21.43	19.14	80.4	37.33	33.33	98.9	13.61	12.15	39.7	35.2
1976	47.6	25.30	22.39	136.5	21.72	19.22	85.2	55.98	49.54	172.6	18.60	16.46	40.4	35.9
Price trend[b] 1976/1965	111	259	128	128	179	89	391	458	227	102	267	132	165	82
Variability (%)[c] 1970–1976	21	34	12	24	32	10	27	50	27	143	34	34	19	12

Source: UNCTAD, "World Market for Bauxite: Statistical Annex," TD/B/IPC/BAUXITE/2/Add. 1 (Geneva: UNCTAD, 1978).
[a]Deflator is U.N. Index of Unit Value of Exported Manufactured Goods.
[b]Ratio between 1965 and 1976.
[c]Coefficient of variation in percent over 1970–1976.

be implemented by native management, as is reflected in Guyana's nationalization of mine and refinery facilities. Thus, armed with confidence, they proceeded to nationalize the rest of the country's bauxite mines and refineries.

Basically, when technology is complex the firm enjoys a strong bargaining position, and if the technology changes notably, then a firm's position remains strong over time. While bauxite mining and refining technology may be complex, it does not change much with time. From examining different agreements, it is apparent that these countries are still dependent, nonetheless, on the construction of such refining and smelting plants by the multinationals. It should also be noted that although the countries enjoy knowledge about mining processes, their knowledge of refining and smelting processes is incomplete.

Marketing Process

In the bauxite and aluminum industry, the marketing process is very important. It stands to reason that a complex marketing structure works to the firm's advantage at the bargaining table and a simple marketing structure favors the host country's position. If bauxite could be sold on the open market in bulk quantities according to undifferentiated specifications, the host country would be in a strong bargaining position. However, the strong vertical structure of the industry has prevented extensive open market sales. Countries can eventually learn the technology involved, but such conditions make it harder for these countries to develop marketing skills.

Control over Resources and Production

Another implication of market structure is the extent to which host governments exercise control over bauxite resources, production, and sales. Girvan, in studying agreements, found that governments previously made no restrictions concerning the firm's use of the resource.[18] However, the former have demanded greater local processing as they have become more aware of value-added. Since the mid-1960s, Jamaica has refused to grant new bauxite concessions unless the companies agree to build local alumina plants. Surinam also required Alcoa to build a refinery and smelter by 1976 in their Brokopondo Agreement of 1958. But in most cases, the companies have retained their right to dispose of the processed bauxite in whatever way they wanted; at least in this way they could avoid any further local processing. This was also the case in Demba's agreement with Guyana in 1957. Although Demba agreed to build a refinery, they still retained the right to dispose of the alumina as they wished.

Historically, host governments have not imposed any restrictions on the discovery and exploitation of bauxite. Girvan indicates that in most of the Caribbean bauxite countries, the holders of exploration rights are not only given first choice to exploitation rights but also may obtain an exclusive exploration permit, which makes them the only explorer and hence exploiter of a region.[19] As an example, Surinam's Brokoponda Agreement with Alcoa in 1958 can be cited. Although bauxite agreements traditionally have involved an exploration permit for three years involving up to 20,000 acres, Alcoa secured a license for ten years covering 500,000 acres. Similar to the case of processing, however, host governments have attempted to regain resource control. Jamaica has required both Kaiser and Reynolds to sell back their bauxite lands with the revoking of automatically granted mining leases. It has also stipulated that any firm that stops mining will suffer an expiration of lease within six months. Although the major firms still have extensive exploration rights in other bauxite-producing countries, this position is gradually being eroded.

Opportunities for Increased Processing

The interest of the host governments in increased processing has been due largely to the substantial gains in value-added that could result from moving to successive stages of aluminum processing. Some examples of export or ex-factory price of aluminum are given below based on the typical experience of OECD countries in 1972.[20] The product classification numbers are that of the Standard Industrial Classification Code (SITC).

SITC Code		Dollars per Ton
283.3	Bauxite	70
513.6 (5)	Alumina	120
684.1	Aluminum, unwrought	500
684.2	Aluminum wire, rod sheets, tubes	1,000
691.2	Finished structures of aluminum	2,000

That there is scope for expanding processing is obvious from the heavy concentration of alumina and aluminum facilities in developed countries. Only about 50 percent of the bauxite produced in Jamaica, Guyana, and Surinam is processed into alumina locally. For Guinea the proportion is only about 20 percent. Among smaller producers, all of the bauxite produced in Ghana, Sierra Leone, Dominican Republic, Haiti, Indonesia, and Malaysia is exported in the same form. The exceptions are Brazil and India, which process most of their bauxite.

Among the factors affecting opportunities for processing, a principal one is the expected growth in the demand for aluminum. For example, aluminum is being increasingly substituted for steel in automobiles in order to reduce the weight of the vehicle and to improve its fuel efficiency. Aluminum is also receiving greater use in the housing and construction industry because of its role in improving insulation, for example, storm windows and aluminum foil-backed insulation materials. World demand for aluminum (including secondary forms) is projected to increase at a rate of about 7.6 percent from 1977 through 1985.[21] This implies an increase in world demand for primary aluminum from 8.9 million tons in 1975 to 22.3 million tons in 1985.

Other important factors include the metal content of bauxite relative to its geographic location. Given that the metal content of bauxite is about 20 percent, there would be substantial cost savings in transporting the processed commodity. Savings would also result from locating aluminum smelters close to alumina plants. The availability of cheap energy also is important because aluminum smelting is an expensive process; electricity accounts for 26 percent of production costs. Opportunities for further processing would thus be enhanced in these developing countries with abundant energy potential such as Ghana, Brazil, India, Malaysia, and Indonesia.

Material Share in Product Prices

Finally, the ability of aluminum refiners to pass cost increases on to consumers has been mentioned. Bauxite costs have been estimated to represent only 3 to 5 percent of fabricated rod and sheet prices.[22] This is based on the export unit value of bauxite from developing countries accounting for 3.9 percent of the wholesale price of aluminum rod in the United States in 1973, and for 5.3 percent of aluminum sheet in the United States and France. With regard to alumina, it constituted 11 percent of the price of aluminum rod and 15 percent of aluminum sheets. The small share of raw material costs in final product price explains why the aluminum companies have succeeded in coping with the near-doubling of bauxite costs resulting from the tax increases.

Obsolescing Bargain

The dynamics of the obsolescing bargain are reflected in the shift in control from the firm's initial dominant position facing investment risk until the host government gradually becomes the more dominant power.[23] This seems to be the pattern in Jamaica, Surinam, and Guyana. Only in Guinea where bauxite development has intensified more recently are foreign firms in a more favorable negotiating position.

The extent to which government revenue can be increased through taxation depends on several factors. On the one hand, the extent of the direct investments made by bauxite consumers tie them to the exporting countries. As these countries exchange information and cartelize their actions, they will be better able to strike bargains and to tap resource rents through taxation. When the threat of nationalization is made, the firm will find it preferable to obtain even a strongly reduced return on investment capital rather than face that alternative. Thus the maximum bauxite cost that the company will accept when threatened by nationalization will equal the level of its demand curve plus the opportunity cost of the capital invested, per unit of bauxite capacity. In this way, the indeterminate range within which the exporting country's returns can vary is widened upward.

On the other hand, there is a limit to the effectiveness of taxation as well as threats of nationalization. Taxation of bauxite production can lead to shifts in supply sources, processing locations, cost structure, or even investment patterns in the long run. For example, the World Bank suggests that the 1975 pattern of bauxite production reflects a reduction in production in the high tax rate nations and shifts in demand away from these producers to the low tax rate producers.[24] Other countries seeking entry to the market could also give better terms of taxation to attract firms. In addition, a production levy could lead to changes in variable costs among different producers. This, in turn, implies that producers have the option to reduce the breakeven levels of production in the higher cost sources by shifts in their supplies, including possible diversification of future supply sources. To some extent, producers did accept the tax increases with the view that they could pass on the tax increases to final consumers.

Nature of Competition

According to the concentration ratios computed for 1973, the eight largest firms account for 54 percent of mine capacity and 67 percent of alumina capacity. This high concentration reflects the ability of the major firms to limit new entrants and to maintain market controls. The history of the aluminum industry indicates that new entrants did appear between 1945 and 1970 but not frequently since then.[25] Although this would suggest that the nature of competition has not changed much recently, there is the noted trend of increased government participation as well as of outright nationalization.

Concerning the ability of the countries to impose bargaining power through threats of nationalization or nationalization itself, the prospects are more limited. Once the foreign assets have been taken over, the threat ceases to exist. Furthermore, a company which is unable to earn the opportunity cost of the capital invested in a bauxite exporting country will be cautious about reinvestments and will certainly avoid new investments to create additional capacity in that country. Despite this fact, the major bauxite-exporting developing countries have moved toward nationalization.

Competition has also been affected by the organization of the International Bauxite Association which has stimulated the indicated tax increases. Whether the association will be able to influence the division of gains further depends on several factors. The amount of clout on either side will ultimately rest on the relatively elasticity of bauxite demand. Each side has its own weak and strong points. For instance, the IBA must regulate taxes so that all prices are the same at the point of delivery; it must determine each member's share and guard against undercutting; and it must discourage new entrants attracted by the high profits.[26] Another problem facing the IBA is that of the vast bauxite reserves of Australia. Australia is a wealthy country compared to most bauxite-producing countries, depends very little on its bauxite-alumina trade, and has close ties with the United States and other developed countries. Any moves on its part to increase taxes might jeopardize its own trade position.

However, the IBA also has a number of factors working in its favor.[27] Since alumina plants handle only certain types of bauxite, sources of supply could only be shifted in the long run. Currently, there are alumina refineries located in high tax countries owned by firms from the United States and other industrialized countries. Thus these firms will continue to depend on these refineries until they become obsolete. Another factor is the influence of inflation. New mines may reach a higher average total cost per ton than presently existing mines in developing countries such as Jamaica. There is also the mentioned inelasticity of bauxite demand.

Despite these possibilities, the IBA cannot continue to raise taxes indefinitely, since bauxite does have some elasticity in the very long run. It has been noted that alternative sources such as clays become economical at $28 per ton in 1974 dollars. Thus, if taxes reach a point of no return, existing plants in Jamaica and Surinam may be abandoned once they have depreciated. But if Australia and Brazil keep imposing moderate taxes, then eventually the high tax countries such as Jamaica and Surinam will be forced to conform. These countries are highly dependent on bauxite and they cannot afford to lose consequent export earnings.

Integration, concentration, and collaboration in the world aluminum industry provide the companies with a high degree of market control which can be used as a counterthreat against the governments. Economies of scale, large absolute costs, lack of technical knowledge, and the availability of cheap power along with institutional factors also have worked to the companies' advantage. As host countries develop their mineral policies and realize their goals and limitations, however, their influence at the bargaining table is bound to increase. There have also been a number of long-term development contracts entered into by Japanese and European firms which benefit the host country by making buyers more competitive. It would appear that sufficient competition has entered of a nature other than just an outright increase in numbers to give the host governments greater bargaining power than they previously possessed.

Government Learning Process

The bauxite-producing countries have hosted investment with little knowledge of industry's behavior, limited negotiating skills, and little technical knowledge. However, as time has passed the governments have brought in foreign experts and have begun demanding that local labor be hired along with being assured that the government will have some say in a firm's transactions. As an example, Jamaica, Surinam, and Guyana had no minister of mines in 1970 even though bauxite constitutes the backbone of their economies. In many cases, the host governments have gone into bargaining sessions uninformed of the industry's cost structure and behavior. Thus it is logical to assume that a new sector of the government should be initiated to monitor the industry. Today all of the countries have either a minister of mines or the equivalent.[28] Jamaica has established, in addition, the Jamaican Bauxite Institute (JBI), which is responsible for briefing the government's negotiating team on costs.[29] It does this by sponsoring research into the technology and economics of processing bauxite and by monitoring and evaluating the aluminum markets. In addition, the JBI is in charge of allocating reserve mining lands to companies. Looking to the other countries, Surinam has established a state trading agency, and Guyana has formed the Bauxite Industry Development Company. The purpose of the latter is similarly to provide information to the minister of mines on the marketing and diversification of the country's bauxite industry. Finally Guinea has established the Office d'Amenagement de Bode (OFAB) for the purpose of overseeing the planning and construction of mining projects.

　　These countries have thus come a long way from their previous level of industry knowledge, and this is confirmed by their success in raising taxes and increasing ownership.

Price Formation

Price Availability

Bauxite and aluminum transactions are normally carried out by (1) transfers within the six major multinationals, (2) long-term contracts, or (3) joint ventures. There are also some thirty smaller aluminum producers in the non-

Socialist world. Their operations are more restricted in scope, and some are allied with governments or with the majors.[30] Most of the smaller producers are nonintegrated and have to procure the bauxite they require from independent mines, mainly in Australia, Greece, and Yugoslavia. Most of the noncaptive bauxite supplies are sold under long-term contracts.

With only very small marginal quantities being traded through commodity dealers, there is no spot market with public prices and no representative posted, or listed, price.[31] For bauxite in particular, pricing is further complicated by the need to account for alumina content, access to shipping terminals, proximity to consuming markets, the nature of impurities, and the quantity and payment terms specified in the purchase arrangements. To some extent, tax and financial arrangements affect the import values used by integrated multinationals. In any case, the bauxite price they report for intercompany transactions is thought to be small compared to the estimated average production cost of bauxite. The price would also vary considerably across different sources of supply.

In arriving at some estimate of bauxite prices, one must determine the stage at which the material is actually traded. Radetzki suggests that the real trading partners are the governments of exporting countries, on the one hand, and the companies, on the other.[32] Taxes and other government levies assume the role ordinarily played by prices in striking a buyer-seller agreement. Any export prices quoted, therefore, do nothing but reflect the transfer prices of the multinationals, adjusted upward or downward to reflect their objectives. For example, they can set prices to minimize their fiscal liabilities, since their operations are carried out in several countries. Of the prices listed in table 5–7, only the U.S. import reference price (CIF) based on Jamaican shipments is considered to reflect bauxite value.

Because of the inadequacy of even this indicator, some attention is given to aluminum prices. In 1974 when the Jamaican government imposed new tax levies on bauxite production, they employed aluminum ingot prices as a base.

Table 5–7
Major Bauxite and Aluminum Price Quotations

Bauxite

U.S. import reference price, based on imports from Jamaica, CIF

Aluminum

Canadian delivered United Kingdom, ingots, minimum purity 99.5%, Al (*Financial Times*).

London, ingots, minimum purity 99.5%, Al (*Metal Bulletin*).

New York, ingots, minimum purity 99.5%, Al, major U.S. producers.

New York, ingots, minimum purity 99.5%, Al (*American Metal Market*).

Federal Republic of Germany, minimum purity Al, 99.5% ingots.

These prices have also been tightly controlled in the world market by the existing oligopoly. The basic ingot price is relatively stable, but rebates and other price deviations occur in contractual relationships. Also important are the small informal markets which exist for noncontract trading in the United Kingdom and the United States. The prices published in the *American Metal Market* are believed to reflect market equilibrium. Even though actual prices have deviated from the quoted or reported price from time to time, this price is followed as a base price by the IBA.

One final possibility for arriving at representative prices for bauxite and subsequently alumina is to impute prices based on export values. Any such prices must be carefully interpreted because of biased accounting practices, overshipments, and other factors. Given the paucity of useful information, export values have been accepted as rough price indicators. Table 5–8 contains export unit values in dollars per ton of bauxite and alumina as well as the import unit value prices mentioned above.

Price-Making Forces

Despite the hidden nature of bauxite pricing, the analysis of market forces can provide insights into price behavior. Naturally, the major firms have always tried to minimize the price which they pay for bauxite.[33] In the past some firms have received agreements from Jamaica which separate their taxes from the value of sales or costs of production. In such a case, the firm pays a fixed tax per LDC of bauxite exported, of which one-half varies with the price of aluminum.[34] Taxes can also be based on profits, but in an agreement between Guyana and Reynolds, the latter did not pay any income taxes between 1953 and 1962, claiming that no profit was made.[35]

The scanty price information available suggests that the accounting prices at which bauxite was shipped from the Caribbean within integrated firms with head offices in the United States have been substantially above the prices quoted for transactions between independent parties in recent years.[36] The explanation to this is primarily to be sought in the tax laws of the United States, which allow full credit against U.S. tax liability for taxes paid by foreign subsidiaries of U.S. corporations.[37] When this rule is applied to a company, minimization of the combined tax payments in the two countries (and hence maximization of combined aftertax profits) will be achieved by internal pricing which splits the profits between the subsidiary and head office so as to equalize the tax payments in each country.[38] The entire tax liability of the subsidiary can then be credited against the tax liability in the United States, and the company can avoid tax payments at home. The peculiar consequences of this tax law can help explain the behavior during the 1970s of the U.S. aluminum companies who are mining bauxite in Jamaica.

Up to 1965, the U.S. companies' transfer prices for Jamaican bauxite were only slightly higher than those in transactions between independent parties. Then in 1970, the Jamaican government, in an effort to increase its tax revenue, demanded a doubling of these transfer prices. This was intended to increase the profitability, and hence the tax liabilities of the subsidiaries operating in the country. The companies agreed not only to the increase but also to making the measure retroactive back to 1966. Since then, a glaring discrepancy between the bauxite prices in transactions within U.S. multinational firms, on the one hand, and in deals between independent parties, on the other, has appeared. In 1974 the Jamaican government increased tax levies on bauxite production again. This time, the levy was determined at 7.5 percent of the aluminum ingot price which nearly doubled the cost of Jamaican bauxite. This time, however, the companies were prepared to go only part of the way toward meeting the Jamaican demands and were quite unwilling to comply with the package as a whole. Eventually, therefore, the new rules had to be forced upon them by the government.

This behavior can also be explained in terms of the companies' efforts to minimize their total tax burden. The new rules, in all probability, pushed the tax payments in Jamaica above the tax payments made in the United States. The companies protested because on the margin the Jamaican tax increase was real and could not be credited against taxes at home. A higher aluminum price would of course have increased the companies tax liabilities in the United States, from which Jamaican taxes could be deducted. But to permit full credit for the new Jamaican levies, prices would have to be increased to levels at which the companies feared to lose sales to competitors less dependent on Jamaican supplies and unwilling to follow in the price rise as well as to substitute materials.

It is clear that the U.S. tax credit regulations provide a competitive advantage to the U.S.-based aluminum companies in relation to companies located in countries without such rules. However, the small share of bauxite in total value-added of aluminum production suggests that this advantage could hardly be of decisive importance for overall competitiveness.

Since prices are commonly a central bargaining issue in commercial relations, the price agreements reached are usually of key importance for determining the benefits accruing to the trading partners. The international bauxite market constitutes an exception in this respect. The ownership structure in the integrated aluminum industry and the artificial nature of most price quotations suggest that the real trading partners are the government of exporting countries, on the one hand, and the companies, on the other, and that taxes and other government levies assume the role ordinarily played by prices in dividing the benefits between buyer and seller. Bargaining power in the bauxite market will, therefore, be reflected in the ability to influence the fiscal conditions on which the foreign investors are permitted to exploit bauxite in producing and exporting countries.

To summarize the forces affecting bauxite price formation, the fiscal conditions cited above in conjunciton with increased nationalization are likely to exert an upward pressure on prices. This pressure could possibly be aug-

Table 5-8
Average Annual Prices of Bauxite, Alumina, and Aluminum, 1955–1976

Year	Bauxite[a] (dollars per ton)		Bauxite[b] (dollars per ton actual weight)		Alumina[b] (dollars per ton of metal content)		Aluminum[c] (cents per pound)	
	Actual Price	Deflated Price	Actual Price	Deflated Price	Actual Price	Deflated Price	Actual Price	Deflated Price
1955	—	—	6.5	13.0	157.1	314.2	20.9	41.8
1956	—	—	6.8	13.1	158.4	304.6	23.8	45.8
1957	—	—	7.8	14.7	158.6	299.2	24.6	46.4
1958	—	—	7.9	15.2	146.3	281.3	23.0	44.2
1959	—	—	8.2	15.9	137.9	265.2	22.5	43.3
1960	8.11	9.65	8.1	15.3	144.3	272.3	23.3	44.0
1961	9.58	11.35	8.3	15.4	143.6	265.9	23.3	43.1
1962	10.22	12.02	9.2	17.0	138.5	256.6	22.6	41.9
1963	11.00	12.94	9.8	18.1	138.1	255.7	22.6	41.9
1963	11.00	12.94	9.8	18.1	138.1	255.7	22.6	41.9
1964	11.23	12.91	9.7	18.0	144.6	267.8	23.9	44.3
1965	11.30	12.84	9.8	17.5	148.1	264.5	24.5	43.8
1966	11.36	12.62	9.9	17.4	142.8	250.5	24.5	43.0
1967	11.54	12.68	9.7	16.7	131.7	227.1	24.5	42.2
1968	11.30	12.42	9.6	16.6	138.7	239.1	25.1	43.3
1969	11.81	12.56	9.8	16.6	133.5	226.3	26.7	45.3

1970	10.74	10.74	9.6	15.5	149.5	241.1	27.9	45.0
1971	10.83	10.31	10.1	15.5	142.7	219.5	28.4	43.7
1972	11.49	10.17	10.5	15.0	141.9	202.7	26.8	38.3
1973	11.17	8.40	10.7	13.0	157.7	192.3	27.2	33.2
1974	11.21	6.92	13.3	13.3	183.6	183.6	34.7	34.7
1975	18.98	10.43	16.0	14.3	236.8	211.4	39.4	35.2
1976	28.74	15.70	19.1	16.9	255.8	226.4	40.4	35.8

Sources: UNCTAD, "The World Market for Bauxite: Statistical Annex," TD/B/IPC/BAUXITE/2 (Geneva: UNCTAD, 1978); and U.S. Trade statistics.

[a]Import value into the United States from Jamaica, CIF.

[b]Bauxite and alumina figures are average FOB unit values of world exports. Prices for alumina in terms of actual weight, rather than metal content, can be approximated by dividing the figures shown in half.

[c]Aluminum prices are for Canadian ingots delivered to the United Kingdom.

[d]The United Nations index of the unit values of manufactured exports of industrialized countries (1974 = 100) was used to deflate actual prices.

mented by further producer coordination within the IBA. Cartellike behavior is more probable in the bauxite industry than in the copper, tin, or iron ore industries. Although this suggests an increase in real prices in the near future, two of the factors analyzed will exert downward pressure. The concentration and strong vertical integration of the major firms together with their strong financial position would permit them to develop new capacity in non-IBA countries. In addition, new technological developments are likely to be forthcoming to offset production from only a limited range of ores as well as from ores of declining quality. Such downward pressure is likely to prevail unless IBA countries find a way to counter these trends.

Notes

1. A complete description of the world aluminum market can be found in M. Brown and J. Butler, *The Production, Marketing and Consumption of Copper and Aluminum* (New York: Praeger, 1968). An updating of some of the facts and figures appears in UNCTAD, "The World Market for Bauxite: Characteristics and Trends," TD/B/IPC/BAUXITE/2 (Geneva: UNCTAD, February 1978).

2. K. Takeuchi, G. Thiebach, and J. Hilmy, "Investment Requirements in the Non-Fuel Mineral Sector in Developing Countries," *Natural Resources Forum,* 1 (1977): 263–75.

3. "1977 E&MJ Survey of Mine and Plant Expansion," *Engineering and Mining Journal* (1977): 59–60.

4. Charles River Associates, *Policy Implications of Producer Country Supply Restrictions: The World Aluminium/Bauxite Market,* a report prepared for the Experimental Incentives Program (Springfield, Va.: National Bureau of Standards, National Technical Information Service, 1977).

5. *Metal Statistics* (Frankfort: Metallgesellshaft A.G., 1963–1972).

6. S. Brubaker, *Trends in the World Aluminum Industry* (Baltimore: Johns Hopkins University Press, 1967).

7. P. Farin and G. Reibsamen, "Aluminum, Profile of an Industry," *Metals Week,* New York, 1967.

8. Charles River Associates, *Policy Implications.*

9. Charles River Associates, *Policy Implications,* p. 58.

10. See John Cornish, "Aluminum and Its Major Competitors: A Summary of Trends Over the Period 1964–1975," *IBA Review,* 1 (1976): 39–47.

11. *Metal Statistics* (Frankfort: Metallgesellshaft A.G., 1966–1974).

12. UNCTAD, "The World Market for Bauxite: Statistical Annex," TD/B/IPC/BAUXITE/2/Add. 1 (Geneva: UNCTAD, 1978), p. 19.

13. A. Dorr, "International Trade in the Primary Aluminum Industry," unpublished Ph.D. thesis, Pennsylvania State University, 1975.

14. Ibid.

15. Charles River Associates, *Policy Implications,* p. 36.

16. A fuller description of bauxite taxation and its likely effects can be found in World Bank, "Market Structure of Bauxite/Alumina/Aluminum," commodity paper no. 24 (Washington, D.C.: Development Policy Staff, World Bank, 1977).

17. See *IBA Quarterly Review,* 1 (1976): 17–24.

18. Girvan,

19. Ibid.

20. OECD, *Foreign Trade Statistics Bulletin,* Series C, *Trade by Commodities* (Paris: Overseas Economic Development Council, 1973).

21. World Bank, *Price Prospects for Major Primary Commodities,* report no. 814/76 (Washington, D.C.: World Bank, 1976), annex III, p. 36.

22. UNCTAD, "Study on the Degree and Scope of Increased Processing of Primary Commodities in Developing Countries," TD/184/Suppl. 3 (Geneva: UNCTAD, 1975), p. 13.

23. T.H. Moran, *Multinational Corporations and the Politics of Dependence: The Case of Copper* (Princeton: Princeton University Press, 1974), pp. 153–224.

24. World Bank, "Market Structure."

25. In 1940, Alcoa held 100 percent of the market in the United States. The government subsequently encouraged the entry of Reynolds and Kaiser. By 1950, these three firms accounted for 100 percent of the U.S. market. During the Korean War the United States again encouraged new firms to enter the industry. The entrance of Anaconda, Harvey, and Ormet, reduced the big three's share to 88 percent by 1960. During the 1960s three additional firms entered the industry, reducing that share further to 70 percent. However it should be noted that many of these new entrants were subsidiaries of major established firms. Since 1970, only Noranda, National Steel, and the South-wire Company have entered the industry, without either government encouragement or involvement with one of the existing firms. See U.S. Council on Wage and Price Stability, *Noncompetitiveness in the World Aluminum Industry* (Washington, D.C., 1976).

26. Charles River Associates, *Policy Implications,* pp. 116–117.

27. Ibid.

28. N. Girvan, "Multinational Economies," *Social and Economic Studies,* 19 (1970), 490–526.

29. The examples are taken from the *Engineering and Mining Journal,* various issues, 1976–1977.

30. *Mineral Facts and Problems,* Bureau of Mines Bulletin 650 (Washington, D.C.: U.S. Department of the Interior, 1970), p. 439.

31. A small amount of aluminum is sold on minor markets such as in New York, but the prices obtained are not considered highly indicative of aluminum value.

32. M. Radetzki, "Market Structure and Bargaining Power: A Study of Three International Mineral Markets," Stockholm: Institute of International Economic Studies, 1976.

33. N. Girvan, "Company-Country Agreements in the Bauxite Industry," Working Paper, Institute of Economic and Social Studies, Kingston, Jamaica, 1975.

34. Ibid.

35. Ibid.

36. World Bank, "Market Structure."

37. J.F. Due, "The Developing Economies, Tax and Royalty Payments by the Petroleum Industry and the U.S. Income Tax," *Natural Resources Journal,* 10(1970):10–26. Foreign taxes can be credited only up to the total amount of the tax liability in the United States, although in principle only income taxes paid abroad receive this favorable tax treatment. In practice many kinds of levies, including royalties, are known to be formulated so as to be treated as income tax by the U.S. authorities.

38. That this is so can be shown by the following formalization. Assume that the integrated firm has earned a given profit which can be allocated between the head office and subsidiary abroad with the help of transfer prices. Let t_1 and p_1 be the profit tax rate and share of total company profit declared in the host country. Let t_2 and p_2 be the corresponding entities for the home country. Total tax claimed will then be $t_1 p_1$ in the host country and $t_2 p_2$ in the home country. Given the U.S. tax credit rules, total tax paid by the company after deducting the tax credits will be

1. $T = t_1 p_1 + t_2 p_2 - t_1 p_1 = t_2 p_2$, when $t_2 p_2 > t_1 p_1$

2. $T = t_1 p_1 + t_1 p_1 - t_1 p_2 = t_1 p_1$, when $t_1 p_1 > t_2 p_2$

3. $T = t_1 p_1$, when $t_1 p_1 = t_2 p_2$

So long as condition (1) is valid, the company can decrease its tax liability by reducing p_2. So long as condition (2) is valid, the company can decrease its tax liability by reducing p_1. Consequently, tax payments will be minimized under condition (3), when the liabilities before tax credit in the two countries are equal. The credit for taxes paid abroad will equal the tax liability in the home country in this case, and in effect, no tax at all will be paid at home. Knowing that $p_2 = 1 - p_1$, and substituting this relationship into equality (3) we obtain:

4. $p_1 = \dfrac{t_2}{t_1 + t_2}$

This tells us that for minimization of its total tax burden, the share of total profits declared by the company in the host country should equal the ratio between the home country's tax rate and the sum total of the tax rates in home and host countries.

6 Iron Ore

Market Conditions

Like the bauxite market, analysis of the iron ore market cannot take place without some attention to processing, in this case steel manufacturing and fabrication.[1] However, there is not the same pattern of dominance and vertical integration by the major multinationals. Figure 6–1, in depicting the structure of the iron ore industry, emphasizes the nature of contracting and the resultant iron ore flows. That is, three separate modalities provide the basis for most transactions: captive mining arrangements, long-term contracts, and annual or short-term contracts. As will be stressed later, the actual proportion of contracts traded in each of these modalities has been changing significantly over time.

The material, as mined in its natural state, is termed crude ore. If sold with only minimal processing or screening, it is called direct-shipping ore. Most of the ore transported in international trade, however, has undergone extensive processing and is called usable ore. This can be of several types: calibrated lumps, concentrates, sinter feed, pellet feed, and pellets. Most iron ore is presently converted to pig iron, which results from smelting the ore in a blast furnace together with a reducing agent, typically coke. Direct-casting pig iron usually refers to ore that has been shaped into ingot molds. Raw steel is then made from hot metal or molten pig iron. Because so much scrap results from making steel mill products, about 40 to 45 percent scrap is used as a raw material with pig iron in open-hearth furnaces and about 30 percent in basic oxygen furnaces.[2] Recently, new technology has made possible the direct reduction of iron ore into raw steel.

The world iron ore industry is just emerging from a period of rapid expansion, mainly because of the substantial increase in world steel demand beginning in the 1960s. Large investments took place in many of the major iron ore mining countries such as west Africa, Australia, Brazil, and Canada. In table 6–1, ore production (Fe content) is shown to have grown from 178.6 million metric tons in 1955 to 325.9 million tons by 1965 and then reaching 501.3 million tons in 1975. About 47 percent of this production was traded internationally in 1975. This amounted to some $4.6 billion, almost four times the amount reached a decade earlier.

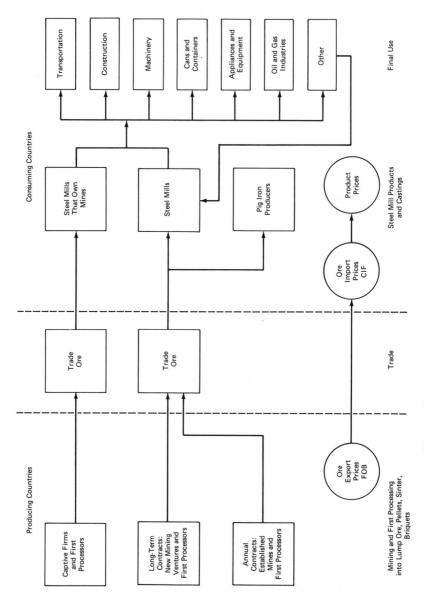

Figure 6–1. Market and Price Structure for Iron Ore

Table 6–1
World Balance Sheet for Iron Ore
(*thousand metric tons*)

Commodity Flow	1955	1960	1965	1966	1967	1968	1969	1970	1971	1972	1973	1974	1975
Ore production (Fe content)	178,593	244,614	325,925	338,639	337,714	367,835	387,885	422,529	423,478	438,350	481,659	510,803	501,301
Pig iron production	190,749	241,670	326,132	335,874	353,500	379,317	409,207	427,370	423,985	449,191	493,962	504,045	469,019
Ore imports (Fe content)	46,517	81,911	120,464	121,848	129,272	147,864	160,576	188,635	187,211	186,477	217,083	236,815	216,475
Ore exports (Fe content)	46,384	79,809	119,337	122,960	128,960	148,308	167,357	190,930	188,473	180,462	228,538	250,218	237,449
Ore consumption (apparent Fe content)	178,726	246,716	327,052	337,527	338,026	367,391	381,095	420,234	422,216	440,765	470,204	497,400	480,327
Kiruna D price (U.S. dollars per metric ton)	13.0	11.5	10.1	9.9	8.7	8.4	8.4	8.3	10.5	10.8	10.1	12.8	19.3

Source: UNCTAD, "Iron Ore: Features of the World Market, Statistical Annex," TD/B/IPC/IRON ORE/2/Add.1 (Geneva: UNCTAD, 1977).

Production

Iron ore is one of the most plentiful raw materials in the world, constituting about 5 percent of the world's crust by weight. Although there are many types of iron-bearing materials, the two most widely distributed are hematite and magnetite. In their natural state, they occur as lumps or fines. A principal characteristic is that the materials are not uniquely identifiable and their quality is influenced by chemical, physical, and metallurgical factors. Most of the iron ore mined is smelted into pig iron, the majority of which is subsequently processed in steel furnaces.

The six continents are known to contain vast resources of iron ore, with recoverable iron sufficient for several centuries at present rates of production. Recent estimates of reserves by the U.S. Bureau of Mines shown in table 6–2 give world reserves at 266.6 billion metric tons, which amounts to 91.5 billion tons of recoverable ore. These estimates are consistent with the 251.3 billion tons suggested by the United Nations in their comprehensive survey of 1967.[3] It should be noted that the definition of reserves used in the two studies differs somewhat; thus the figures are not directly comparable.

Even so both estimates are probably conservative because potential ore deposits in many parts of the world are poorly estimated. There are several reasons for this. First, objective and complete statistical data from the

Table 6–2
Estimated World Iron Ore Reserves, 1973

Country	Reserves (million metric tons)	Percent World Total	Recoverable Iron (million metric tons)	Percent World Total
United States	10,000	3.75	1,814	1.98
Australia	20,000	7.50	11,340	12.40
Brazil	42,000	15.76	14,431	15.77
Canada	33,600	12.60	11,078	12.11
France	8,000	3.00	2,449	2.68
India	9,000	3.38	5,625	6.15
Liberia	700	0.26	363	0.40
Sweden	3,300	1.24	1,996	2.18
Venezuela	3,700	1.39	2,087	2.28
U.S.S.R., eastern Europe (except Yugoslavia)	116,000	43.51	31,298	34.21
	20,300	7.61	8,998	9.84
World total	266,600	100.0	91,479	100.0

Source: U.S. Bureau of Mines, *Mineral Facts and Problems, 1975* (Washington, D.C.: U.S. Department of the Interior, 1975); Department of Energy, Mines and Resources, *Iron Ore*, Bulletin No. MR 148 (Ottawa: Canadian Department of Energy, Mines and Resources, 1976).

Communist bloc countries are woefully lacking. When available, they are both speculative and subject to some question as to their validity. Second, we have the problem of subjectivity in estimation and the lack of extensive exploration expenditures in the less developed countries. Third and last, developing countries tend to overstate their reserve and resource estimates in the hopes of attracting development projects. The reported reserve levels suggest that any possibility of a supply shortage in the near future appears to be nonexistent. At the current level of consumption, world resources are projected to last for over two hundred years. Adjusting this consumption for an exponential rate of growth in the demand for iron ore, these resources should still last for well over a hundred years.[4] This, coupled with likely new discoveries, will certainly be sufficient to satisfy any foreseeable increase in world steel production.

Iron ore reserves and resources display a wide geographic distribution. However, there is a heavy degree of concentration among those countries listed as having reserves of over 2 billion metric tons, that is, those countries which have undergone extensive exploratory surveys. The major countries reported in table 6–2 account for approximately 92 percent of the world's known reserves. Concerning the geographic distribution of these reserves, there are two marked irregularities. Although both Japan and western Europe are major consumers of the world's total production of iron ore, Japan has virtually no resources; and domestic quantities available to western Europe are inadequate to meet even short-run requirements, except for Sweden.

The largest concentrations of the world's iron ore reserves are in the Soviet Union (31.1 percent) followed by Brazil (15.8 percent), Canada (12.6 percent), and Australia (7.5 percent). Russia alone has nearly one-third of the world's reserves and is endowed with nearly twice the quantities of its nearest competitor, Brazil. From this data, one can confirm that the reserve concept is a dynamic one, subject to changes in technology, economics, and politics. As an example, Australia's reserves were not even estimated in the 1967 study made by the United Nations. Today their reserves are believed to be about 10 percent of the world's total. Since 1970, Australia has been the free world's leading exporter.

The cost of investment in advancing from iron ore exploration to mining and extraction is indeed high. In iron ore, even more than in bauxite, the advantages of scale are very important. Practically all new capacity established in the 1950s and early 1960s has come from mines with an initial output in excess of 2 million tons of ore per year.[5] Currently about 10–15 million tons of capacity are required for an inland mine, if the costs of establishing a railway and a harbor are to be carried by that mine. However, capacity figures have risen to as high as 50 million tons, as is the case for a new mine at the Carajas iron ore deposit in Brazil. In the mid-1960s the investment costs required to open up a mine in the 10-million-ton range were $15–20 per ton, if the plant was to include facilities for beneficiation.[6] More recent estimates are much higher. Takeuchi, Thiebach, and Hilmy have arrived at the following figures of capital costs per metric ton of annual production capacity in 1975 dollars.[7]

Iron ore mining	65–115
Iron ore pelletizing	20–35
Iron ore mining-pelletizing	75–125

Such figures could easily result in a total investment cost of $1 billion for a 10-million-ton mine.

Very sizable additional investments are required to establish rail transport and special harbor installations for the rational handling of the huge amounts of ore material. For example, out of the total LAMCO investments to open up the Nimba mine in Liberia in the early 1960s, almost one-half were spent on harbor and railroad facilities.[8] But it must be noted that LAMCO was the first sizable mining venture in the country, and this may have increased the relative share of investments in infrastructural installation.

In view of the size of financial requirements, foreign financial participation has frequently been solicited and secured in opening new iron ore mines. This has been true not only in developing countries with small financial markets but also in large countries like Australia. With the growth of economic size in individual projects, the importance of foreign investments in iron ore, whether directly or through long-term loans, is likely to continue also in future years.

A great spurt in mining developments around the globe took place in the early 1960s. Among the causes for this were unsatisfactory economic returns from domestic ore production in many industrial countries with lean ores, a fast expansion of steel production in areas with insufficient ore reserves, and greatly improved transport and handling facilities for seaborne iron ore. Only in the early 1970s did the consequences of these changes become fully apparent. Australia and Brazil have acquired a prominence as iron ore exporters, and their importance is likely to increase still more in coming years. Canada, Liberia, India, Mauritania, Chile, and Peru are other important iron ore exporters.

The iron content of produced ores has risen considerably as a result of the opening up of new mines in virgin territories. Up to about 1960, the world average was below 50 percent. It rose to 56 percent in 1970, and reached 57 percent in 1973.[9] The wider introduction of cleaning and concentrating facilities at mines further increased the iron content of shipped materials from 57 percent in 1960 to 62 percent in 1973.

The average hauls over which ores are transported almost doubled from 1960 to 1973 to reach an average of 8,700 kilometers in the later years.[10] Today it is common for the large mines to deliver even to the most distant continents. Thus, one single world market is gradually replacing the somewhat isolated regional iron ore markets of the past. This is to some extent true also of eastern Europe which even now meets its requirements predominantly from the U.S.S.R.

Regarding mining technology, the need for improved blast furnace burden as well as the increased availability of ore fines require that practically all iron ore receive some form of beneficiation. Beneficiation is a process involving the simple washing, sizing, and grading or more complex grinding, concentrating, and agglomerating of lower-grade ores. Most often found is agglomeration to produce high-grade pellets or sinters. Pelletizing involves controlling the shape and dimensions of iron particles to roughly 10–30 millimeters in diameter with an iron content between 62–66 percent. Sinter similarly involves particularization; but its shapes and dimensions are much more variable. Finally, rich ores can be converted directly to a product called "sponge iron," which replaces pig iron and thus enables steel producers to bypass the blast furnace stage.

The location of the world's iron ore capacity together with production for 1973 is given in Table 6–3. The share of production of the major countries reported for 1973 is the U.S.S.R., 25.8 percent; Australia, 11.0 percent; the United States, 11.0 percent; Brazil, 7.6 percent; China, 6.7 percent; and Canada, 6.5 percent. The location of capacity has also been affected by the highly concentrated nature of the iron and steel industries. Prior to 1970, the production of iron ore was more restricted geographically than were the locations of deposits. Most facilities were located in the industrialized countries also having domestic iron ore supplies. Until the 1950s, it was also a function of the local or regional market structure. Sweden and France supplied the major portion of western Europe's iron ore needs. The Soviet Union provided for eastern Europe, and the United States and Canada accounted for nearly all of North America's requirements.

It was not until the late 1950s that this regional structure of the production and trade in iron ore was broken. With Japan's becoming a major producer of steel and hence a major consumer of iron ore, the production of iron ore took on a more international perspective. Since Japan was located a great distance from the already existing suppliers of iron ore, new supply sources had to be created.

During this same period, western Europe's demand for iron ore and iron and steel vastly surpassed the abilities of Germany, France, and Great Britain to provide an adequate supply. It became obvious that provisions for an adequate future supply of iron ore would necessarily be met from other than the traditional sources.

It was these two situations which gave the impetus for the rapid and enormous expansion of the world base for iron ore production. Especially evident are production changes as reflected by the exploitation of deposits in India, Brazil, Australia, and Venezuela. In 1955, 85 percent of iron ore production was accounted for by western Europe, Canada, and the United

Table 6–3
World Iron Ore Production and Capacity, 1973–1980
(million short tons of contained iron)

	Production	Production Capacity		
Area	*1973*	*1973*	*1974*	*1980*[b]
North America				
United States				
Pellets	43.4	45.7	50.0	71.0
Natural ore and other	16.5	30.0	30.0	9.0
Subtotal	59.9	75.7	80.0	80.0
Canada	35.6	43.0	44.0	56.0
Mexico	3.4	3.6	4.6	11.0
Total	98.9	122.3	128.6	147.0
South America				
Brazil	41.5	47.0	57.0	87.0
Venezuela	14.6	21.0	21.0	24.0
Other	13.1	17.3	18.0	23.0
Total	69.2	85.3	96.0	134.0
Europe				
France	18.4	20.0	20.0	20.0
Sweden	23.4	30.0	31.0	32.0
Other (except U.S.S.R.)	20.2	26.0	25.0	26.0
Total	62.0	76.0	76.0	78.0
U.S.S.R.	140.5	150.0	155.0	180.0
Africa				
India	24.2	28.0	32.0	37.0
People's Republic of China	36.4[a]	37.0	37.0	38.0
Other (includes				
Middle East)	10.0	13.0	12.0	17.0
Total	70.6	78.0	81.0	92.0
Oceania				
Australia	59.8	69.0	79.0	107.0
Other	1.4	2.0	2.0	2.0
Total	61.2	71.0	81.0	109.0
World total	544.1	632.0	669.0	803.0

Source: *Mineral Facts and Problems, 1975* (Washington, D.C.: U.S. Department of the Interior, 1976).

[a]Revised figure of 30.8 used in later publication (1974 Minerals Yearbook). Capacity figures for 1973 and 1974 revised to 31 and 33, respectively.

[b]Estimated.

States. By 1975, production by the same regions had fallen to about 55 percent.

Of particular significance is the change in the share of production in iron ore enjoyed by the developing countries. In 1955, they were responsible for only about 10 percent of iron ore production. By 1975, the developing countries accounted for about 30 percent of the world's iron ore production and capacity, including slightly more than 50 percent of the export market.

An additional feature of today's production has been the noted improvements in technological methods of beneficiation and agglomeration. Whereas the production of iron ore in terms of actual weight increased by 2.3 times between 1955 and 1975, production in terms of estimated iron content increased by 2.8 times. This increase can be seen in terms of the increase in pellet and sinter production since 1955, as shown in table 6–4. Pellet production has grown from 1.5 million tons in 1955 to 167.1 million tons in 1975. Sinter production has also risen sharply from 104.4 million tons in 1955 to 508.5 million tons in 1975. Major sinter producers are the United States, Canada, and the U.S.S.R.; its use has been greater in Japan and the U.S.S.R. than in the United States. The global output of sinter is growing more rapidly than that of pellets, even though the latter has certain advantageous physical properties and can be more easily shipped.

In view of the lack of readily documentable information on the costs of producing iron ore, cost inferences are often made on the basis of FOB values. The latter consists of a number of components including mining costs, internal transport costs, port charges, financial charges, and in some cases beneficiation charges. The largest of these components appear to be financial charges which are composed of amortization interest payments, taxation, and royalties. Next in importance are mining costs, of which labor and energy are the major components. As will be shown later, the export values of iron ore for the major countries have increased between 40 and 100 percent between 1970 and 1975. It can be inferred that iron ore production costs have risen at a similar rate.

Consumption

World demand for iron ore is a derived demand, almost entirely dependent on the demand for steel. One ton of steel uses approximately 0.7 tons of pig iron, and each ton of pig iron requires 1.7 tons of iron ore; thus it takes about 1.19 tons of iron ore to produce 1 ton of steel. Most of the world's production of iron ore is used in the production of steel. As a major raw material in the production of pig iron, iron ore is so essential that it has virtually no substitutes. However, the iron employed in steel making can be obtained either from pig iron or from ferrous alloy scrap. Since steel production technology allows for a wide variation in the amounts of scrap used, ferrous scrap consumption in the steel industry is highly related to the availability and price of pig iron. Ferrous scrap thus represents the greatest competitor to iron ore and to pig iron in the

Table 6–4
Change in Iron Ore Production and Processing
(million tons)

Country	Total Iron Ore[a]			Pellets			Sinters			Pig Iron		
	1955	*1965*	*1975*	*1955*	*1965*	*1975*	*1955*	*1965*	*1975*	*1955*	*1965*	*1975*
Brazil	2.1	14.1	49.4	0.0	0.0	4.2	0.7	1.7	6.1	—	—	73.8
United States	53.0	50.9	48.7	0.9	32.1	70.0	26.3	48.5	38.4	70.6	80.6	—
Canada	8.2	21.8	25.3	0.2	10.3	24.5	3.0	3.6	2.5	—	—	—
France	17.8	18.1	14.5	—	—	—	1.7	18.5	30.8	—	—	—
Federal Republic of Germany	3.9	2.9	1.2	0.1	1.8	7.0	14.0	29.9	36.8	—	—	—
Japan	0.8	1.4	0.5	—	—	—	3.4	25.2	108.8	5.2	27.5	86.6
U.S.S.R.	39.5	81.0	127.3	0.0	0.0	27.2	33.8	110.0	151.9	33.3	66.2	102.4
Developing countries	21.7	83.4	150.5	0.0	1.0	15.8	1.0	4.9	19.0	4.6	14.2	25.8
World	178.6	325.9	501.3	1.5	46.5	167.1	104.4	319.0	508.5	190.5	326.1	469.0

Source: UNCTAD, *Iron Ore: Features of the World Market*, Statistical Annex, TD/B/IPC/IRON ORE/2/Add. 1 (Geneva: UNCTAD, 1977).
[a] Metal content.

production of steel. Since 1955, pig iron has accounted for 70–75 percent of the raw material input to steel production.

As shown in table 6–5, the major consumers of iron are the EEC, Japan, the Soviet Union, and the United States. In 1975, the latter three alone accounted for 53.6 percent of world consumption. Regarding the pattern of this consumption, some change has taken place since 1975. Japan has increased her share from 3 percent to more than 16 percent; the EEC has decreased its share from 26 to 17 percent; and the share of the United States has declined from 36 to 16 percent. Although not shown, India, North Korea, South Korea, Brazil, Mexico, and Argentina account for approximately 90 percent of iron ore consumption in developing countries.

These changes generally have been associated with an increased dependence on imports by the major consumer countries. This, however, has not been the case with the U.S.S.R. which has been able to provide for nearly all of its domestic consumption needs. Only the import of high-grade ores has enabled western Europe, the United States, and Japan to maintain a semblance of stability in providing for domestic steel consumption. France, Spain, the United Kingdom, and the United States have displayed major declines in domestic production of iron ore in relation to domestic consumption. For example, the United States and France still rank in the top ten as major producers of iron ore, yet both are heavily dependent on imported ore to meet consumption requirements.

In 1975, the developing countries' share of pig iron production was 5.5

Table 6–5
World Apparent Consumption of Iron Ore[a]
(million tons)

Country	1955	1960	1965	1970	1971	1972	1973	1974	1975
Belgium, Luxembourg	7.4	9.2	11.6	15.0	14.1	14.0	14.4	16.1	12.4
France	14.0	15.0	14.1	18.3	17.3	17.9	17.8	20.2	17.7
Germany	11.8	22.5	22.7	29.6	25.0	25.1	29.1	34.8	26.7
India	0.8	1.0	7.2	6.9	10.0	9.1	7.9	8.7	12.0
Japan	3.9	10.1	23.8	64.1	72.0	69.8	84.7	84.7	78.9
U.S.S.R.	35.1	56.3	68.9	86.2	89.7	91.9	94.9	98.3	102.9
United Kingdom	11.9	15.2	15.3	16.2	13.5	13.1	14.1	13.0	10.9
United States	64.0	62.6	74.4	77.4	71.6	66.7	78.4	79.5	75.9
Rest of world	29.8	54.8	89.1	106.5	109.0	133.2	128.9	141.3	142.9
Total	178.7	246.7	327.1	420.2	422.2	440.8	470.2	497.4	480.3

Source: UNCTAD, "Iron Ore: Features of the World Market," Statistical Annex, TD/B/IPC/ IRON ORE/2/Add. 1 (Geneva: UNCTAD, 1977).

[a]No data are available regarding iron ore consumption in most countries. To obtain a rough idea of growth in consumption, apparent consumption was used instead, that is, production plus imports minus exports, all in iron content. Obvious errors are involved regarding countries or years with substantial stocks or stock changes.

percent. This, combined with the high level of iron ore stocks believed to be held in those countries, suggests that their share of world iron ore consumption has been overstated, since some of it represents ore in sinter. Similarly the growth of sinter in Japan depends on blast furnace practice employing 68 percent sinter, 19 percent crude ore, and 12 percent pellets. Finally, blast furnaces in western Europe require 70 percent sinter, 16 percent pellets, and 14 percent lump ore. Although the latter suggests a strong demand for sinter, increasing environmental control legislation is likely to shift some demand to pellets.

Capacity Adjustment

One of the more pronounced problems of the world market for iron ore, iron, and steel has been the existence of surplus capacity since 1958. As indicated by Manners, many parts of the world were suffering from a shortage of iron ore and iron and steel products in 1950, but by 1965 steel makers were embarrassed by what suddenly became a surplus of productive capacity.[11] Although these remarks were addressed primarily to the production of iron and steel, they would also seem to be relevant for the iron ore market. During most of the 1950s, the growth in production of iron ore and iron and steel roughly matched the growth in demand. But by 1958, capacity began suddenly to exceed production levels commensurate with demand. Although the amounts of excess capacity created are difficult to estimate precisely, it is generally agreed that production capacities outstripped demand for ore and metal products by about 15 percent annually over the period 1965 to 1975, with the exception of 1974.

Four reasons are cited for the existence of surplus capacity. First, productive capacity and self-sufficiency have increased in those countries (especially developing ones) which have traditionally relied on western Europe, the Soviet Union, Canada, and the United States for imports. More significantly in building the productive capacity, these new producers have not been able to adjust investment such that production would just equal domestic demand.

Second, while these new producers have increased output, the demand for iron ore and iron and steel in the developed countries did not match projections for the period. Along with the generally slow pace of the world economy from 1970 through 1977, several specific factors caused excess supply in the developing countries: a nearly 700 percent increase in prices of fuel and of coking coal, the consequent reduction in iron and steel demand growth, and overly optimistic projections of future demand levels. These optimistic projections of increased demand for iron and steel induced the iron and steel industries to boost production capacity levels to new highs in the 1960–1964 period and the 1970–1973 period. These capacity increases were just prior to inventory stock reductions by major users as a result of the rapidly increasing inflation rate and dramatic rise in the cost of fuels.

A third cause of surplus capacity was that technological advancements in virtually all branches of the industry induced many countries and companies to expand capacity greater than required in order to benefit from the economies of scale. Manners states that this would have been a successful strategy had it been undertaken by only a few producers. However, that many followed this notion compounded the problem.

Fourth, the greatest degree of influence on the disequilibrium between production capacity and consumption was the change in technology, markets, and raw material sources that took place. These changes attracted new production capacity to the industry and aggravated the problem still further.

Trade

Before the Second World War, only small quantities of iron ore were transported internationally because of the prevalence of adequate iron ore reserves in most industrialized nations and high transportation costs. In the 1950s and early 1960s, the trade which took place had a regional character, with Venezuela and Canada covering the deficient supplies of the United States. Sweden was the major exporter to the west European users, and Japan satisfied its somewhat limited needs at that time from diverse sources in south and east Asia.

Since then, trade in iron ore has accelerated from 26 percent of world iron ore production in 1955 to about 47 percent of production in 1975. Over the same period the value of exports rose from $701 million to $5,300 million, an average annual rate of growth of 10.6 percent. With regard to the developing countries' share in world exports, the proportion estimated is sensitive to the measure selected. As shown below the percentage is highest in terms of metal content and lowest in terms of value:

LDC Exports	1955	1965	1970	1973	1975
Metal content (percent LDC share)	36	50	46	43	46
Actual weight (percent LDC share)	32	47	44	41	45
Value (percent LDC share)	32	43	40	37	41

The proportion is shown to vary between 32 and 36 percent in 1955 and between 41 and 46 percent in 1975.

The principal exporters among the developed countries in 1975 were Australia, 9 percent; Canada, 12 percent; and U.S.S.R., 12 percent. Among the developing countries, the leaders were Brazil, 17 percent; Liberia, 6 percent; and Venezuela, 5 percent. The principal importers in the same year were Japan, 33 percent; Federal Republic of Germany, 13 percent; and the United States, 13 percent. Although this could be described as a direct trade flow from south to north, the presence of developed countries as exporters adds variations to the pattern. In addition, several of the exporting countries slipped from a position of dominance in 1955 to one of insignificance by 1975, among them Algeria, Tunisia, and Morocco and some of them have become major importers, namely Spain and France. Finally Australia, Liberia, India, and Venezuela rose from the ranks of minor importers to major exporters.

By any standard, the rate of growth of exports achieved has been substantial. Among the factors contributing to this growth, the world demand for steel rose from 270 million net tons in 1955 to 710 million tons in 1974.[12] There has also been an increase in the exploitation of ore deposits with higher iron ore content; the average grade of ores entering international trade was 51 percent iron in 1950, 53 percent in 1960 and an estimated 59 percent in 1975. Economies of scale have also increased in ocean transportation, principally through the development of larger ore carriers. New importing countries also have appeared such as Japan, which is one of the world's principal steel producers and is almost totally dependent on imported iron ore. Finally, technological improvements have been important, such as in the beneficiation of certain lower-grade ores, notably taconites.

Market Structure

The structure of the iron ore industry can be characterized as follows:[13]

1. The policies pursued by major steel companies to assure foreign supplies of iron have resulted in shifts in the magnitudes of transactions among the three major trading modalities.
2. Such policies resulted in an overexpansion of production capacity, despite falling iron ore prices in real terms since the 1960s.
3. Somewhat dispersed and competing sources of supply are normally confronted by more concentrated demand markets.
4. These demand markets contain monopsonistic elements such as purchase organizations that coordinate iron ore purchases in any one country.
5. Efforts by some exporting countries to improve the price situation have resulted in changes in the demand and supply relationship as well as in the formation of the Association of Iron Ore Exporting Countries.

Recent Evolution

Because of the rapid growth of the iron ore industry since the 1960s, the underlying market structure has been undergoing continuous change. There are three aspects of this change that seem best to typify it. First, the development of the new large mines has been dependent on substantial investment contributions from international sources. To safeguard their capital, the international investors required the new mining firms to sign delivery contracts with steel producers in the industrialized world for periods of ten to fifteen years or even longer. This supposedly assured the mines of the cash flow required for their debt service. These contracts commonly specified not only volumes but also prices in U.S. dollars for a substantial part of the duration of the contract. The contracts invariably failed in anticipating the accelerated world inflation which occurred in the late 1960s and early 1970s as well as the repeated dollar devaluations. From 1970 onward, therefore, a sharply widening gap emerged between the prices established for long periods of time and the prices which were negotiated annually.

The Japanese buyers have been particularly keen on entering into long-term supply arrangements with the new mines. They were consequently the ones who benefited most from the emerging price gap. Apart from the inflation and weakness of the dollar, three other important factors worked to the advantage of the Japanese in their arrangements. First was the unawareness among the new Australian mining companies of the growth prospects of Japan's steel industry. Fearing that there might not be sufficient markets for Australia's greatly expanded iron ore supplies, each mining company was very keen to assure itself of steady sales through long-term contractual arrangements. This obviously strengthened the Japanese bargaining position. Retrospectively, the Japanese ore needs turned out to be so great that there was no problem whatever in absorbing the expanding Australian output. Recently, however, there have been indications that it may be difficult for Australia to further increase its exports to Japan.

Second, the Japanese seem to have modified the long-term contract system to their own advantage. The usual contract stipulates an offtake of ±10 percent of the contracted volume. The Japanese, however, have generally purchased only the minimum 90 percent of the volume (and sometimes less), opening a margin of underused capacity of about 20 percent which serves to depress prices.

The third factor was their preparedness to buy the ore on an FOB basis and to provide their own facilities for shipping it to the steel mills. This arrangement then appeared advantageous to the miners, who thus felt relieved of the uncertainties of fluctuating freight rates. Again, their suppliers, failed to anticipate the fast reduction in freight costs which followed with increasing ship sizes and further mechanization of port facilities. This cost reduction was thus entirely reaped by the Japanese buyers.

Thus, from the late 1960s the contractual arrangements entered into by the Japanese steel industry not only neutralized, but even reversed its earlier disadvantageous position vis-à-vis its main competitors. Japan has continued its efforts in this regard, despite the renegotiations of many of the contracts imposed upon the Japanese in the early 1970s as a condition for keeping their suppliers viable.

A second aspect of change in market structure has been a gradual weakening of the price leading role of the annual German-Swedish negotiations. This has resulted from the decreasing importance of Sweden in the world market for iron ore. Its place has been taken by Brazil which is posed for a major expansion of its market shares. Substantial investments are being made in mining, infrastructure, and ports in Brazil, where foreign capital inflows are constantly increasing. On the whole, one might say that today there is much more competition in the annual negotiations where sales volumes and prices for the following year are determined.

The third aspect has to do with the increasing involvement of governments in the iron ore sectors of almost all major exporting countries. Thus, outright nationalizations of iron ore mines in countries like Mauritania, Peru, and Venezuela have reduced the output share of captive mines, that is, those owned by steel-producing firms. The output of such mines found primarily in Canada and Liberia has decreased to less than 25 percent of world exports. In addition, increasing government control has led to a considerable coordination of the mines' sales efforts at the national level. Conditions for exports from countries like Brazil, Peru, Venezuela, Mauritania, and India are now in effect agreed upon by the exporting mines under the supervision of each national government. In Australia, the government's role is less direct but probably equally important in that all major export contracts require government approval. Only in Canada and Liberia among the major exporting countries are the private mines free to enter into contractual agreements quite independent of the government.

These major changes have led to the depiction of market structure given in figure 6–1. If some division of the proportion of trade now transacted can be made, the following is probably the closest: (1) 20 percent or less of international ore trade is captive. (2) 40 percent or more of the trade is transacted under contractural arrangements of ten to fifteen years' duration. (Note that the traumatic inflationary experience of recent years has caused prices to be commonly negotiated in these contracts every two years.) (3) The remaining 40 percent of world iron ore exports are sold under short-term contracts with both quantities and prices renegotiated each year.

In the early 1970s, iron ore prices such as the Kiruna D quotation have been about 50 percent below those of the late 1950s in real terms. This fall is partly the result of cost-reducing technological progress. The price depressing influence of the new large-scale mines anxiously seeking market outlets as well as a generally easy supply situation are important in explaining this decline. During long periods, the price levels fixed in the long-term contracts not only remained below those of the one-year agreements, but also tended to pull down the levels of the latter.

Organization and Concentration

A further essential aspect of the market structure for iron ore is the degree of concentration found. The allegation has often been made that the iron ore industry is an oligopoly on the supply side and an oligopsony on the demand side. In fact it is difficult to exemplify the market as such, based on table 6–6. The four largest firms are shown to account for 34.3 percent of total iron ore shipments and the eight largest for 57 percent. To the extent that the market contains a large number of small producers, particularly many of those

Table 6–6
Concentration in the World Iron Ore Industry

Firm	Shares (%)	Shipments (gross tons)
Largest four		
Cia Vale Do Rio Doce (Brazil)	12.2	51,600,677
The Hanna Mining Co. (U.S.)	7.5	31,830,365
Hamersley Iron Pty. Ltd. (Australia)	7.5	31,810,800
Mt. Newman Mining Co. Pty. Ltd. (Aus.)	7.1	30,252,197
Subtotal	34.3	145,494,039
Indexes (4)		
CR = 0.343; HH = 0.031;		
HG = 0.177; GR = 0.149		
Lesser four		
U.S. Steel Corporation (U.S.)	6.5	27,391,002
The Cleveland Cliffs Iron Co. (U.S.)	6.1	25,955,516
C.V.G. Ferromineria Orinoco C.A. (Venez)	4.9	20,826,054
Luossavaara-Kiirunavaara (Sweden)	4.8	20,266,400
Subtotal	56.6	239,933,011
Indexes (8)		
CR = 0.566; HH = 0.044;		
HG = 0.209; GR = 0.176		
All other	43.4	184,084,000
Total	100.0	423,980,736

Sources: *Skilling's Mining Review,* London, 1976; and *Metal Bulletin,* London, 1977.

organized as state trading enterprises in exporting developing countries, it is only a weak oligopoly. At the same time, one receives the image of an industry somewhat dominated by the major multinationals, with the organization of the major ore suppliers becoming more centralized and increasingly more oligopolistic in nature.

Like copper, tin, and bauxite, it is difficult to measure concentration on the demand side. Here concentration is believed to be reflected in the bargaining power of the purchase organizations in the major importing countries. For example, the British Steel Corporation contracts for all iron ore imports; it then distributes receipts according to needs. In the Federal Republic of Germany, two companies purchase practically all iron ore imports, Rohstoffhandle GmbH and Erzkontor-Ruhr GmbH. In Italy, Italsider, a subsidy of the state holding company Finsider, imports all domestic requirements. In France, the same role is played by two steel companies, Wendel-Sidelor and Sinor. Finally, Hoogoverus, the only iron and steel producer in the Netherlands, contracts for all of the country's ore needs.

Even where purchase organizations do not exist, such as in the United States, the iron ore purchase contracts agreed upon by one of the major mills such as United States Steel will strongly influence the negotiations of other steel producers. The difficulty of obtaining data on iron ore purchases by the above companies and countries has prevented estimating concentration on the demand side. But the purchasing power reflected in the above examples does suggest a strong oligopsony.

Nationalization

With regard to the increasing nationalization of iron ore mines, its major effect to now has been the reduction in share of total trade due to captive mining. Between 1964 and 1975, the government of Venezuela through direct nationalization and a restructured tax base managed to take over majority control of its entire extractive industry. The more immediate effect has been the reduction of Venezuela's percentage share of the world iron ore market and the loss of foreign investment capital. However, the government has attempted to improve the position of the industry since 1976 through increased investment. The more lasting effect of the nationalization has been the possibility of the United States curtailing severely its imports from Venezuela. This could be a result of the bitter litigation which took place over company taxing between the government and its major firms, U.S. Steel (Orinoco Mining Company) and Bethlehem Steel (Iron Mines Company of Venezuela).[14]

In contrast to Venezuela, Brazil has pursued nationalization more stringently. Since the late 1960s, the government of Brazil, through its national conglomerate, Companhia Vale do Rio Doce (CVRD), has managed to gain control of most production facilities. In fact, CVRD accounted for 78 percent of total iron ore exports in 1974. The conglomerate is permitted to mine and exploit raw materials, but it must do this on its own account rather than as a service contractor.[15] Not operating strictly as a monopoly, CVRD operates under the same regulations as other companies. Its main purpose is to participate in such a manner as to safeguard national interests and development goals. Meanwhile Brazil believes a certain amount of private capital is essential to stimulate competition, and it attempts to provide a favorable environment for foreign investment.

In addition to lessening traditional ownership ties, nationalization also reflects a movement by the exporting developing countries toward greater control of the industry as a whole. Although substantial foreign ownership still remains, governments have acquired a strong equity interest in the iron ore mines of these countries. In many cases, the governments coordinate and take an active part in the negotiations at which the sales price of the mines situated within their borders are determined.

Producer Coordination

There has also been a reaction by these countries to the problems of falling terms of trade and oversupply of iron ore. An Iron Ore Exporters Association was agreed upon in 1975 by Algeria, Australia, Chile, India, Mauritania, Peru, Sweden, Tunisia, and Venezuela. Refraining from membership were Canada, Brazil, and the United States. The goals of the association are to promote country cooperation in assuring healthy growth of the industry, to secure remunerative prices, to expand processing downstream including iron and steel, and to provide a forum for exchange and problem slving. Because of the differing philosophies of the member nations, attempts to secure iron ore agreements have failed. This factor together with substantial existing reserves and the availability of scrap imply that no substantial changes in the marketing of iron ore will occur in the short run.

Despite the costs and risks of stockpiling iron ore, it should be mentioned that several attempts are being made to assure future supplies. The Kawaski Steel Corporation of Japan is planning to construct a stockpile in the Philippines and in Sweden. And the Swedish state-owned iron ore company (Luossavaara Kiirunavaara Aktibolag) is financing stockpiling at both producer and consumer locations.[16]

Market Implications

Export Dependence

There is a mixed pattern in the contribution of iron ore exports to total export earnings in developing countries. Those with the largest export quantities tend to have the smallest export shares. Brazil and Venezuela have had shares in

1974 of 7.2 percent and 3.6 percent only. The exception is Liberia where iron ore has constituted 65.0 percent of total exports. In contrast, Mauritania, with relatively low iron ore export levels, also tended to have a high dependency, the share being some 73.1 percent. Among the iron ore exporting developed countries, iron ore exports represent only a small share of total exports. Some examples are Sweden, 2.7 percent; Australia, 5.7 percent; and Canada, 7.2 percent.

The substantial growth in iron ore production experienced by Brazil, Liberia, and Venezuela can be viewed in table 6–8. Brazil's exports increased from $30 million in 1955 to $996 million in 1976, Liberia from $18 million to $332 million, and Venezuela from $49 million to $266 million. The decrease in growth of exports from Sweden is shown in contrast. Their iron ore exports rose from $158 million in 1955 to $428 million in 1974 and remained at that level during 1975 and 1976.

That these countries have experienced falling prices in their exports is also reflected in table 6–7. The deflated unit values have decreased from 1960 to 1976 for each of the countries shown except Sweden. However, an upturn did occur in 1975, partially because of rising input costs and partially because of pressures by the developing countries to reverse the downward price trend. Brazil is shown to have a unit value more stable than that of the other countries with a variability of 22 percent. The finished steel deflated price index with a variability of 6 percent proved to be more stable. The levels of variability found are lower than that of copper or tin unit values.

Magnitude of Fixed Investment

Fixed investments in iron ore mining and processing facilities are indeed large. This would suggest that firms willing to make such investments have stronger bargaining power initially relative to the host government. For the three developing countries of interest, gross domestic product (GDP), contribution made to that product from the mining sector (MS), and gross domestic investment (GDI) are provided in millions of dollars for 1973.[17]

	GDP	MS	GDI
Brazil	49,910	10,003	118
Venezuela	12,500	3,548	2,323
Liberia (1972)	419	71	118

Investment costs in iron ore mining given earlier amount to $65–115 per metric ton of annual capacity in 1975 dollars. At $100 per ton, a mine of the current typical size of 10 million tons would cost $1 billion. This represents 35

Iron Ore

Table 6-7
Trend and Variability of Iron Ore Export Values and Unit Values
(millions of dollars and dollars per metric ton)

Year	Brazil Export Value	Brazil Unit Value	Brazil De-flated[a]	Liberia Export Value	Liberia Unit Value	Liberia De-flated	Sweden Export Value	Sweden Unit Value	Sweden De-flated	Venezuela Export Value	Venezuela Unit Value	Venezuela De-flated	Finished Steel Price Index (Iron Ore) Price ¢/lb	Finished Steel Price Index (Iron Ore) De-flated
1955	30	11.70	—	18	10.14	—	158	10.12	—	49	6.24	—	—	—
1960	54	10.23	12.18	35	11.68	13.90	186	9.39	11.18	166	8.57	10.20	6.20	7.38
1965	103	8.09	9.19	96	6.26	7.11	218	8.93	10.15	138	8.11	9.22	6.37	7.24
1970	210	7.47	7.47	151	6.40	6.40	230	8.22	8.22	177	8.40	8.40	7.65	7.65
1971	237	7.65	7.29	161	7.78	7.41	246	9.39	8.94	166	8.68	8.27	8.25	7.86
1972	232	7.59	6.72	183	7.95	7.04	286	10.36	9.17	142	8.58	7.59	9.00	7.96
1973	363	8.07	6.07	197	7.69	5.78	350	10.64	8.00	166	7.56	5.68	9.38	7.05
1974	571	9.61	5.93	262	10.25	6.33	428	12.94	7.99	252	9.47	5.85	11.14	6.88
1975	909	12.53	6.88	303	16.30	10.06	482	20.89	11.48	257	12.93	7.10	13.10	7.20
1976	996	14.84	8.11	332	14.84	8.06	444	21.13	11.55	266	15.21	8.31	14.21	7.76
Trend[b] 1976/1965	967	183	88	346	237	113	204	237	114	193	188	90	223	107
Variability (%)[c] 1970–1976	66	30	11	32	38	20	29	40	17	26	28	16	24	6

Source: UNCTAD, "Iron Ore: Features of the World Market," Statistical Annex, TD/B/IPC/IRON ORE/2/Add. 1 (Geneva: UNCTAD, 1977).
[a]Deflater is U.N. Index of Unit Value of Exported Manufactured Goods.
[b]Ratio between 1965 and 1976.
[c]Coefficient of variation in percent over 1970–1976.

percent of Venezuela's gross domestic investment for one year and 22 percent of the product of the mining sector. For Liberia the proportions are in fact a multiple. When one considers the capital required for an integrated steel works in developing countries, even the above figures seem modest. Figures with the lower figure applying to larger-scale operations in the vicinity of 12 million tons and above.

Nature of Technology

The nature of mining and pelletization technology is stable, with the latter being slightly more complex. This produces demands for certain technologically related skills. Although pellets have the advantage of constituting a standard product, they must be produced subject to a fairly sophisticated level of quality control. Where the pellets fail to meet product standards, steel makers will change sources of supply. The experiences of producing developing countries that have nationalized such as Brazil, however, show that to some extent skills can be improved and these difficulties overcome.

It is worth adding that the increasing adoption of direct-reduction technology might change the relationship between the nature and amounts of iron ore required in steel production. This would facilitate the expansion of steel production in developing countries and make them less dependent on steel imports.

Marketing Process

The variety of marketing arrangements in iron ore make it difficult to generalize as to whether the firm or the host government have a greater advantage in the division of gains. The division of marketing transactions suggested was: 20 percent captive arrangements, 40 percent or more under contracts of ten to fifteen years duration, and the remaining 40 percent under short-term contracts with quantities and/or prices renegotiated each year. This pattern tends to vary across different regions of the world. For example, most U.S. iron ore requirements are on a captive basis. In western Europe, about one-half of the requirements are captive, with the remainder met through long- and short-term contracts. Japan, with no iron ore at all, tends to use trading houses as an intermediary between the steel industry and iron ore producers. In this way, trading houses can spread the risk of acquisition by contracting ore from a wide variety of foreign ore-producing countries and a wide range of mining firms within a single country.

Firms have an advantage in using long-term contracting only when they can cutback purchases below their minimum contractual levels in times of recession. Otherwise they must hold to their purchase agreement. Such obligations must also be met by state-owned firms which have agreed to supply given amounts at contract prices.

Control over Resources and Production

The recent formation of the Association of Iron Ore Exporting Countries reflects the interest of these countries in obtaining greater control over iron ore resources and production. Nationalization has been one means of achieving this goal, and Venezuela and Brazil have moved in this direction. India and Bolivia also have nationalized industries. Attempts to increase steel production in the ore-producing developing countries will result in an increase of the vertical structure of their industries. Changes in the nature of long-term contractural arrangements, particularly to obtain more control over initial capital and annual takeoff levels will add to their advantage. Increased movement in this direction together with the decrease in captive mining arrangements should also lead to more control. However, this tendency is presently being tempered by the lack of availability of capital for project development and the subsequent dependency of the government on foreign investors.

Opportunities for Increased Processing

Possibilities for increased processing in the developing countries are likely at the iron ore beneficiation and agglomeration stage as well as at the steel-making stage. Concerning the first of these, both the production of pellets and sinter has grown between 1965 and 1975. As previously shown, pellets produced in developing countries accounted for 9.5 percent of world production in 1975 and sinter for 3.7 percent. Among the principal pellet-exporting countries in this group are Peru, Liberia, and Brazil.

It would appear that there are benefits to be derived by the production of pellets in developing countries. Because pellet prices have been rising faster than ore prices and require more input, countries with abundant energy will experience greater foreign exchange earnings. Between 1970 and 1976, the contract prices of lumpy ores (64 percent Fe) rose between 44 and 51 percent, while the prices for 64 percent pellets rose by 75 percent.[18] Exporting pellets would also reduce unit costs of transport, especially shipping. And the current trend in direct reductions may reduce costs of production for domestic steel processing.

One disadvantage of pellet production is that pelletization facilities cannot easily be added to existing plants. In adding them to new mining facilities, however, the capital required for the scale of operation required is not excessive. Earlier, an investment cost of $20–35 per metric ton of annual capacity was cited. For a 3-million-ton facility, this implies a capital requirement of about a $100 million in 1975 dollars. A recent survey has indicated that as of January 1977 there were almost forty direct production plants in operation with a combined annual productive capacity of 8.5 million tons of prereduced pellets.[19] Developing countries had a share of 2.8 million tons or 33 percent, all of which is concentrated in Latin America. When some twenty-eight new direct reduction plants reach full production by 1980, this will increase capacity to 31.6 million tons. Some 50 percent of this would be located in eleven developing countries.

The possibilities for investment in steel making are less, based on the high capital costs involved. Given the $250–400-per-ton investment figure quoted, this implies $3 billion for a 12-million-ton faculty. Among factors that are likely to increase steel making are increased domestic demand, the availability of lower-cost smaller-scale production technology, and the substantial value-added to be gained. In the first case, an estimated 5 million metric tons of annual demand would be required, given the minimum size of an integrated iron and steel facility (blast furnace and basic oxygen).[20] Second, for annual demand below that level, direct reduction facilities could be employed because of their low required scale of operation. Finally, although facilities of this size may not provide a base for exporting steel, the gains in gross value-added to be experienced in steel production are substantial: from some 13 percent for iron ore mining and 24 percent for briquette production to 63 percent for steel making.

Among factors working against increased steel production in developing countries, these mainly affect export potential. Of importance here is the growing protectionism in the United States, new attempts by the steel industry in the United States to modernize, and the depressed world steel market. Steel consumption is only expected to grow at 3.3 percent annually over the next several years, a figure considerably less than that of the previous decade.[21]

Material Share in Product Prices

The extent to which an increase in iron ore prices would affect final product prices is not thought to be substantial. Estimates of the proportion of iron ore costs are about 7–15 percent of the wholesale price of steel merchant bars and 5–13 percent of the wholesale price of heavy steel plates.[22] These proportions have varied somewhat over time, following a slightly declining trend. The fact that iron ore accounts for only a small proportion of the prices of semi-fabricated steel products can be partially explained by the costs already prevalent at the pig iron stage, notably freight costs, the dual costs of coke as a reducing agent and fuel, and labor charges.

With regards to passing on an increase in iron ore prices, a 10 percent increase in the raw material cost would add about 1 percent to the cost of producing steel. Although such a cost rise could be absorbed by the steel industry as a whole, certain firms in the industry would experience a relatively substantial profit decline. This might very well develop into a general resistance against such a price increase.

Obsolescing Bargain

Investment in iron ore mining has been shown to involve substantial initial capital outlays. Not only does this make risk and uncertainty an important consideration in iron ore mining decisions, but the uncertainty is compounded by the timing of investment programs, which take about ten years from exploration to completion. Thus, the investing firm has an initial bargaining advantage, given the host governments' attempts to attract the substantial amounts of capital required for iron ore projects.

An approach which has been recently practiced to secure adequate finance has been to negotiate a long-term contract for the purchase of the ore, the contract then being used as a collateral against a loan to finance the production facilities and infrastructure.[23] Such contracts also have included an obligation of minimum deliveries at specified prices in order to guarantee a minimum revenue flow to the mining enterprise. Contracts such as these have formed the bases of an increasing number of investment projects in Australia, Latin America, and Africa. Increased market uncertainty as found in the early 1970s, however, has caused some contract violations. For example, some purchasers requested renegotiation to decrease their quantities below minimum stated contractual levels. Given that the iron ore could not be sold elsewhere, the mining enterprises were forced to reduce output.

This dependence of the host governments is not likely to change in the near future, given the foreseen shortages of capital together with increasing economies of large-scale operations. One tendency among firms appears to be that of expanding production capacity rather than of initiating new projects. This practice would tend to increase the market shares of existing producers, preserving existing trade patterns.

Nature of Competition

Another aspect of the dynamics of adjustment in the iron ore industry concerns the changing nature of competition. In this respect, the degree of bargaining power held by either the producers or consumers depends on the (1) extent of the nationalization in host countries, (2) presence of government-sanctioned privately owned monopolies, (3) degree of government financial participation,

(4) extent of vertical integration, (5) amount of export capacity, and (6) presence of cartel-type practices.

The structure of the iron ore industry has been characterized as a weak oligopoly. Iron ore producers are many and dispersed at the firm level, reflecting only a small amount of concentration. However, in the developing countries most are state owned or controlled with national or state-owned monopoly characteristics. Iron ore consumers tend to be more concentrated at the purchase organization level. In addition, the purchase organizations themselves represent a form of cartel. As an example, the European Coal and Steel Community is a power structure serving as an umbrella over the purchasing cartels in western Europe. Their control is more apparent at the steel product level where crises such as recessions permit them to intervene directly in steel pricing. In the United States, a single firm has been regarded as a price leader from time to time.

Regarding the geographic concentration of iron ore trade, exports as well as imports have tended to remain concentrated in the major countries. Canada, Sweden, and the Soviet Union have remained the major exporters since 1960, although now Australia and Brazil have become important. Japan, the United States, and the Federal Republic of Germany have remained the major importers. Any perceptible shift in the competitive structure has resulted from the adjustment in marketing arrangements, with long-term contracts becoming more important. At the same time, the reduction in captive arrangements has accompanied an increase in nationalization. The formation of the Association of Iron Ore Exporting Countries, on the other hand, has not affected competition or marketing structure to any notable extent.

Government Learning Process

It would appear that some host governments, such as that of Brazil, have demonstrated an ability to cope with the problems of attracting foreign capital and dealing with complex technological processes. However, this has not involved substantial changes in rates of taxation or similar methods of increasing control. The example of Brazil appears to be unique, nonetheless; the country reflects a higher state of economic development than does that of other large iron ore exporters such as Liberia, Mauritania, and Angola. Even with its state-owned enterprises such as Cia Ferro e Oco de Vitoria and Cosim, Brazil has enjoyed a high reputation among foreign investors. Given the difference in evolution of this industry from that of bauxite and tin, a state of dominant government control has not yet been reached.

In fact, the tendency to employ the latest technique in iron and steel projects gives those countries possessing recent investment a technological advantage over others. The encouragement of new investment, therefore, gives host governments the opportunity to stay abreast of technology and to facilitate its transfer.

Price Formation

Price Availability

Since iron ore is not traded on any of the world's commodity exchanges, there is no market as such where price quotations provide an indicator of market equilibrium. Iron ore prices are usually considered as arising from the three trading modalities: captive mining, spot sales, and long-term contracts. However, there is an increasingly important variation of the captive modality which differs sufficiently to have implications for price formation. In its usual form, captive mining suggests some form of vertical integration. However, in recent years the increased scale of activity and its financial requirements have led steel companies (especially European, but also in the United States) into cooperative joint ventures for the mining of ore. Although the control of mining still rests with the steel companies, pricing policy may be different in a joint venture than in a captive situation. Indeed, these new joint ventures may be closer in behavior to the traditional ore merchant companies in the United States.

In examining available price data, there are additional factors which complicate any interpretation of what might be considered a representative price.[24] First, prevailing market forces reflect themselves differently in each of the three different modalities. Long-term contracts may offer some protection against short-run influences on prices, but the prices stemming from supplies of captive mines do not necessarily reflect supply and demand conditions. They are intended more to cover production costs and normal profits. Second, since iron ore is a relatively heterogeneous commodity, each contract requires the sale and purchase of specific grades of ore, requiring a variety of prices to reflect adequately these quality differences. Third, the loading conditions (size of ships and loading rates) are important in determining prices. And finally, prices are quoted in FOB and CIF terms, depending on which of the parties are responsible for shipment. Since the latter prices are generally about 25–50 percent higher than the former, this distinction is an important one.

A selection of the more important international price quotations are provided in table 6–8. One problem in analyzing any of these prices over time is that they are likely not to be representative over any long-run period. This is a consequence of changes in the physical composition of ores from a specific location, together with the depletion of supplies over the period and the emergence of new producers. With respect to related contract prices, there is a general formula in which the prices are related to a stated percentage of iron in the ore (Fe basis), and a sliding scale is agreed for any deviation from this basis ("tel quel" price, or effective price).

An example of the use of this formula for a price quoted on an FOB or CIF basis is as follows:[25]

Iron ore of grade "x" is sold at a basis (FOB) price, with basis 60 percent Fe raw with a scale of U.S. $0.30 Fe parts in proportion.		$ 8.00 per ton

1. At an analysis of 58.5 percent Fe raw, the penalty
    would be 1.5 percent (Fe) by $0.30 $ 0.45
    and the "tel quel" price (FOB)   7.55
    with a freight rate of   2.00
    the "tel quel" price would be (CIF)   9.55

2. At an analysis of 62.5 percent Fe raw, the
    premium would be 1.5 percent (Fe) by $0.30 $ 0.75
    and the "tel quel" price   8.75
    with a freight rate of   2.00
    the "tel quel" price would be (CIF)   10.75

Of course there are a number of other factors which enter the FOB price that are not explicitly included in the formula. Among these are internal transport costs, port charges, financial charges, and sometimes beneficiation charges.

Among the quotations given in table 6–8, there are several established ones which serve to indicate the general movement in iron ore prices. This is largely the situation in North America where the major steel companies and the leading merchants or firms have established a base in terms of a fixed iron (Fe) content price schedule for a number of major types of ore, following to some extent the formula shown. Such is the case in particular for the Lake Superior Mesabi price and the Lake Superior pellet price. The former is expressed in dollars per long ton for different qualities of iron ore containing a base composition of 51.5 percent natural iron, delivered CIF at rail or vessel lower lake ports. The latter is quoted somewhat differently, based on a long ton natural unit (1 percent of a ton or 22.4 pounds equals 1 long ton unit).

It should be noted that these prices do not necessarily reflect demand and supply conditions. They are designed more to reflect production costs plus normal profits, since most ore traded is captive. Only about 10–15 percent of the iron ore produced in North America in the Great Lakes region is traded at "arms length" or merchant ore.[26] Price changes are normally announced at a specific date and apply only to merchant ores; but since they are based on changing cost conditions, they also generally apply to captive ores. These prices constitute a basis for the pricing of Canadian exports to the United

Table 6–8
Iron Ore Price Quotations

Algeria,
　FOB Bône

Angola,
　FOB Moçâdemes

Australia,
　Cliffs Western Australian Mining Co. (Robe River), FOB
　Hamersley (Mt. Tom Price), FOB King Bay, ROM

Brazil,
　FOB Brazilian Ports Lump Ore, 68–69% Fe.
　CIF North Sea ports, 65%.

Canada,
　Lake Jeannine, CIF North Sea ports, c. 65% Fe.

Chile,
　FOB Cruz Grande

Japan,
　Goa Ore, CIF Japanese Ports, 58% Fe.

Liberia,
　FOB Buchanan, Lamco ROM
　Bong Range, CIF North Sea ports, c. 62% Fe.

Sweden,
　Kiruna D. FOB Narvik
　Kiruna D, 60%, CIF Rotterdam Fe, 1.8%P,

U.S.S.R.,
　FOB Jllichutsk, Krivoy Rog fines

United Kingdom,
　Average Import Price, CIF, United Kingdom Ports

United States,
　Lake Superior Mesabi at Lake Erie Docks
　Lake Superior pellets, 63% Fe basis

Venezuela,
　FOB Puerto Ordaz, Orinoco I, 58% Fe.

States, as well as prices paid for west African and South American ores and for former captive ore supplies from Chile and Venezuela.

　Another price watched carefully in the past has been the Kiruna D. However, this quotation has been declining in interest because the mine itself is becoming depleted and Swedish exports are also decreasing relatively. More significantly, the high cost of Swedish production relative to that of Brazil simply is making the Kiruna mine highly unprofitable. To some extent, the price now more closely watched as an international reference is the Brazil, CIF North Sea ports. In Japan, the relative competitive advantage of Australian exports make its price the leader for iron ore quotations. In addition, the calculation of unit import values from trade data can reflect the general trend in prices as well as their relation to a particular importing or exporting country.

An approach useful for determining real trends in ore values has been to compare the prices of ore with the prices of the final output of the industry using the ore. In one case, an attempt has been made to compare iron ore prices to prices for steel.[27] Some covariation was found by comparing a number of FOB and CIF prices to the *Iron Age* Finished Steel Composite Price. However, the method has not been accepted for pricing by the industry.

Price-Making Forces

A major consideration in interpreting this price information is that the nature and importance of the trading modalities themselves have changed. In particular, contract sales have become more dominant than spot sales. However, the annual contract-spot market still accounts for possibly 40 percent of world exports and is very important in western Europe, where for some countries up to 50 percent of purchases may be made this way. With respect to the nature of contract sales not originating from captive mines, Radetzki has suggested the emergence of a new pattern.[28] First, the large investment needed to secure long-term contracts which act as collateral for a project loan to finance mining has caused the contract term to extend from ten to fifteen years, if not longer. In this regard there also has been an interest in equity investment in mining by consumers or groups of consumers. This consortium approach to mining may be regarded as almost as important as the trend to longer-term contracting. On the consumer side it is of growing importance in Europe and more recently in the United States. On the producer side it is of significance in South America, west Africa, and Australia.

Second, rising inflation and its effects have influenced long-term contract negotiations such that prices and quantities are renegotiated each year. Generally quantities have remained fixed for long periods (five years or more), but the price element has been subject to more frequent revision. In some cases, this has been as often as every three months, but more generally it would seem to be every two years. It has been suggested that such long-term contracts have become merely long-term quantitative arrangements, but even the quantitative element has been subject to renegotiation when there has been supply pressure.

And finally, increased nationalism has resulted in only a small amount of export flows emanating from captive mines. With regard to spot sales, these are now occurring less frequently and in such cases represent either supplement tonnage already agreed upon or marginal sales designed to launch a new grade of ore.

Another important factor underlying iron ore price formation is that iron ore acquires its value only when delivered to the market area where it is to be consumed. There is, therefore, a natural tendency toward equalization of the CIF prices in each market, irrespective of the origin of the shipments. On the other hand, depending on its location, a mine delivering to several destinations may have to charge different FOB prices, so as to keep its CIF price competitive in each market. The FOB prices from a mine can vary quite substantially in view of the high proportion of freight in total delivered costs. Out of the average CIF prices for ores imported from overseas to Germany in 1962, freight amounted to a minimum of 28 percent for shipments from Canada, Liberia, and Sweden, and a maximum of 56 percent for ore supplied from Peru.[29] The Japanese CIF prices for major deliveries in 1965 contained freight costs of less than 25 percent for shipments from Malaysia and the Philippines, while freight constituted almost half the CIF price for supplies from Brazil.[30] In any of these cases the percentage figures mentioned will be strongly affected by the great variations in freight rates from year to year.

For long periods of time, the CIF prices quoted in Japan tended to be above those in western Europe and North America. This was primarily because the Japanese market was further away from its major ore suppliers than the other markets. Since the mid-1950s, however, the CIF prices in Japan have declined relative to the other markets. This has three explanations. First, the opening up of the large Australian mines has brought Japan closer to its material supplies. Second, the recent establishment of improved port facilities in Japan has enabled the use of larger and more economical ships. Finally, the Japanese steel industry, by skillful bargaining involving joint buying techniques, has succeeded in obtaining highly advantageous long-term deals with its major ore suppliers.

A final major price influence has been the opening of the large mines of Australia, South America, and Africa in the mid-1960s. Up to that time, about one-third of total ore was supplied by captive mines in which steel concerns owned more than 50 percent of the capital.[31] As in the case of bauxite, not much significance can be attached to the prices quoted in such transactions internal to the firm. Most of the remaining 70 percent of exports were sold under annual contracts entered into in unregulated markets between independent buyers and sellers.

The Swedish ore exporters played a very influential role in the international price formation process during that time. As late as 1960, Sweden was by far the most important supplier of iron ore in the west European market. The autumn negotiations between the Swedish sales cartel and the German buying agencies, which determined quantities and prices for the coming year, were taken as a significant indication of the state of the iron ore market and exerted a strong influence on the deals between other parties, concluded soon afterward.

To conclude, this wide range of price influences illustrates the complexities surrounding iron ore price formation. That price formation will be slightly different in the three different trading modalities has been emphasized. The principal impact that market structure will have on future price formation can be summarized in terms of the three aspects considered. The organization and concentration of the market suggests a downward pressure on prices because of relative strength on the buyers side. Although we have witnessed a decade of large mine openings, new investment must offset the decline in investment caused by nationalization for this new capacity also to represent a downward pressure on prices. For the moment, producer coordination is not likely to exert an upward movement on prices. And this fact is to some extent confirmed by a relative lack of power to pass on raw material price increases. Upward pressure on prices will thus have to come from increasing freight costs, energy costs, labor costs, and the inflated prices of new capital.

Notes

1. A more complete description of the iron ore industry appears in G. Manners, *The Changing World Market for Iron Ore 1950–1980* (Baltimore: Johns Hopkins University Press, 1967). One source of updating is UNCTAD, "Iron Ore: Features of the World Market," TD/B/IPC/IRON ORE/2 (Geneva: UNCTAD, 1977).

2. H.T. Reno and D. Desy, "Iron and Steel," in *Mineral Facts and Problems, 1975* (Washington, D.C.: U.S. Department of the Interior, 1975), p. 526.

3. United Nations, *Survey of World Iron Ore Resources* (New York: United Nations, 1970).

4. *Commodity Data Summaries 1975* (Washington, D.C.: U.S. Bureau of Mines, 1976), p. 81.

5. *Report on Iron Ore—Past Trends 1950–1973* (Stockholm: Malmexport, 1975), chap. 1, table 3.

6. Manners, *Changing World Market,* p. 167.

7. K. Takeuchi, G. Thiebach, and J. Hilmy, "Investment Requirements in the Non-Fuel Mineral Sector in Developing Countries," *Natural Resources Forum* 1 (1977): 269.

8. Manners, *Changing World Market,* p. 154.

9. *Report on Iron Ore,* chap. 1, fig. 1A.

10. Ibid.

11. Manners, *Changing World Market.*

12. See *Iron Ore,* MR 148 (Ottawa: Canadian Department of Energy, Mines and Resources, 1977), pp. 21–22.

13. Ibid., pp. 20–21.

14. J. Tilton, *The Future of the Nonfuel Minerals* (Washington, D.C.: Brookings Institution, 1977), p. 46.

15. B. Lloyd and E. Wheeler, "Brazil's Mineral Development," *Resources Policy* 3 (1977): 39–59.

16. *Iron Ore,* p. 29.

17. Given at average 1967–1969 market prices, World Bank, *World Tables 1976* (Washington, D.C.: World Bank, 1976).

18. UNCTAD, "Iron Ore," p. 12.

19. *Skillings Mining Review,* London, January 1967, p. 67.

20. Takeuchi et al., "Investment Requirements," VI–3.

21. World Bank, *Price Prospects for Major Primary Commodities,* report no. 814 (Washington, D.C.: World Bank, 1975), annex III, p. 2.

22. Based on iron ore export unit values and wholesale steel prices averaged between 1955 and 1973 for major consuming countries. See UNCTAD, "Proportions between Export Prices and Consumer Prices of Selected Commodities Exported by Developing Countries," TD/184/Suppl. 3 (Geneva: UNCTAD, 1976), p. 7.

23. UNCTAD, "Iron Ore," p. 29.

24. Ibid., p. 22.

25. United Nations, *The World Market for Iron Ore,* E 69LL/E10 (New York: United Nations, 1968).

26. *Iron Ore,* p. 14.

27. See UNCTAD, "A Comparison of World Prices of Iron Ore and Steel 1950–1970," UNCTAD/CD/Misc. 58 (Geneva: UNCTAD, 1974).

28. M. Radetzki, "Market Structure and Bargaining Power: A Study of Three International Mineral Markets," working paper (Stockholm: Institute of International Economic Studies, 1976).

29. Manners, *Changing World Market,* p. 264.

30. United Nations, *World Market For Iron Ore,* p. 69.

31. Ibid., p. 88.

7   Conclusions

The purpose of this study has been to develop a framework suitable for analyzing price formation on international minerals markets. Past experience with the application of economic theory to mineral price analysis has suggested that mineral price formation involves determinants and institutions much more complex than those employed in conventional microeconomic analysis. It is thus worthwhile to pursue a framework capable of deciphering the complex array of price influences. The framework selected features market conditions, market structure, and market implications as they impinge on price formation. Some details of the framework are summarized in table 7–1.

Market conditions refer to the microeconomic forces of supply and demand as they determine prices. These forces are essential to the framework, since in the long run they affect the major economic decisions of mineral industries such as investment in exploration, development and production, substitution and the development of technology, and others as previously mentioned.

Market structure suggests how these basic price-making forces are affected as the mineral industries become more highly concentrated or achieve a higher degree of vertical integration. Most important in the analysis of market structure is the inclusion of concentration on the demand side. In short, the present approach accommodates changes in bargaining power between mineral producers and consumers as well as between host governments and foreign investors in explaining price behavior.

Market implications relate to the dependence of many of the producing nations on minerals for their income together with the goals of foreign mineral-investing firms. Essential to interactions between these two parties is the changing nature of the division of gains or the bargaining situation confronted. The effect of the latter on price formation is indeed difficult to untangle. Among the implications deemed most important are: mineral export dependence, magnitude of fixed investment, nature of technology, control over resources and production, opportunities for increased processing, material share in product prices, obsolescing bargain, nature of competition, and government learning process.

In table 7–1, the attempt has been to show how the application of the framework can provide insights into price formation for copper, tin, bauxite, and iron ore. The summary of market structure indicates whether firm size and concentration implies greater bargaining power over prices on the supply or the

Table 7-1
Market Structure and Its Implications for Mineral Price Formation

| Commodity | Market Structure and Power[a] | | Bargaining and Structural Implications[b] | | | | | | | | | Price Formation | |
	Supply	Demand	Export Dependence	Initial Investment	Nature of Technology	Resource Control	Processing Opportunity	Material Share	Obsolescing Bargain	Changes in Competition	Increases in Learning	Process Stage[c]	Major Determinants
Copper	Homogeneous oligopoly with relatively large competitive fringe (57%)	Many fabricators but concentrated	S	M	D	S	M	S	M	MC	S	Refined metal (LME wirebars)	Contract prices linked to prices on LME, a marginal but competitive market
	Limited MTN domination; limited producer-country action	Limited MTN domination											
Tin	Oligopoly (77%)	Oligopsony	N	N	D	M	N	N	M	MC	M	Smelting/metal (Penang, Grade A)	Prices formed in Penang, a competitive market; some control via ITC buffer stock
	Partially MTN domination; joint national interest producer-country action	Increasing											
Bauxite	Tight oligopoly (56%)	Tight oligopsony	S	S	D	M	S	N	S	LC	M	Ore (U.S. imports CIF Jamaica)	Price formed primarily in company-government deals over extraction; beyond that transfer pricing used
	Dominated by six firms; limited producer-country action	Dominated by six firms											

Iron ore	Weak oligopoly with competition; increasing coordination at the national level (57%)	Oligopsony; national bargaining units typical, except in U.S.	M	S	A	N	N	N	M	MC	M	Concentrates (Brazil CIF North Sea)	Prices formed according to captive, short-, or long-term contracts
	Vertical MTN integration; limited producer- country action	Concentration among steel producers											

Source: Summarized from the text.

[a]Figures in brackets are concentration ratios for the largest eight firms.

[b]S = substantial, M = moderate, N = negligible, A = advanced, D = standard, MC = more competitive, LC = less competitive.

[c]Major price quotation also cited.

demand side of the market. For example, recent tendencies toward concentration among suppliers in the bauxite and iron ore markets are likely to improve their ability to negotiate better contract terms.

The market implications summarized indicate how the evolution of the markets affect the welfare of the host governments as well as the foreign mineral investors. These impacts, in turn, have a substantial influence on price formation. Let us turn again to some examples. The higher export dependence of the copper-exporting countries makes them more vulnerable in bargaining. The high initial investment costs, particularly of bauxite, make the dependent countries more flexible in attracting investment. The stable as well as relatively simple nature of tin processing technology makes it easier for host governments to increase their profit share. Resource ownership and control is well advanced in copper, affording greater bargaining power to the governments. Because the share of raw materials in aluminum products is low, the host governments have more latitude for increasing taxes and prices. Similarly, the much higher share of value-added for aluminum products makes it desirable for governments to bargain for increased processing of bauxite. The long period of development of costly iron ore and bauxite deposits implies a higher risk which a firm is more able to accept than a government. The degree of competition in iron ore is increasing, which gives greater advantage to nationalized firms in developing countries. Finally, the government learning process which has advanced most in copper is reaching the point where nationalization is nearly complete in many countries, but favorable ownership and leasing terms must again be offered to attract investment.

The ways in which the factors underlying market conditions, structure, and performance affect price formation are indeed complex. Even though nationalization of the copper industry is fairly complete in the developing producing countries, the availability of other sources of supply as well as of substitutes has kept the real price from increasing noticeably over the long run. In the case of bauxite, attempts by countries to increase taxes have been successful, but the substantial control, integration, and efficiency of the major firms has kept real prices low. Although declining tin reserves have forced tin production costs and prices upward, increases in substitution by consumers have kept price increases moderate. Iron ore prices have risen in real terms, largely because of increases in costs of production. But changes in contractural arrangements and the geographic dispersion of production still keep prices competitive with those of possible substitutes.

These simple conclusions about price formation of course neglect many of the complexities discussed so far. In particular, it has proven difficult to apply the oligopolistic pricing methods described in detail in chapter 2 to the four minerals markets studied. But the availability of a framework with a wide range of price-making explanations should permit us to focus on the essentials of mineral price formation. I would be the last one to suggest that the proposed framework is comprehensive or conclusive in its ability to apply economic and institutional forces to the process of mineral price formation. But I do think that it provides a starting point for dealing with the many questions surrounding mineral price formation today. The extent to which the framework is further applied will determine its ultimate worth.

Bibliography

General

Adam, R.G. "Currency Exchange Fluctuations: Their Impact on the Mining Industry." *Engineering and Mining Journal,* 175(1974):19–81.

_____. "Secondary Supply." In W.A. Vogely (ed.), *Economics of the Mineral Industries.* New York: American Institute of Mining Engineers, 1976.

Adelman, M.A. "Economics of Exploration for Petroleum and Other Minerals." *Geoexploration,* 8(1970):131–50.

_____. *The World Petroleum Market.* Baltimore: Johns Hopkins Press, 1972.

Agria, S.R. "Special Tax Treatment of Mineral Industries." In A.C. Harberger and M.J. Bailey (eds.), *Taxation of Income from Capital.* Washington: The Brookings Institution, 1969.

Aharoni, Y. *The Foreign Investment Process.* Boston: Division of Research, Graduate School of Business Administration, Harvard University, 1966.

Alexander, W.O. "The Competition of Materials." *Scientific American,* 217 (1967):254–66.

Allais, M. "Method of Appraising Economic Prospects of Mining Exploration Over Large Territories: Algerian Sahara Case Study." *Management Science,* 3(1957):285–347.

American Bureau of Metal Statistics. *Yearbook.* New York, annual.

Anderson, K.P. "Optimal Growth When the Stock of Resources is Finite and Depletable." *Journal of Economic Theory,* 4(1972):256–67.

Arrow, K.J., and Fisher, A.C. "Environmental Preservation, Uncertainty and Irreversibility." *Quarterly Journal of Economics,* 88(1974):312–19.

Arrow, K.J., and Lind, R.C. "Uncertainty and the Evaluation of Public Investment Decisions." *American Economic Review,* 60(1970):364–78.

Australia, Bureau of Mineral Resources, Geology and Geophysics. *The Australian Mineral Industry Review.* Melbourne, annual.

Australia, Bureau of Statistics. *Foreign Ownership and Control of the Mining Industry.* Canberra, 1971–1972.

Ayres, R.U., and Kneese, A.V. "Production, Consumption, and Externalities." *American Economic Review,* 59(1969):282–97.

Bailey, P.A. "The Problem of Converting Resources to Reserves." *Mining Engineering,* 28(1976):27–37.

Bain, J.S. *Industrial Organization.* New York: John Wiley & Sons, 1968.

_____. *Barriers to New Competition.* Cambridge: Harvard University Press, 1956.

Baldwin, R.E. *Economic Development and Export Growth.* Berkeley: University of California Press, 1966.

Banks, F.E. "A Note on Some Theoretical Issues of Resource Depletion." *Journal of Economic Theory,* 9(1974):238–44.

Baran, P.A. *The Political Economy of Growth.* New York: Monthly Review Press, 1957.

Barger, H., and Schurr, S.H. *The Mining Industries, 1899–1939.* New York: National Bureau of Economic Research, 1944.

Barkman, K. "The International Tin Agreements." *Journal of World Trade Law,* 9(1975):495–524.

Barnett, H.J. *Energy Use and Supplies, 1939, 1947, 1965.* Bureau of Mines Information Circular, 7482. Washington, D.C.: U.S. Department of Interior, October 1950.

Barnett, H.J., and Morse, C. *Scarcity and Growth: The Economics of Natural Resource Availability.* Baltimore: Johns Hopkins University Press, 1963.

Bator, F. "The Anatomy of Market Failure." *Quarterly Journal of Economics,* 72(1958):351–79.

Baumol, W.J. "On Taxation and the Control of Externalities." *American Economic Review,* 62(1972):307–22.

Baumol, W.J., and Bradford, D.F. "Detrimental Externalities and Non-Convexity of the Production Set." *Economica,* 39(1972):160–76.

Baumol, W.J., and Oates, W.E. "The Use of Standards and Prices for Protection of the Environment." *Swedish Journal of Economics,* 73 (1971):52–54.

Beckerman, W. *In Defense of Economic Growth.* London: Jonathan Cape, 1974.

Beckmann, M.J. "A Note on the Optimal Rates of Resource Exhaustion." *Review of Economic Studies,* Symposium on the Economics of Exhaustible Resources, 41(1974):121–22.

Beddington, J.R., Watts, C.M., and Wright, W.D. "Optimal Cropping of Self-Reproducible Natural Resources." *Econometrica,* 43(1975):789–802.

Beerman's Financial Yearbook of Europe. New York: International Publishers Service, 1970.

Behrman, J.N. *National Interests and Multinational Enterprise.* Englewood Cliffs, N.J.: Prentice-Hall, 1970.

Behrman, J.R. *International Commodity Agreements.* Washington, D.C.: Overseas Development Council, 1976.

————. "International Commodity Market Structures and the Theory Underlying International Commodity Market Models." In F.G. Adams and J.R. Behrman (eds.), *Econometric Modeling of World Commodity Policy.* Lexington, Mass.: Lexington Books, D.C. Heath, 1978.

Bell, F.W. "Technological Externalities and Common Property Resources: An Empirical Study of the U.S. Northern Lobster Fisher." *Journal of Political Economy,* 80(1972):148–58.

Bergsten, C.F. *The Future of the International Economic Order.* Lexington, Mass.: Lexington Books, D.C. Heath, 1973.

_____. "The Threat From the Third World." *Foreign Policy,* 11(1973): 102–124.

_____. "The New Era in World Commodity Cartels." *Challenge,* 17(1974): 34–42.

_____. "The Threat is Real." *Foreign Policy,* 14(1974):84–90.

Bernstein, M.D. *The Mexican Mining Industry, 1890–1950.* Albany: State University of New York, 1965.

Bosson, R., and Varon, B. *The Mining Industry and the Developing Countries.* Oxford: Oxford University Press, 1977.

Bosworth, B. "Capacity Creation in Basic Materials Industries." *Brooking's Papers on Economic Activity,* 6(1976):297–341.

Boulding, K.E. "The Economics of the Coming Spaceship Earth." In H. Jarrett (ed.), *Environmental Quality in a Growing Economy.* Baltimore: The Johns Hopkins Press, 1966, pp. 3–14.

Bradley, P.G. *The Economics of Crude Petroleum Production.* Amsterdam: North-Holland Publishing Co., 1967.

Brannon, G.M. *Energy Taxes and Subsidies.* Cambridge, Mass.: Ballinger Publishing, 1975.

British North American Committee. *Mineral Development in the Eighties: Prospects and Problems.* Report No. 19, Washington, D.C., 1976.

Brobst, D.A., Pratt, W.P., and McKelvey, V.E. *Summary of United States Mineral Resources.* Geological Survey Circular 682. Washington, D.C.: U.S. Government Printing Office, 1973.

Brodsky, D., and Sampson, G., "Social Shadow Process, Externalities, and Depletion of Natural Resources Exploited by Developing Countries." Working Paper. Geneva: UNCTAD, 1976.

Brooks, D.B. "Minerals: An Expanding or a Dwindling Resource." Mineral Resources Branch, Information Canada. *Mineral Bulletin* 134 (1973).

_____. "Mineral Supply as a Stock." In W.A. Vogely (ed.), *Economics of the Mineral Industries.* New York: American Institute of Mining, Metallurgical and Petroleum Engineers, 1976.

Brooks, D.B. (ed.), *Resource Economics: Selected Works of Orris C. Herfindahl.* Baltimore and London: Johns Hopkins University Press, 1974.

Brooks, D.B., and Andres, "Mineral Resources, Economic Growth and World Population." *Science,* 185(1974):13–19.

Brown, C.P. *The Political and Social Economy of Commodity Control.* London: Macmillan, 1979.

_____. *Primary Commodity Control.* Kuala Lumpur: Oxford University Press, 1975.

Brundenius, C. "The Anatomy of Imperialism: Multinational Mining Corporations in Peru." *Journal of Peace Research,* 1972.

Burrows, J. "Econometric Models of Mineral Markets for Intermediate and

Long Term Forecasting." Presented at the Conference on Commodity Markets, Models, and Policies in Latin America, Lima, Peru, 1978.

_____. *Cobalt: An Economic Analysis.* Lexington, Mass.: Lexington Books, D.C. Heath, 1971.

_____. *Tungsten: An Industry Analysis.* Lexington, Mass.: Lexington Books, D.C. Heath, 1971.

Burt, O.R. "Optimal Use of Resources Over Time." *Management Science,* 11(1964):80–93.

Burt, O.R., and Cummings, R.G. "Production and Investment in Natural Resources Industries." *American Economic Review,* 60(1970):576–90.

Cameron, E. (ed.). *The Mineral Position of the United States, 1975–2000.* Madison: University of Wisconsin, 1973.

Cameron, J.I. "Investment Theory and Mineral Investment Practice." Presented at the Meetings of the Council of Economics of the AIME, Washington, D.C., 1977.

_____. "Investment Theory and Mineral Investment Practice." Presented at the 1977 Meetings of the Council of Economics of the AIME, Washington, D.C., 1977.

Canada, Government of, Department of Energy, Mines and Resources. *Canadian Minerals Yearbook,* Ottawa, annual.

_____. "Departmental Terminology and Definitions of Reserves and Resources: Interim Document." Ottawa, 1975.

_____. *Mineral Area Planning Study: Mineral Development Sector,* Mineral Policy Series, Ottawa, 1975.

_____. "Geological Survey." In A.R. Berger (ed.), *Geoscientists and the Third World: A Collective Critique of Existing Aid Programs.* Ottawa, 1975.

_____. *Towards a Mineral Policy for Canada: Opportunities for Choice,* Ottawa, 1974.

_____. *Transfer Pricing, the Multinational Enterprise and Economic Development,* Ottawa, 1976.

Canadian Mines Handbook, Toronto: Northern Miner Press, annual.

Capen, E.C., Clapp, R.V., and Campbell, W.M. "Competitive Bidding in High-Risk Situations." *Journal of Petroleum Technology,* 23(1971): 641–53.

Carlisle, D. "The Economics of a Fund Resource with Particular Reference to Mining." *American Economic Review,* 44(1954):595–616.

Carlson, J.W. "Reliable Minerals Supply for the Future." *Mining Congress Journal,* 61(November 1975):42–47.

Carman, J.S. "Forecast of United Nations Mineral Activities." Paper presented at the World Mining Congress, Lima, Peru, 1974.

_____. "Notes and Observations on Foreign Mineral Ventures." *Mining Engineering,* 19(September 1967):46–73.

———. "Notes on Impediments to Mining Investments in the Developing World." Paper prepared for Association of Geoscientists for International Development, Bagauda, Nigeria, September 1975.

Charles River Associates. *Impact of Supply Restrictions on the Nonferrous Metals Markets: Summary Volume.* Washington, D.C.: ETIP, National Bureau of Standards, 1976.

Cicchetti, C.J. *Alaskan Oil: Alternative Routes and Markets.* Baltimore: Johns Hopkins Press, 1972.

Cicchetti, C.J., Fisher, A.C., and Smith, V.K. "An Econometric Evaluation of a Generalized Consumer Surplus Measure: The Mineral King Controversy." *Econometrica,* 44(1976):1259–76.

Ciriacy-Wantrup, S.V. *Resource Conservation: Economics and Politics.* Berkeley: University of California Press, 1952.

Clarfield, K.W., Jackson, S., Keeffe, J., Noble, M.A., and Ryan, A. *Eight Mineral Cartels: The New Challenge to Industrialized Nations.* New York: McGraw-Hill, 1975.

Clark, C.W. and Munro, G.R. "The Economics of Fishing and Modern Capital Theory." *Journal of Environmental and Economic Management,* 2(1975):92–106.

Coase, R.H. "The Problem of Social Cost." *Journal of Law Economics,* 3(1960):1–44.

Cockcroft, J.D., Frang, A.G., and Johnson, D.L. (eds.). *Dependence and Underdevelopment: Latin America's Political Economy.* Grove City, N.Y.: Doubleday, 1972.

Connelly, P. "Resources: The Choice for Importers." *International Affairs,* 50(October 1974):599–610.

CONSAD Research Corporation. "The Economic Factors Affecting the Level of Domestic Petroleum Reserves." In U.S. Treasury Department, *Tax Reform Studies and Proposals.* Part 4 of Testimony before the Committee on Ways and Means, U.S. Congress. Washington, D.C.: U.S. Government Printing Office, March 1969.

Cooper, R.N., and Lawrence, R.Z. "The 1972–75 Commodity Boom." *Brookings Papers on Economic Activity,* 3(1975):671–723.

Corry, A.V., and Kiessling, O.E., *Grade of Ore.* Report No. E-6, Mineral Technology and Output Studies. Philadelphia: Works Progress Administration, 1938.

Courtney, L.H. "Jevon's Coal Question: Thirty Years After." *Journal of the Royal Statistics Society,* 15(1897):789–810.

Cox, D.P., et al. "Copper." In D.A. Brobst and W.P. Pratt (eds.), *United States Mineral Resources.* Geological Survey Professional Paper 820. Washington, D.C.: U.S. Government Printing Office, 1973, pp. 163–90.

Cox, J.C., and Wright, A.W. "The Cost-Effectiveness of Federal Tax Subsidies for Petroleum Reserves." In G.M. Brannon (ed.), *Studies in*

Energy Tax Policy. Cambridge, Mass.: Ballinger Publishing, 1975, pp. 177–202.

Cranstone, D.A., and Martin, H.S. "Are Ore Discovery Costs Increasing?" *Canadian Mining Journal,* 94(April 1973):53–64.

Crommelin, M., and Thompson, A.R. (eds.). *Mineral Leasing as an Instrument of Public Policy.* Vancouver: University of British Columbia Press, 1976.

Cumberland, J.H. "A Regional Interindustry Model for Analysis of Development Objectives." *The Regional Science Association Papers,* 17(1966): 75–94.

Cumberland, J.H., and Korback, R.J. "A Regional Interindustry Environmental Model." *The Regional Science Association Papers,* 30(1973): 61–75.

Cummings, R.G., and Norton, V. "The Economics of Environmental Preservation: Comment." *American Economic Review,* 64(1974):1021–24.

_____. "Some Extensions of the Economic Theory of Exhaustible Resources." *Western Economic Journal,* 7(1969):201–10.

d'Arge, R.C., and Kogiku, K.C. "Economic Growth and the Environment." *Review of Economic Studies,* 40(1973):61–78.

Dales, J.H. *Pollution, Property and Prices.* Toronto: University of Toronto Press, 1968.

Dasgupta, P., and Heal, G. "The Optimal Depletion of Exhaustible Resources." *Review of Economic Studies,* Symposium on the Economics of Exhaustible Resources, 41(1974):3–28.

Dasgupta, P., and Stiglitz, J.E. "Uncertainty and the Rate of Extraction under Alternative Institutional Arrangements." Mimeographed, Stanford University, Palo Alto, 1975.

Davidson, P. "Public Policy Problems of the Domestic Crude Oil Industry." *American Economic Review,* 53(1963):85–108.

Davis, O.A., and Whinston, A.B. "Externalities, Welfare, and the Theory of Games." *Journal of Political Economics,* 70(1962):241–62.

Dayal, R. *Models of Trade and Development: A Theoretical Review.* Research Monograph 13. Zurich: Center for Economic Research, Swiss Federal Institute of Technology, 1975.

Dewhurst, J.F., et al. *America's Needs and Resources.* New York: Twentieth Century Fund, 1947. Revised 1955.

Dolbear, F.T. "On the Theory of Optimum Externality." *American Economic Review,* 57(1967):90–103.

Dorfman, R. "The Technical Basis for Decision Making." In E.T. Heafele (ed.), *The Governance of Common Property Resources.* Baltimore: The Johns Hopkins Press, 1975.

Downer, H.C. "The Impact of Marine Slurry Transportation on World

Mineral Development." In N.W. Dirshenbaum and G.O. Argall, Jr. (eds.), *Minerals Transportation.* Vol. 1. San Francisco: Freeman, 1972, pp. 244–265.

Drake, P.J. "Natural Resources versus Foreign Borrowing in Economic Development." *Economic Journal,* 82(September 1972):951–62.

Due, J.F. "The Developing Economies, Tax and Royalty Payments by the Petroleum Industry and the U.S. Income Tax." *Natural Resources Journal,* 10(January 1970):10–26.

Dunn, J.R., and Moffel, H.L. "Mineral Explorations in the U.S.: Problem and an Answer." *Mining Congress Journal* (November 1975).

Eckbo, R. "OPEC and the Experience of Previous Commodity Cartels." Working Paper. Cambridge, Mass.: MIT Energy Laboratory, 1975.

Elliott, W.Y. *International Controls in Non Ferrous Metals.* New York: Macmillan, 1937.

Engineering and Mining Journal. "Survey of Mine and Plant Expansions." January Issues, 1973–1975. New York: McGraw-Hill.

Erb, G.F. "Hard Rocks, Hard Choices: Trade and Investment Policies for Non-Fuel Minerals." Working Paper. Washington, D.C.: Overseas Development Council, 1975.

Erickson, G.K. "Alaska's Petroleum Leasing Policy." *Alaska Review of Business and Economic Conditions,* 7(1976).

Fischman, L., and Landsberg, H. "Adequacy of Nonfuel Minerals and Forest Resources." In G. Ridker (ed.), *Population, Resources and the Environment.* Washington, D.C.: U.S. Government Printing Office, 1972.

Fisher, A.C. "Environmental Externalities and the Arrow-Lind Public Investment Theorem." *American Economic Review,* 63(1973):722–25.

Fisher, A.C., and Krutilla, J.V. "Valuing Long Run Ecological Consequences and Irreversibilities." *Journal of Environmental and Economic Management,* 1(1974):96–108.

Fisher, A.C., and Krutilla, J.V. "Resource Conservation, Environmental Preservation, and the Rate of Discount." *Quarterly Journal of Economics* 89(1975):358–70.

Fisher, A.C., Krutilla, J.V., and Cichettie, C.J. "The Economics of Environmental Preservation: A Theoretical and Empirical Analysis." *American Economic Review,* 62(1972):605–19.

Fisher, A.C., and Peterson, F.M. "The Environment in Economics." *Journal of Economic Literature,* 14(1976):1–33.

Fisher, F.M. *Supply and Costs in the U.S. Petroleum Industry.* Washington, D.C.: Resources for the Future, 1964.

Franko, L.G. "Strategy Choice and Multinational Corporate Tolerance for Joint Ventures with Foreign Partners." D.B.A. Thesis, Graduate School of Business Administration, Harvard University, 1969.

Gabriel, P. *The International Transfer of Corporate Skills: Management*

Contracts in Less Developed Countries. Boston: Division of Research, Graduate School of Business Administration, Harvard University, 1967.

Gaffney, M. "Concepts of Financial Maturity of Timber and Other Assets." Agricultural Economcis Information Series No. 62. Raleigh: North Carolina State College, 1960.

_____. *Extractive Resources and Taxation.* Madison: University of Wisconsin Press, 1967.

Galbraith, J.K. *American Capitalism: The Concept of Countervailing Power.* Boston: Houghton Mifflin, 1956.

Garg, P.C., and Sweeney, J.L. "Optimal Growth with Depletable Resources." Mimeographed. Palo Alto: Stanford University, 1974.

Gaskins, D.W., and Teisberg, T. "An Economic Analysis of Pre-Sale Exploration in Oil and Gas Lease Sales." In R. Masson and P.D. Qualls (eds.), *Essays in Industrial Organization in Honor of Joe S. Bain.* Cambridge, Mass.: Ballinger Publishing Co., 1978.

Gaskins, D.W., and Vann, B. "Joint Buying and the Sellers Return: The Case of OCS Lease Sales." Mimeographed. Berkeley: University of California, 1975.

Georgescu-Roegen, N. *The Entropy Law and the Economic Process.* Cambridge: Harvard University Press, 1971.

Gilbert, R. "Decentralized Exploration Strategies for Nonrenewable Resource Deposits." Mimeographed. Palo Alto: Stanford University, 1975.

_____. "Resource Depletion Under Uncertainty." Mimeographed. Palo Alto: Stanford University, 1975.

Girvan, N. "Multinational Economies." *Social and Economic Studies* 19(1970):490–526.

Goldsmith, O.S. "Market Allocation of Exhaustive Resources." *Journal of Political Economy,* 62(1954):124–42.

Gordon, H.S. "The Economic Theory of a Common Property Resource." *Journal of Political Economy,* 62(1954):124–42.

Gordon, R.L. "A Reinterpretation of the Pure Theory of Exhaustion." *Journal of Political Economy,* 75(1967):274–86.

Gould, J.R. "Extinction of a Fishery by Commercial Exploitation: A Note." *Journal of Political Economy,* 80(1972):1031–38.

Goundry, G.K. "Forest Management and the Theory of Capital." *Canadian Journal of Economics and Political Science,* 26(1960):439–51.

Gray, L.C. "Rent under the Assumption of Exhaustibility." *Quarterly Journal of Economics,* 29(1914):466–89.

Griffin, J.M. "An Econometric Evaluation of Sulfur Taxes." *Journal of Political Economy,* 82(1974):669–88.

_____. "Recent Sulfur Tax Proposals: An Econometric Evaluation of Welfare Gains." In M.S. Macrakis (ed.), *Energy: Demand, Conservation, and Institutional Problems.* Cambridge, Mass.: MIT Press, 1974.

Grillo, H. "The Importance of Scrap." *The Metal Bulletin,* special issue on copper (1965).

Guccione, E. "Mine Financing: From Bad to Worse." Paper presented at the Rocky Mountain Energy-Minerals Conference, sponsored by the U.S. Bureau of Land Management, Billings, Mont., October 15–16, 1975.

Haberler, G. "Terms of Trade and Economic Development." In H.S. Ellis (ed.), *Economic Development for Latin America.* London: Macmillan, 1961.

Harberger, A.C. "The Taxation of Mineral Industries." In Joint Committee on the Economic Report, *Federal Tax Policy for Growth and Stability,* U.S. Congress. Washington, D.C.: U.S. Government Printing Office, 1955, pp. 439–49.

Harris, D. "Geostatistics in the Appraisal of Metal Resources." In W. Vogely (ed.), *Minerals Material Modeling.* Washington, D.C.: Resources for the Future, 1975.

Harris, D.P. "A Probability Model of Mineral Wealth." *American Institute of Mining, Materialogical and Petroleum Engineers Transactions,* 235(1966):199–216.

Harris, D.P. "An Application of Multivariate Statistical Analysis to Mineral Exploration." Ph.D. Dissertation, Pennsylvania State University, 1965.

Heal, G. "The Influence of Interest Rates on Resource Prices." Cowles Foundation Research Paper No. 407. New Have Conn.: Yale University, 1975.

Henry, C. "Investment Decisions Under Uncertainty: The 'Irreversibility Effect.' " *American Economic Review,* 64(1974):1006–12.

_____. "Option Values in the Economics of Irreplaceable Assets." *Review of Economic Studies,* Symposium on the Economics of Exhaustible Resources, 41(1974):89–104.

Herfindahl, O.C. "The Process of Investment in Mineral Industries." In D.B. Brooks (ed.), *Resource Economics.* Baltimore: Johns Hopkins University Press, 1974.

_____. *Three Studies in Mineral Economics.* Washington, D.C.: Resources for the Future, 1961.

Herfindahl, O.C., and Kneese, A.V. *Economic Theory of Natural Resources.* Columbus, Ohio: Charles Merrill, 1974.

_____. "The Long-Run Cost of Minerals." In *Three Studies in Mineral Economics.* Washington, D.C.: Resources for the Future, 1961.

Higgins, C.I. "An Econometric Description of the U.S. Steel Industry." In L.R. Klein (ed.), *Essays in Industrial Economics.* Vol. II. Philadelphia: Wharton School of Finance and Commerce, 1969.

Hotelling, H. "The Economics of Exhaustible Resources." *Journal of Political Economy,* 39(1931):137–75.

Hubbard, D.A. "Nickel in International Trade." Master's Thesis, Pennsylvania State University, 1975.

Hubbert, M.K. "Energy Resources." In *Resources and Man.* National Academy of Sciences-National Resource Council. San Francisco: Freeman, 1969, pp. 157–242.

Hudson, E.A., and Jorgenson, D.W. "U.S. Energy Policy and Economic Growth, 1975–2000." *Bell Journal of Economics and Management Science,* 5(1974):461–514.

Hufbauer, G.C. *Synthetic Materials and the Theory of International Trade.* London: Duckworth, 1966.

Hughart, D. "Informational Asymmetry, Bidding Strategies, and the Marketing of Offshore Petroleum Leases." *Journal of Political Economy,* 83(1975):969–85.

Humphrey, D.B., and Moroney, J.R. "Substitution Among Capital, Labor, and Natural Resource Products in American Manufacturing." *Journal of Political Economy,* 83(1975):57–82.

Hymer, S. "The International Operations of National Firms: A Study of Direct Foreign Investment." Ph.D. Thesis, Massachusetts Institute of Technology, 1960.

Ingham, A., and Simmons, P. "Natural Resources and Growing Population." *Review of Economic Studies,* 42(1975):191–206.

International Economic Policy Association. "Interim Report of the Study on U.S. Natural Resources, Requirements and Foreign Economic Policy." Washington, D.C.: IEPA, July 1974.

International Financial Statistics. Washington, D.C.: International Monetary Fund, monthly.

Ise, J. "The Theory of Value as Applied to Natural Resources." *American Economic Review,* 64(1974):284–91.

Jane's World Mining: Who Owns Whom. New York: McGraw-Hill, annual.

Johnson, C.J. "Cartels in Minerals and Metal Supply." *Mining Congress Journal,* 62(1976);30–34.

Johnson, H.G. *Economic Policies toward Less Developed Countries.* Washington, D.C., Brookings' Institution, 1967.

Kahn, A.E. "Economic Issues in Regulating the Field Price of Natural Gas." *American Economic Review,* 50(1960):506–17.

Kalter, R.J., Stevens, T.H., and Bloom, O.H. "The Economics of Outer Continental Shelf Leasing." *American Journal of Agricultural Economics,* 5(1975):251–58.

Kalter, R.J., and Tyner, W.E. "An Analysis of Contingency Leasing Options for Outer Continental Shelf Development." Mimeographed. Ithaca, N.Y.: Cornell University, 1975.

Kay, J.A., and Mirrlees, J.A. "The Desirability of Natural Resource Depletion." In D.W. Rose (ed.), *The Economics of Natural Resource Depletion.* New York: John Wiley & Sons, 1975, pp. 140–90.

Keeler, E., Spence, M., and Zeckhauser, R. "The Optimal Control of Pollution." *Journal of Economic Theory,* 4(1972):19–34.

Kirshenbaum, N.W., and Argall, G.O., Jr. *Minerals Transportation.* San Francisco: Freeman, 1974.

Kneese, A.V., Ayres, R.U., and D'Arge, R.C. *Economics and the Environ-*

ment: A Materials Balance Approach. Washington, D.C.: Resources for the Future, 1970.

Knight, F.H. "Some Fallacies in the Interpretation of Social Cost." *Quarterly Journal of Economics,* 38(1924):582–606.

Knudsen, O., and Parnes, A. *Trade Instability and Economic Development.* Lexington, Mass.: Lexington Books, D.C. Heath, 1975.

Kohn, R.E. "Price Elasticities of Demand and Air Pollution Control." *Review of Economics and Statistics,* 54(1972):392–400.

Koopmans, T.C. "Proof for a Case where Discounting Advances Dooms-day." *Review of Economic Studies,* Symposium on the Economics of Exhaustible Resources, 41(1974):2.

_____. "Some Observations on 'Optimal' Economic Growth and Exhaustible Resources." In H.C. Bos, H. Linnemann, and P. de Wolff (eds.), *Economic Structure and Development: Essays in Honor of Jan Tinbergen.* Amsterdam: North-Holland Publishing Co., 1973, pp. 239–55.

Koopmans, T.C., and Beckmann, M. "Assignment Problems and the Location of Economic Activities." *Econometrica,* 25(1957):53–76.

Krasner, S.D. "Oil is the Exception." *Foreign Policy,* 14(Spring 1974):68–83.

Krutilla, J.V. "Conservation Reconsidered." *American Economic Review,* 57(1967):777–86.

Krutilla, J.V., and Fisher, A.C. *The Economics of Natural Environments: Studies in the Valuation of Commodity and Amenity Resources.* Baltimore: Johns Hopkins Press, 1975.

Kuller, R.G., and Cummings, R.G. "An Economic Model of Production and Investment for Petroleum Reservoirs." *American Economic Review,* 64(1974):66–79.

Labys, W.C. "Commodity Modeling Approaches to Resources, Energy and Regional Planning." In M. Chatterji and P. Van Rompuy (eds.), *Energy, Regional Science and Public Policy.* Berlin: Springer-Verlag, 1976.

_____. *Dynamic Commodity Models: Specification, Estimation and Simulation.* Lexington, Mass.: Lexington Books, D.C. Heath, 1973.

_____. "Foreign Investment in the U.S. Minerals Industry: The Case of West Virginia Coal." In E. Wunderlick (ed.), *A Study of Alien Investment in U.S. Lands.* Washington, D.C.: U.S. Department of Agriculture, 1976.

_____. "Interactions between the Commodity Export Sector, the Developing Economy and the Environment." Working Paper. Geneva: Project on the Study of the Environmental Component in the Social Evaluation and Pricing of Natural Resources, UNCTAD, 1977.

_____. "Environmental Trade Strategies for Resource Exporting, Developing Countries: A Case Study of Copper, Tin, Bauxite and Iron Ore." Working Paper. Geneva: Project on the Environmental Component in the Social Evaluation and Pricing of Natural Resources, UNCTAD, 1978.

_____. "Interactions between the Resource Commodity Sector, the Developing Economy, and the Environment: The Case of Malaysia." Working Paper. Geneva: UNCTAD, 1978.

_____. "Nature of Commodity Markets and Stabilization Problems." Subcommittee Hearings on International Reactions of the 94th Congress. Washington, D.C.: U.S. Government Printing Office, 1976.

_____. "The Problems and Challenges for International Commodity Markets and Model Builders." *American Journal of Agricultural Economics,* 57 (1975):873–78.

_____. "Commodity Models Bibliography." College of Mineral and Energy Resources, West Virginia University, Morgantown, W.V., 1978.

Labys, W.C. (ed.), *Quantitative Models of Commodity Markets.* Cambridge, Mass.: Ballinger Publishing Co., 1975.

Labys, W.C., and Granger, C.W.J. *Speculation, Hedging and Commodity Price Forecasts.* Lexington, Mass.: Lexington Books, D.C. Heath, 1970.

Labys, W.C., and Hunkeler, J. "Survey of Commodity Price Elasticities," Research Memorandum, UNCTAD, Geneva, 1974.

Labys, W.C., and Thomas, H. "Speculation, Hedging and Commodity Price Behavior: An International Comparison." *Applied Economics,* 7(1975): 287–301.

Lall, S. "Transfer-Pricing by Multinational Manufacturing Firms." *Oxford Bulletin of Economics and Statistics,* 35(1973):173–93.

Landsberg, H.H., Fischman, L.L., and Fisher, J.L. *Resources in America's Future.* Baltimore: The Johns Hopkins Press, 1963.

Lantz, E. "Impact of Environmental Regulations on Mining." *Mining Congress Journal,* 61(1975):48–51.

Lanzilotti, R.F. "Pricing Objectives in Large Companies." *American Economic Review,* 48(1958):923–29.

LaQue, F.L. "Deep Ocean Mining: Prospects and Anticipated Short-Term Benefits." In *Pacem in Maribus.* Santa Barbara, Calif.: The Center for the Study of Democratic Institutions, 1970.

Law, A. *International Commodity Agreements.* Lexington, Mass.: Lexington Books, D.C. Heath, 1975.

Leary, R.J., and Larwood, G.M. "Potential Effects of Direct Reduction in Mineral Supply." In *Proceedings of the 46th Annual Meeting of the Minnesota Section, AIME, and the 34th Annual Mining Symposium of the University of Minnesota, January 15–17, 1973.* Duluth: University of Minnesota Press, 1973, pp. 72–83.

Leland, H.E., Norgaard, R., and Pearson, S. "An Economic Analysis of Alternative Outer Continental Shelf Petroleum Leasing Policies." Mimeographed. Berkeley: University of California, 1974.

_____. "Optimal Risk Sharing and the Leasing of Natural Resources." Working Paper No. 38. Berkeley: Institute of Business and Economic Research, University of California, 1975.

Leontief, W.W. "Environmental Repercussions and the Economic Structure: An Input-Output Approach." *Review of Economics and Statistics,* 52(1970):262–71.

_____. "Domestic Production and Foreign Trade: The American Capital Position Re-examined." In R. Heller (ed.), *International Trade Theory and Empirical Evidence.* Englewood Cliffs, N.J.: Prentice-Hall, 1953, pp. 68–71.

_____. *The Structure of the American Economy, 1919–1929.* Cambridge: Harvard University Press, 1941.

Lewis, J.P. "Oil, Other Scarcities, and the Poor Countries." *World Politics,* 27(October 1974):63–86.

Long, W.V. "Resource Extraction Under Uncertainty about Possible Nationalization." *Journal of Economic Theory,* 7(1975):42–53.

Lovering, T.S. *Minerals in World Affairs.* Englewood Cliffs, N.J.: Prentice-Hall, 1943.

Lovesay, G. "Forecasting Inflation Effects on Prices of Primary Products." Working Paper. Washington, D.C.: World Bank, 1973.

Lownie, H.W., Jr. "Perspectives on Direct Reduction Process." *Proceedings of the 46th Annual Meeting of the Minnesota Section, AIME, and the 34th Annual Mining Symposium of the University of Minnesota, January 15–17, 1973.* Duluth: University of Minnesota Press, 1973, pp. 85–88.

MacGregor, W., and Vickers, E. "Capital and the U.S. Resources Crunch." *Engineering and Mining Journal,* 175(September 1974):110–15.

Maizels, A. *Exports and Economic Growth of Developing Countries.* Oxford: Oxford University Press, 1963.

Malenbaum, W. "Report of Panel on Demand for Fuel and Mineral Resources: A Minority View." In *Mineral Resources and the Environment.* Washington, D.C.: National Academy of Sciences, 1975, pp. 310–16.

Malinvaud, E. "Capital Accumulation and Efficient Allocation of Resources." *Econometrica,* 21(1953):233–68.

Malmgren, H.B. "The Raw Material and Commodity Controversy." In *Contemporary Issues.* No. 1. Washington, D.C.: International Economic Studies Institute, 1975.

Mann, H. "Seller Concentration, Barriers to Entry, and Rates of Return in Thirty Industries, 1950–1960." *Review of Economics and Statistics,* 48 (1966):296–307.

Marglin, S.A. "The Social Rate of Discount and the Optimal Rate of Investment." *Quarterly Journal of Economics,* 77(1963):95–112.

Mason, E.S. *Economy Concentration and the Monopoly Problem.* Cambridge: Harvard University Press, 1957.

McInnes, D.F. "Estimates of World Metals Depletion: Background for

Metals Policy Planning." Center for the Study of Alternative Societies, Firbank Fell, December 1973.

McKelney, V.E. "Mineral Resource Estimates and Public Policy." United States Mineral Resources, Geological Survey Professional Paper 820, U.S. Department of the Interior. Washington, D.C.: U.S. Government Printing Office, 1973.

————. "Mineral Potential of the United States." In E. Cameron (ed.), *The Mineral Position of the United States, 1975–2000.* Madison: University of Wisconsin Press, 1973.

McKewan, W.M., and Frommer, D.W. "The Changing Fuel Situation for the Mineral Industries." *Mining Congress Journal,* 61(1975):24–28.

McKie, J.W. "Market Structure and Uncertainty in Oil and Gas Exploration." *Quarterly Journal of Economics,* 74(1960):543–71.

McKinstry, H. *Mining Geology.* Englewood Cliffs, N.J.: Prentice-Hall, 1948.

Mead, W.J. "Natural Resource Disposal Policy: Oral Auctions versus Sealed Bids." *Natural Resources Journal,* 7(1967):194–224.

Meadows, D.H., et al. *The Limits to Growth.* New York: Universe Books, 1972.

Metal Bulletin. London: Metal Bulletin, Ltd., annual.

Metal Statistics. Frankfurt am Main: Metallgesellschaft Aktiengesellschaft, annual.

Metal Statistics. New York: Fairchild Publications, annual.

Mikdashi, Z. *The International Politics of Natural Resources.* Ithaca, N.Y.: Cornell University Press, 1976.

————. "Collusion Could Work." *Foreign Policy,* 14(Spring, 1974):57–67.

Mikesell, R. (ed.). *Foreign Investment in the Petroleum and Mineral Industries: Case Studies in Investor-Host Country Relations.* Baltimore: Johns Hopkins Press, 1971.

————. "Financial Considerations in Negotiating Mine Development Agreements." *Mining Magazine,* 130(April 1974):257–71.

————. *Foreign Investment in Copper Mining: Case Studies of Mines in Peru and Papua-New Guinea.* Baltimore and London: Johns Hopkins Press, 1975.

————. "More Third World Cartels?" *Challenge,* 17(November–December 1974):24–31.

————. "Nonfuel Minerals: U.S. Investment Policies Abroad." In *The Washington Papers.* Beverly Hills and London: Sage, 1975.

————. "Rate of Exploitation of Exhaustible Resources: The Case of an Export Economy." Presented at the Second Trans-Pacific Seminar on Minerals Across the Pacific: Bridge or Barrier, sponsored by the Australian Society for Latin American Studies, Melbourne, June 20–22, 1975.

Mining Companies of the World, 1975. London: Mining Journal Books, Ltd., 1975.

Mining Journal. London: Mining Journal Ltd., weekly.

Mishan, E.J. "The Postwar Literature on Externalities: An Interpretative Essay." *Journal of Economic Literature,* 9(1971):1–28.

Moran, T.H. "Multinational Corporations and the Changing Structure of Industries that Supply Industrial Commodities." Working Paper. Washington, D.C.: Institute for International Studies, 1977.

_____. *Multinational Corporations and the Politics of Dependence.* Princeton: Princeton University Press, 1974.

_____. "New Deal or Raw Deal Materials." *Foreign Policy,* 5(Winter 1971–72):119–38.

_____. "Transnational Strategies of Protection and Defense by Multinational Corporations: Spreading the Risk and Raising the Cost for Nationalization in Natural Resources." *International Organization,* 27(1973).

_____. "The Evolution of Concession Agreements in Underdeveloped Countries and the U.S. National Interest." U.S. Senate Foreign Relations Subcommittee on Multinational Corporations Testimony and Report. Washington, D.C.: U.S. Government Printing Office, July 1973.

_____. "A Model of National Interest, Balance of Power, and International Exploitation in Large Natural Resource Investments." In J. Kurth and S. Rosen (eds.), *Testing the Theory of Economic Imperialism.* Lexington, Mass.: Lexington Books, D.C. Heath, 1974.

Musgrove, P. "The Distribution of Metal Resources Tests and Implications of the Exponential Grade-Size Relation." *Proceedings of the Council of Economics of the American Institute of Mining, Metallurgical and Petroleum Engineers,* New York, 1971, pp. 340–71.

National Academy of Sciences, National Academy of Engineering. *The Costs and Benefits of Automobile Emission Control.* Washington, D.C.: U.S. Government Printing Office, 1975.

National Commission on Materials Policy. *Material Needs and the Environment Today and Tomorrow.* Washington, D.C.: U.S. Government Printing Office, June 1973.

Narver, J.C., and Savitt, R. *The Marketing Economy: An Analytic Approach.* New York: Holt, Rinehart and Winston, 1971.

Netschert, B.C. *The Future Supply of Oil and Gas.* Baltimore: The Johns Hopkins Press, 1958.

Netschert, B.C., and Landsbergh, H.H. *The Future Supply of the Major Metals.* Baltimore: The Johns Hopkins Press, 1961.

Newcomb, R.T. "Mineral Industry Demands and General Market Equilibrium." In W. Vogely (ed.), *The Economics of the Mineral Industries.* New York: American Institute of Mining and Petroleum Engineers, 1976.

_____. "The Economic Implications of Environment Quality and Materials Policy." In *Man, Materials, and Environment.* Chap. 2. National Academy of Sciences. Cambridge: MIT Press, 1973.

_____. "Toward a Dynamic Theory of Substitution and Technical Change." *Proceedings of the Council of Economics.* American Institute of Mining and Petroleum Engineers, New York, 1969.

Noll, O.G., and Trijonis, J. "Mass Balance, General Equilibrium, and Environmental Externalities." *American Economic Review,* 61(1971): 730–35.

Non-Ferrous Metal Works of the World. London: Metal Bulletin Books, annual.

Nordhaus, W.C. "Resources as a Constraint on Growth." *American Economic Review,* 64(1974):22–26.

_____. "The Allocation of Energy Resources." *Brookings Papers on Economic Activity,* 3(1973):529–70.

Nordhaus, W.C., and Tobin, J. "Is Growth Obsolete?" In M. Moss (ed.), *The Measurement of Economic and Social Performance.* New York: National Bureau of Economic Research, 1973.

Novick, D. *A World of Scarcities.* London: Halsted Press, 1976.

Page, R.T., and Ferejohn, J. "Externalities as Commodities: Comment." *American Economic Review,* 64(1974):454–59.

Paterson, N.R. "Geophysics Leads Mineral Exploration." Survey and Directory Number. *World Mining Catalog,* 1974.

Payer, C. *Commodity Trade of the Third World.* London: Halsted Press, 1975.

Peach, W.N., and Constantin, J.A. *Zimmerman's World Resources and Industries.* New York: Harper & Row, 1972.

Pearce, D.W. *The Economics of Natural Resource Depletion,* edited with the assistance of J. Rose. London: Macmillan, 1975.

Pearson, S., and Cownie, J. *Commodity Exports and African Economic Development.* Lexington, Mass.: Lexington Books, D.C. Heath, 1974.

Peck, M.G. *Competition in the Aluminum Industry.* Cambridge: Harvard University Press, 1961.

Penrose, E.T. *The Large International Firm in Developing Countries: The International Petroleum Industry.* London: Allen and Unwin, 1968.

Peterson, F.M. "A Theory of Mining and Exploring for Exhaustible Resources." Mimeographed. College Park: University of Maryland, 1975.

_____. "An Economic Theory of Mineral Leasing." In M. Crommelin and A.R. Thompson (eds.), *Mineral Leasing as an Instrument of Public Policy.* Vancouver: University of British Columbia Press, 1976.

_____. "The Economics of Natural Resources." Working Paper. College Park: University of Maryland, 1976.

_____. "The Long Run Dynamics of Minerals Taxation." Mimeographed. College Park: University of Maryland, 1975.

_____. "The Theory of Exhaustible Natural Resources: A Classical Variational Approach." Ph.D. Thesis, Princeton University, 1972.

_____. "Two Externalities in Petroleum Exploration." In G.M. Brannon (ed.), *Studies in Energy Tax Policy.* Cambridge, Mass.: Ballinger Publishing Co., 1975, pp. 101–13.

Peterson, F.M., and Fisher, A.C. "The Economics of Natural Resources: A Review and Synthesis of the Literature." Mimeographed. College Park: University of Maryland, 1975.

Plourde, C.G. "A Simple Model of Replenishable Natural Resource Exploitation." *American Economic Review,* 60(1970):518–22.

_____. "Exploitation of Common Property Replenishable Natural Resources." *Western Economic Journal,* 9(1971):256–66.

Polinsky, A.M., and Rubinfeld, D.L. "Property Values and the Benefits of Environmental Improvements: Theory and Measurement." Discussion Paper, Harvard Institute of Economic Research, 1975.

Popkin, J. "Price Behavior in Primary Manufacturing Industries, 1958–74." Paper presented at the Annual Meetings of the Eastern Economic Association, 1976.

Potter, N., and Christy, F.T. *Trends in Natural Resource Commodities: Statistics of Prices, Output, Consumption, Foreign Trade and Employment in the United States 1870–1957.* Baltimore: The Johns Hopkins Press, 1962.

President's Materials Policy Commission. *Resources for Freedom.* Washington, D.C.: U.S. Government Printing Office, 1952.

Pryor, F. "An International Comparison of Concentration Ratios." *Review of Economics and Statistics,* 54(1972):130–40.

Pullianinin, K "A World Study: An Econometric Model of the Pattern of the Commodity Flows in International Trade in 1948–1960." *Ekonomiska Samfundets Tidskrift,* 2(1963):78–91.

Quirk, J.P., and Smith, V.L. "Dynamic Models of Fishing." In A.D. Scott (ed.), *Economics of Fisheries Management: A Symposium.* Vancouver: Institute of Animal Resource Ecology, University of British Columbia, 1970, pp. 3–32.

Radetzki, M. "Market Structure and Bargaining Power: A Study of Three International Mineral Markets." Working Paper. Stockholm: Institute for International Economic Studies, 1976.

Rayment, P.B.W. "On the Analysis of the Export Performance of Developing Countries." *Economic Record,* 47(1971):270–76.

Resources for the Future. "Resource Terminology: An Examination of Concepts and Terms and Recommendations for Improvement." Washington, D.C., 1975.

Ridge, J.D. "World Trade in Metal Raw Materials." Mimeographed. College of Mineral Industries, Pennsylvania State University, 1953.

Ridker, R.G. *Changing Resource Problems of the Fourth World.* Baltimore: Johns Hopkins Press, 1976.

Root, F.R. *International Trade and Investment.* 3rd ed. Chicago: South-Western Publishing Co., 1973.

Rosenberg, N. "Innovative Responses to Materials Shortages." *American Economic Review,* 63(1973):111–18.

Roth, A. (ed.). "The Crisis in World Materials, A U.S.-Japanese Symposium." Newark, N.J.: Rutgers University, Graduate School of Business Administration, 1974.

Rothschild, M. "Models of Market Organization with Imperfect Organization: A Survey." *Journal of Political Economy,* 81(1973):1283–1308.

Rowe, J.W.F. *Primary Commodities in International Trade.* Cambridge: Cambridge University Press, 1965.

Russell, C.S. "Model for Investigation of Industrial Response to Residuals Management Actions." *Swedish Journal of Economics,* 73(1971):134–56.

Sherer, F.M. *Industrial Market Structure and Economic Performance.* Chicago: Rand McNally, 1971.

Scherer, F.M. *Industrial Pricing.* Chicago: Rand McNally, 1970.

Schulze, W.C. "The Optimal Use of Non-Renewable Resources: The Theory of Extraction." *Journal of Environmental Economic Management,* 1(1974):53–73.

Schurr, S.H., and Netschert, B.C. *Energy in the American Economy, 1850–1975: An Economic Study of its History and Prospects.* Baltimore: The Johns Hopkins Press, 1960.

Scitovsky, T. "Two Concepts of External Economies." *Journal of Political Economy,* 62(1954):143–51.

Scott, A.D. *Natural Resources: The Economics of Conservation.* Toronto: University of Toronto Press, 1955.

Sheridan, J.H. "Reserve Mining: A Decision with Broad Implications." *Industry Week,* 181(1974):11–12.

Singer, D.A. "Mineral Resource Models and the Alaskan Mineral Resource Assessment Program." In W. Vogely (ed.), *Non-Fuel Mineral Models: A State of the Art Review.* Baltimore: The Johns Hopkins Press, 1976.

Singer, D.A., Cos, D.P., and Drew, L.V. "Grade and Tonnage Relationships among Copper Deposits." Geological Survey Professional Paper 907-A, U.S. Geological Survey. Washington, D.C.: U.S. Government Printing Office, 1975.

Smith, D., and Wells, A. *Negotiating Third World Mineral Agreements.* Cambridge: Ballinger Publishing Co., 1975.

Smith, F.A. "The Economic Theory of Industrial Waste Production and Disposal." Ph.D. Thesis, Northwestern University, 1968.

Smith, F.A. "Waste Material Recovery and Reuse." In R.G. Ridker (ed.),

Population, Resources and the Environment. Washington, D.C.: U.S. Government Printing Office, 1972.

Smith, V.K. "Detrimental Externalities, Nonconvexities, and Technical Change." *Journal of Public Economics,* 4(1975):289–95.

_____. "Re-Examination of the Trends in the Prices of Natural Resource Commodities, 1870–1972." Working Paper No. 44. Binghamton: Economic Growth Institute, State University of New York, November 1974.

_____. *Technical Change, Relative Prices, and Environmental Resource Evaluation.* Baltimore: Johns Hopkins Press, 1974.

_____. "An Optimistic Theory of Exhaustible Resources." *Journal of Economic Theory,* 9(1974):384–96.

_____. "Dynamics of Waste Accumulation: Disposal Versus Recycling." *Quarterly Journal of Economics,* 86(1972):409–31.

_____. "Economics of Production from Natural Resources." *American Economic Review,* 53(1968):409–31.

Solow, R.M. "Intergenerational Equity and Exhaustible Resources." *Review of Economic Studies,* Symposium on the Economics of Exhaustible Resources, 41(1974):29–46.

_____. "Richard T. Ely Lecture: The Economics of Resources or the Resources of Economics." *American Economic Review,* 64(1974):1–14.

Spangler, M.B. *New Technology and Marine Resources Development.* New York: Praeger, 1970.

Spendlove, M. "Opportunities in the Produciton of Secondary Non-Ferrous Metals." Working Paper. UNIDO, Vienna, 1969.

Stapleton, J.H.D. "Bulk Ships for Transporting Minerals in the Year 1980." In N.W. Kirshenbaum and G.O. Argall, Jr. (eds.), *Mineral Transportation.* San Francisco: Freeman, 1974, pp. 118–26.

Starrett, D., and Zeckhauser, R.J. "Treating External Diseconomies: Markets or Taxes?" In J.W. Pratt (ed.), *Statistical and Mathematical Aspects of Pollution Problems.* New York: Marcel Dekker, 1974, pp. 65–84.

Steiner, P.O. "Percentage Depletion and Resource Allocation." In U.S. Congress, House Committee on Ways and Means, *Tax Revision Compendium.* Washington, D.C.: U.S. Government Printing Office, 1959.

Stiglitz, J.E. "Growth with Exhaustible Natural Resources: Efficient and Optimal Growth Paths." *Review of Economic Studies,* Symposium on the Economics of Exhaustible Resources, 41(1974):123–37.

_____. "Growth with Exhaustible Natural Resources: The Competitive Economy." *Review of Economic Studies,* Symposium on the Economics of Exhaustible Resources, 41(1974):139–52.

_____. "Monopoly and the Rate of Extraction of Exhaustible Resources." *American Economic Review,* 66(1976):655–61.

_____. "The Efficiency of Market Prices in Long Run Allocations in the Oil

Industry." In G.M. Grannon (ed.), *Studies in Energy Tax Policy.* Cambridge, Mass.: Ballinger Publishing Co., 1975, pp. 87–94.

Strotz, R.H. "The Use of Land Rent Changes to Measure the Welfare Benefits of Land Improvements." In J.E. Haring (ed.), *The New Economics of Regulated Industries: Rate Making in a Dynamic Economy.* Los Angeles: Economic Research Center, Occidental College, 1968.

Subcommittee on Antitrust and Monopoly of the Committee on the Judiciary, Concentration Ratios in Manufacturing Industry, 1958, and Concentration Ratios in Manufacturing Industry, 1963. Reports prepared by the Bureau of the Census for the Subcommittee on Antitrust and Monopoly of the Committee on the Judiciary. U.S. Senate. 87th Congress. 2nd Session. Washington, D.C.: U.S. Government Printing Office, 1962; 89th Congress. 2nd Session. Washington, D.C.: U.S. Government Printing Office, 1966.

Sumitomo Shoji Kaisha, Ltd. *Survey of Non-Ferrous Metals Industries in China.* Tokyo, 1972.

Sutulov, A. *Minerals in World Affairs.* Salt Lake City: The University of Utah Printing Services, 1972.

Sweeney, J.L. "Economics of Depletable Resources: Market Forces and Intertemporal Bias." *Review of Economic Studies,* in press.

Takeuchi, K. "CIPEC and the Copper Export Earnings of Member Countries." *Developing Economies,* 10(1972):3–29.

Takeuchi, K., and Varon, B. "Commodity Shortage and Changes in World Trade." *Annals of the American Academy of Political and Social Science,* 420(1975):46–59.

Thoburn, J. *Primary Commodity Exports and Economic Development.* New York: John Wiley & Sons, 1977.

Tilton, J.E. "The Choice of Trading Partners: An Analysis of International Trade in Aluminum, Bauxite, Copper, Lead, Manganese, Tin and Zinc." Ph.D. Thesis, Yale University, 1966.

_____. "Past and Future Patterns of World Trade in Mineral and Mining Products." Paper Prepared for the Conference Sponsored by the Foreign Affairs Association on the Politics of Strategic Raw Materials. Department of Mineral Economics, Pennsylvania State University, 1976.

_____. "The Choice of Trading Partners: An Analysis of International Trade in Aluminum, Bauxite, Copper, Manganese, Tin and Zinc." *Yale Economic Essays,* 6(1966):419–74.

_____. *The Future of Nonfuel Minerals.* Washington, D.C.: The Brookings Institution, 1977.

Tilton, J.E., and Dorr, A.L. "An Econometric Model of Metal Trade Patterns." In W. Vogely (ed.), *Mineral Materials Modeling: A State-of-the-Art Review.* Washington, D.C.: Resources for the Future, 1975, pp. 150–79.

Treadgold, M.L. "Bougainville Copper and the Economic Development of Papua-New Guinea." *Economic Record,* 47(1971):186–202.

Uhler, R.S., and Bradley, P.G. "A Stochastic Model for Determining the Economic Prospects of Petroleum Exploration over Large Regions." *Journal of the American Statistical Association,* 65(1970):623–30.

United Nations. "Small Scale Mining in the Developing Countries." New York: ST/ECA/155, 1972.

_____. "Natural Resources of Developing Countries: Investigation, Development and Rational Utilization." New York: E.70.11.B.2, 1970.

_____. *Permanent Sovereignty over Natural Resources.* New York: E/C.7/53, 1975.

_____. "Comprehensive Plan of Action for Coordination of Programmes within the United Nation Systems in the Field of Natural Resources Development." New York: E/C.7/47/add.2, 1975.

_____. "United Nations Revolving Fund for Natural Resources Exploration: Operational Procedures and Administrative Arrangements." New York: DP/142, October 24, 1975.

_____. "Economic Implications of Seabed Mineral Development in the International Area." New York: A.Conf.62/65, 1974.

_____. "Evolution of Basic Commodity Prices Since 1950: Study of the Problems of Raw Materials and Development." New York: A/9544, 1974.

_____. "Implications of the Exploitation of the Mineral Resources of International Area of the Seabed: Issues of International Commodity Policy." New York: TD/B/C.1/170, 1975.

_____. "Interregional Seminar on the Application of Advanced Mining Technology." New York: DP/UN/INT-72-064, 1975.

_____. "Financial Considerations in Negotiating Mining Development Agreements." New York: ESA/RT/AC.7/4, 1973.

_____. "Nationalization." New York: ESA/RT/AC.7/18, 1973.

_____. "Processing." New York: ESA/RT/AC.7/12, 1973.

_____. "Social Considerations and Environmental Protection." New York: ESA/RT/AC.7/7, 1973.

_____. "Taxation and Incentives." New York: ESA/RT/AC.7/9, 27.9.73, 1973.

_____. "Mineral Resources of the Sea." New York: E/4973, 1974.

_____. "Multinational Corporations in World Development." New York: ST/ECA/190, 1973.

_____. "Nonferrous Metals: A Survey of their Production Potential in the Developing Countries." New York: E.72.11.B.18, 1972.

_____. "Projections of Natural Resources, Reserves, Supply and Future Demand." New York: E/C.7/40/add.2, 1972.

_____. "The Impact of Multinational Corporations on Development and on International Relations." New York: ST/EDA/11 and ST/ESA/6, 1974.

U.N. Conference on Trade and Development. "An Integrated Programme for Commodities: Specific Proposals for Decision and Action by Governments." Geneva: TD/B/C.1/193, 1975.

————. "Measures to Expand Processing Primary Commodities in Developing Countries." Geneva: TD/B/C.7/197, 1975.

————. "Problems of Raw Materials and Development." New York: TD/B/488, 1974.

————. "Proportions between Export Prices and Consumer Prices of Selected Commodities Exported by Developing Countries." Geneva: TC/184/Suppl., 1976.

————. "Social Valuation and Pricing of Natural Resources." Research Memorandum No. 58, Geneva: Research Division, UNCTAD, 1976.

United States Congress. House Committee on Banking and Currency. Report of Ad Hoc Committee on the Domestic and International Monetary Effects of Energy and Other Natural Resource Pricing. *Meeting America's Resource Needs: Problems and Policies.* 93rd Congress, 2nd Session, November, 1974.

————. Joint Committee on Defense Production. *Potential Shortages of Ores, Metals, and Minerals, Fuels and Energy Resources.* 92nd Congress, 1st Session, August 2, 1971.

————. *Meeting America's Resource Needs: Problems and Policies.* Report of the House Committee on Banking and Currency. House of Representatives. 93rd Congress, 2nd Session, 1974.

United States Council on International Economic Policy. *Critical Imported Materials.* Washington, D.C.: U.S. Government Printing Office, 1974.

United States Department of Agriculture, Forest Service. *Anatomy of a Mine From Prospect to Production.* Tech. Rep. No. INT-35, 1977.

United States Department of the Interior, Bureau of Mines. *Commodity Data Summaries,* Washington, D.C.: U.S. Government Printing Office, annual.

————. *Minerals in the U.S. Economy: Ten-Year Supply-Demand Profiles for Mineral and Fuel Commodities.* Washington, D.C.: U.S. Government Printing Office, annual.

————. *Minerals Yearbook.* Washington, D.C.: U.S. Government Printing Office, annual.

————. Office of Minerals Policy Development. *Critical Materials: Commodity Action Analyses: Aluminum, Chromium, Platinum and Palladium.* Washington, D.C.: U.S. Government Printing Office, 1975.

————. *United States Mineral Resources.* Geological Survey Professional Paper 820. Washington, D.C.: U.S. Government Printing Office, 1973.

————. *Mineral Trade Notes.* Washington, D.C.: U.S. Government Printing Office, annual.

————. *Mineral Facts and Problems.* Bulletin No. 667. Washington, D.C.: U.S. Government Printing Office, 1975.

————. *Mineral Facts and Problems.* Bulletin No. 650. Washington, D.C.: U.S. Government Printing Office, 1970.

United States Department of State, Bureau of Public Office, Office of Media Services. "Special Report: International Collusive Action in World Markets of Nonfuel Minerals." Washington, D.C.: U.S. Government Printing Office, 1974.

United States National Commission on Material Needs and the Environment Today and Tomorrow. "Final Report of the Commission." Washington, D.C.: U.S. Government Printing Office, 1973.

_____. "Materials Requirements in the United States and Abroad in the Year 2000." Prepared by the Wharton School, University of Pennsylvania. Washington, D.C.: U.S. Government Printing Office, 1973.

Varon, B., and Takeuchi, K. "Developing Countries and Non-Fuel Minerals." *Foreign Affairs,* 52(April 1974):497–510.

Verlage, H.C. *Transfer Pricing for Multinational Enteprrises.* Rotterdam: Rotterdam University Press, 1975.

Vernon, R. "Foreign Enterprises and Developing Nations in the Raw Materials Industries." *American Economic Review,* Proceedings 60 (1970):122–26.

_____. "Long Run Trends in Concession Contracts." *Proceedings of the American Society of International Law,* 1967.

_____. *Sovereignty at Bay: The Multinational Spread of U.S. Enterprises.* New York: Basic Books, 1971.

_____. "International Investment and International Trade in the Product Cycle." *Quarterly Journal of Economics,* 80(1966):190–209.

Vogely, J. (ed.). *Economics of the Mineral Industries.* New York: American Institute of Mining and Petroleum Engineers, 1976.

_____. *Mineral Material Modeling.* Baltimore: Johns Hopkins Press, 1975.

Wakesburg, S. "Scrap: Myths and Realities of the U.S. Market." *Metal Bulletin* (Special Issue 1974).

Walter, I. "A Discussion of the International Economic Dimensions of Secondary Materials Recovery." Washington, D.C.: International Economic Studies Institute, 1975.

Walthier, T.N. "Problems of Foreign Investment in Natural Resources." Presented at the International Minerals Acquisition and Operations Institute, Denver, Col., 1974.

Wang, K.L. "Interindustry Analysis." In W.A. Vogely (ed.), *Economics of the Mineral Industries.* New York: American Institute of Mining, Metallurgical and Petroleum Engineers, 1976, pp. 322–36.

Weinstein, M.C., and Zeckhauser, R.J. "Use Patterns for Depletable and Recycleable Resources." *Review of Economic Studies,* Symposium on the Economics of Exhaustible Resources, 41(1974):67–88.

Wells, L.T. "A Product Life Cycle for International Trade?" In R. Baldwin and D. Richardson (eds.), *International Trade and Finance.* Boston: Little, Brown, 1974, pp. 34–43.

Wilson, T., Shina, R.P., and Castree, J.R. "The Income Terms of Trade of Developed and Developing Countries." *Economic Journal,* 79(December 1969):813–32.

Worcester, D.A. "Why Dominant Firms Decline." *Journal of Political Economy,* 65(1957):338–47.

World Bank. *Commodity Trade and Price Trends.* Washington, D.C., annual.

_____. "Report on the Limits to Growth." A Study by a Special Task Force of the World Bank. Washington, D.C., 1972.

_____. *Price Prospects for Primary Commodities.* Report No. 814, Washington, D.C., 1975.

Zeckhauser, R.J. "Resource Allocation with Probabilistic Individual Preferences." *American Economic Review,* 59(1969):546–52.

Copper

Adams, F.G. "The Impact of Copper Production from the Ocean Floor: Application of an Econometric Model." Philadelphia: Economics Research Unit, University of Pennsylvania, 1973.

American Metal Market Company. *Metal Statistics: The Purchasing Guide of the Metal Industries.* New York: American Metal Market Co., annual.

Annual Copper Data Summary. New York: Copper Development Association, annual.

Banks, F.E. *The World Copper Market: An Economic Analysis.* Cambridge, Mass.: Ballinger Publishing Co., 1974.

Bennett, H., Moore, L., Welborn, L., and Toland, J. *An Economic Appraisal of the Supply of Copper from Primary Domestic Sources.* Bureau of Mines Information Circular, Washington, D.C.: U.S. Department of the Interior, 1973.

Bohm, P. *The Pricing of Copper in International Trade.* Stockholm: Economic Research Institute, Stockholm School of Economics, 1968.

Bottelier, J.C. "A Case Study of the World Copper Industry." Study prepared for UNCTAD, 1968.

Brown, M.S., and Butler, J. *The Production, Marketing and Consumption of Copper and Aluminum.* New York: Praeger, 1968.

Charles River Associates. "Forecasts and Analysis of the Copper Market." Cambridge, Mass., 1973.

_____. "Economic Analysis of the Copper Industry." Washington, D.C.: U.S. Department of Commerce Publication, PB 189 927, March 1970.

_____. *Policy Implications of Producer Country Supply Restrictions: The World Copper Market.* Springfield, Va.: E.T.I.P., National Bureau of Standards, 1977.

CIPEC. "The Role of Copper Stocks and their Effect on Prices." Intergovernmental Council of Copper Exporting Countries, Paris, 1977.

_____. "The Marketing and Pricing of Copper." Intergovernmental Council of Copper Exporting Countries, Paris, 1977.

_____. "Capital Requirements and Probable Costs of Future Copper Operations." Intergovernmental Council of Copper Exporting Countries, Paris, 1977.

Copper Development Association. *Copper Supply and Consumption 1948–1967.* New York: Copper Development Association, 1968.

Dammert, A., and Kendrick, D. "A World Copper Model." Discussion Paper No. 8076. Austin: Department of Economics, University of Texas, 1976.

Ertek, Tumay. "The World Demand for Copper, 1948–63: An Econometric Study." Ph.D. Thesis, University of Wisconsin, 1967.

Fisher, F.M., Cootner, P.H., and Baily, M.N. An Econometric Model of the World Copper Industry. *Bell Journal of Economics and Management Science,* 3(1972):568–609.

Girvan, N. "Copper in Chile: A Study in Conflict between Corporate and National Economy." Ph.D. Thesis, University of the West Indies, 1970.

Grillo, H. "The Importance of Scrap." *The Metal Bulletin* (Special Issue on Copper, 1965).

Herfindahl, O.C. *Copper Costs and Prices: 1870–1957.* Baltimore: Johns Hopkins Press, 1959.

Houthakker, H.S. "Report of the Subcommittee on Copper to the Cabinet Committee on Economic Policy." Mimeographed. Washington, D.C.: The White House, 1970.

_____. "Copper: The Anatomy of a Malfunctioning Market." Lecture Presented at Duke University, March 1970.

International Wrought Copper Council. "Survey of Planned Increases in World Copper Mine, Smelter and Refinery Capacity 1974–1980." London, 1975.

Knight, C.L. *Secular and Cyclical Movements in the Production and Price of Copper.* Philadelphia: University of Pennsylvania Press, 1935.

Labys, W.C., Rees, H.J.B., and Elliott, C.M. "Copper Price Behavior and the London Metal Exchange." *Applied Economics,* 3(1971):99–113.

Mamalakis, M. "The American Copper Companies and the Chilean Government, 1920–1967: Profile of an Export Sector." Discussion Paper No. 37. New Haven, Conn.: Economic Growth Center, Yale University, 1967.

_____. "An Analysis of the Financial and Investment Activities of the Chilean Development Corporation: 1939–1964." *Journal of Development Studies,* 5(1969):118–37.

Mamalakis, M., and Reynolds, C.W. *Essays on the Chilean Economy.* Homewood, Ill.: Richard D. Irwin, 1965.

Marcosson, I.F. *Anaconda.* New York: Dodd, Mead, 1957.

Materials System Policy Making, A Case Study of Copper. Final Report by Pugh-Roberts Associates to the Science and Technology Policy Office, September 1976.

McCarthy, J.L. "The American Copper Industry, 1947–1955." *Yale Economic Essays,* 4(1964):65–132.

McDonald, J. "The World of Kennecott." *Fortune,* 44(November 1951): 84–97.

McMahon, A.D. *Copper: A Materials Survey.* U.S. Department of Interior, Bureau of Mines. Washington, D.C.: U.S. Government Printing Office, 1964.

McNicol, D.L. "The Two-Price System in the Copper Industry." *Bell Journal of Economics,* 6(1975):50–73.

Moran, T.H. *Multinational Corporations and the Politics of Dependence: Copper in Chile.* Princeton: Princeton University Press, 1977.

Newhouse, J.P., and Sloan, F.A. "An Econometric Study of Copper Supply." Unpublished Report, Rand Corporation, 1966.

O'Hanlon, T. "The Perilous Prosperity of Anaconda." *Fortune* (May 1966): 117–21.

Prain, R. *Copper, The Anatomy of an Industry.* London: Mining Journal Books, 1976.

Radetzki, M. "Copper Dependent Development." Working Paper UNCTAD-UNEP Project 005. Geneva: UNCTAD, 1977.

Saez, R. *Chile y el cobre.* Santiago: Departmento del Cobre, January 1965.

Stewardson, B.R. "The Nature of Competition in the World Market for Refined Copper." *Economic Record,* 46(1970):169–81.

Survey of Planned Increases in World Copper Mine, Smelter and Refinery Capacities 1974–1980. London: International Wrought Copper Council, 1975.

Takeuchi, K. "CIPEC and the Copper Export Earnings of Member Countries." *The Developing Economies,* 4(1972):1–29.

Underwood, J. "Optimizing Rules for Producer Groups in a Stochastic Market Setting with Applications to the Copper and Tea Markets." Ph.D. Thesis, University of Minnesota, 1976.

United Nations. "Future Demand and the Development of the Raw Materials Base for the Copper Industry." New York: E/C.7/65, 1977.

United Nations Conference on Trade and Development. "Long-Term Trends in the Demand and Supply of Copper." TD/B/IPC/COPPER/AC/L.23. Geneva: UNCTAD, 1977.

———. "Marketing and Pricing Methods for Copper." TD/B/IPC/COPPER/AC/L.15, Geneva: UNCTAD, 1977.

———. "Substitution including the Relative Stability of Supplies and Prices of Copper and Competing Metals." TD/B/IPC/COPPER/AC/L.25, Geneva: UNCTAD, 1977.

United Nations Economical Social Council. *Future Demand and the Development of the Raw Materials Base for the Copper Industry.* E/C.7/65. Geneva: U.N. Economic and Social Council, 1977.

United States, Bureau of Mines: *An Economic Appraisal of the Supply of Copper from Domestic Primary Sources.* IC 8598. Washington, D.C.: U.S. Department of the Interior, 1972.

United States Federal Trade Commission. "Report of the Federal Trade Commission on the Copper Industry." Washington, D.C.: U.S. Government Printing Office, 1947.

Whitney, J. "Analysis of Copper Production, Processing and Trade Patterns, 1950–1972." Ph.D. Thesis, Pennsylvania State University, 1976.

Wimpfen, S.P., and Bennett, H.J. "Copper Resources Appraisal." *Resources Policy* (March 1975):126–41.

Tin

Banks, R.E. "An Econometric Model of the World Tin Economy: A Comment." *Econometrica,* 40(1972):749–52.

Barry, B.T. *In Every Sphere.* London: Tin Research Institute, 1977.

Desai, M. "An Econometric Model of the World Tin Economy: A Reply to Mr. Banks." *Econometrica,* 40(1972):753–55.

Fox, W. *Tin: The Working of a Commodity Agreement.* London: Mining Journal Books, 1974.

Geer, T. "The Post-War Tin Agreements: A Case of Success in Price Stabilization of Primary Commodities." *Schweizerische Zeitschrift fur Volkwirtschaft and Statistik,* 2(1970):78–96.

Gilmore, G.A. "Mining Investment in Indonesia." *Mining Magazine,* 125(October 1971):331–46.

Harris, D. "Tin." In *Mineral Facts and Figures, 1975.* U.S. Department of the Interior, Bureau of Mines. Washington, D.C.: U.S. Government Printing Office, 1975.

Hedges, E.S. *Tin and Its Alloys.* London: Edwin Arnold, 1961.

Hoong, Y.Y. "The Development of the Tin Mining Industry of Malaya." Ph.D. Thesis, London School of Economics, 1969.

Hoong, Y.Y. "The Marketing of Tin Ore in Kampa." *Malayan Economic Review,* 4(1959).

International Tin Committee. "International Tin Control and Buffer Stocks." London: Tin Producers' Association, 1941.

International Tin Council Statistical Year Book. London: International Tin Council, annual.

Knorr, K. *Tin Under Control.* Stanford: Stanford University Press, 1945.

Ley, R. "Bolivian Tin and Bolivian Development." Ph.D. Thesis, Washington State University, 1977.

Liaqat, Ali. "The Principle of Buffer Stock and its Mechanism and Operation in the International Tin Agreement." *Weltwirtschaftliches Archives,* 96(1966).

Lim, K.K. "The Economics of Gravel Pump Mining in Malaysia." Paper Presented at the International Tin Symposium, LaPaz, November 1977.

Robbins, D.A. *Technological Developments in Tin Consumption Combat Substitution.* London: International Tin Research Institute, 1977.

Rogers, C. "Commodity Case Study—Tin." Working Paper. Geneva: Commodities Division, UNCTAD, 1978.

Sainsbury, C.L. *Tin Resources of the World.* U.S. Geological Survey Bulletin No. 1301. Washington, D.C.: U.S. Government Printing Office, 1969.

Smith, G.W., and Schink, G.R. "The International Tin Agreement: Reassessment." *Economic Journal,* 86(1976):715–28.

Thoburn, J. "Commodity Prices and Appropriate Technology: Some Lessons from Tin Mining." *Journal of Development Studies,* 14(1977):35–52.

———. "Malaysia's Tin Supply Problems." *Resources Policy,* 4(1978):31–34.

Bauxite and Aluminum

Brown, M., and Butler, J. *The Production, Marketing and Consumption of Copper and Aluminum.* New York: Praeger, 1968.

Brubaker, S. *Trends in the World Aluminum Industry.* Baltimore: Johns Hopkins University Press, 1967.

Charles River Associates. *Economic Analysis of the Aluminum Industry.* Cambridge, Mass., 1971.

———. *Policy Implications of Producer Country Supply Restrictions: The World Aluminum/Bauxite Market.* A Report Prepared for the Experimental Incentives Program. Springfield, Va.: National Bureau of Standards, National Technical Information Service, 1977.

Cornish, J. "Aluminum and Its Major Competitors: A Summary of Trends over the Period 1964–1975." *IBA Review,* 1(1976):39–47.

Dorr, A. "International Trade in the Primary Aluminum Industry." Ph.D. Thesis, Pennsylvania State University, 1975.

Farin, P., and Reibsamen, G. "Aluminum, Profile of an Industry." *Metals Week* (1967).

Fisher, E.C. "Annotated Bibliography of the Bauxite Deposits of the World." U.S. Geological Survey, Bulletin No. 221. Washington, D.C.: U.S. Government Printing Office, 1955.

Girvan, N. "Company-Country Agreements in the Bauxite Industry." Working Paper. Kingston, Jamaica, 1975.

Huang, A.C. "Prospects for World Import Demand for Bauxite, Alumina, Aluminum from Developing Countries in the Seventies." Washington, D.C.: World Bank, 1974.

Peck, M.J. *Competition in the Aluminum Industry: 1945–1958.* Cambridge: Harvard University Press, 1961.

United Nations. *Pre-investment Data on the Aluminum Industry.* New York, ST/ECLA/Conf.II/L 24, 1963.

United Nations Conference on Trade and Development. "The World Market for Bauxite: Characteristics and Trends." TD/B/IPC/BAUXITE/2. Geneva: UNCTAD, February 1978.

_____. "The World Market for Bauxite: Statistical Annex." TD/B/IPC/BAUXITE/2/Add. 1. Geneva: UNCTAD, 1978, p. 19.

United States, Bureau of Mines. *1950 Materials Survey—Bauxite.* Washington, D.C.: U.S. Government Printing Office, 1953.

_____. *1950 Materials Survey—Aluminum.* Washington, D.C.: U.S. Government Printing Office, 1956.

_____. *Revised and Updated Cost Estimates for Producing Alumina from Domestic Raw Materials.* Information Circular 8648. Washington, D.C.: U.S. Department of the Interior, 1974.

United States Council on Wage and Price Stability. *Noncompetitiveness in the World Aluminum Industry.* Washington, D.C., 1976.

Von Salmuth, C.F. *Die Aluminum Industrie der Welt.* Dusseldorf, West Germany: Aluminum Verlag GmGH, 1969.

World Bank. "Prospects for Exports of Bauxite/Alumina/Aluminum from Developing Countries." Commodity Paper No. 12. Washington, D.C.: World Bank, 1974.

_____. (R. Vedavalli.) "Market Structure of Bauxite/Alumina/Aluminum." Commodity Paper No. 24. Developing Policy Staff. Washington, D.C.: World Bank, 1977.

Iron Ore

Aiken, G.E., Bertram, J.M., and Greenwalt, R.B. "Streamlining the North American Taconite Industry." *Mining Engineering,* 24(1973):35–39.

Boylan, M.G. *Economic Effects of Scale Increases in the Steel Industry: The Case of U.S. Blast Furnaces.* New York: Praeger, 1975.

Burn, D.L. *The Economic History of Steelmaking 1867–1939: A Study in Competition.* London: Cambridge University Press, 1940.

Carr, J.C., and Taplin, W. *History of the British Steel Industry.* Cambridge: Harvard University Press, 1962.

Cockerill, A., and Silberston, A. *The Steel Industry: International Comparisons of Industrial Structure and Performance.* London: Cambridge University Press, 1974.

Cordero, R., and Serjeantson, R. *The Iron and Steelworks of the World 1974.* London: Metal Bulletin Books, 1975.

Earney, F.C. *Researcher's Guide to Iron Ore: An Annotated Bibliography on the Economic Geography of Iron Ore.* Colorado: Libraries Unlimited, 1974.

Engineering and Mining Journal. "Canadian Iron Mines with Changing Politics and Restrictive Taxes." 175(1974):72.

_____. "U.S. Steel and Bethlehem Iron Ore Holdings in Venezuela Will Be Nationalized." 175(1974):27.

_____. "1975 EM/J Survey of Mines and Plant Expansion." 176(1975):73–88.

_____. "Compensation Agreement for U.S. Steel and Bethlehem Signed in Caracas." 176(1975):36–37.

_____. "Exploration on the Decline in Australia." 176(1975):17.

_____. "Capacity Surge Slated for Direct Reduced Iron." 176(1976):132.

Fetters, K.L. "The Rivalry between Oxygen and Electric Furnace Steel Making." *Proceedings of the 34th Annual Mining Symposium of the University of Minnesota, January 15–17, 1973.* Duluth: University of Minnesota Press, 1973.

Fujita, K., and Chiba, T. "Handling Iron Ore Slurry at Hirohata Steelworks." In N.W. Kirshenbaum and G.O. Argall, Jr. (eds.), *Minerals Transportation.* San Francisco: Freeman, 1972, pp. 340–46.

Gomez, H. "Venezuela's Iron Ore Industry." In R. Mikesell (ed.), *Foreign Investment in the Petroleum and Mineral Industries.* Baltimore: Johns Hopkins Press, 1971, pp. 312–44.

Greaves, M.J. "Merchant Iron Plants, the Case for Importing Energy in the Form of Direct Reduced Iron." *Engineering and Mining Journal,* 176(1976):68–73.

Guccione, E. "Do We Really Want a Domestic Iron and Steel Industry?" *Mining Engineering,* 27(1975):17.

Hogan, W.T. *Economic History of the Iron and Steel Industry in the United States.* Lexington, Mass.: Lexington Books, D.C. Heath, 1972.

Japan's Iron and Steel Industry. Tokyo: Kawata Publicity, annual.

Lloyd, B., and Wheeler, E. "Brazil's Mineral Development." *Resources Policy,* 3(1977):39–59.

Manners, J. *The Changing World Market for Iron Ore 1950–1980.* Baltimore: Johns Hopkins University Press, 1967.

Margueron, C. "A Quantitative Analysis of the Supply-Demand Patterns in Iron Ore: The Future Possibilities of Brazil." Ph.D. Thesis, Columbia University, 1969.

Mikesell, R. "Iron Ore in Brazil: The Experience of Hanna Mining Company." In R. Mikesell (ed.), *Foreign Investment in the Petroleum and Mineral Industries.* Baltimore: Johns Hopkins Press, 1971, pp. 345–64.

Miller, J.R. "The Inevitable Magnitudes of Metallized Iron Ore." *Iron and Steel Engineer,* 49(1972):41–45.

Mining Engineering. "Billion Dollar Expansion of U.S. Iron Pellet Facilities is Underway." 27(1975):30–31.

Molin, V.J. "Mideast Nations Plan for Self-Sufficiency in Steel." *Steel Facts* (1975):5–7.

Reno, H.T., and Brantley, F.E. *Iron: A Materials Survey.* U.S. Department of the Interior, Bureau of Mines. Washington, D.C.: U.S. Government Printing Office, 1973.

Reno, H.T., and Desy, D. "Iron and Steel." In *Mineral Facts and Problems, 1975.* Washington, D.C.: U.S. Department of the Interior, 1975.

Ross, G.W. *The Nationalization of Steel.* London: MacGibbon and Kee, 1965.

Russel, C.S., and Vaughan, W.J. "A Linear Programming Model of Residuals Management for Integrated Iron and Steel Production." *Journal of Environmental and Economic Management,* 1(1974):17–42.

Santos, A. "International Trade in Iron Ore: An Econometric Analysis of the Determinants of Trade Patterns." Ph.D. Thesis, Pennsylvania State University, 1976.

Sisselman, R. "Iron Ore in the United States: A Profile of Major Mining and Processing Facilities." *Mining Engineering,* 25(1973):45–64.

Szekely, J. (ed.). *The Steel Industry and the Environment.* New York: Marcel Dekker, 1974.

United Nations. "Problems of Air and Water Pollution Arising in Iron and Steel Industry." New York: ST/ECE/STEEL/32, 1970.

_____. "Problems Relating to Iron and Steel Scrap." New York: ST/ECE/STEEL/33, 1971.

_____. "World Iron Ore Resources and Their Utilization." New York: ST/ECE/11, 1950.

_____. "Survey of World Iron Ore Resources: Occurrence, Appraisal and Use." New York: ST/ECE/27, 1955.

_____. "Long-Term Trends and Problems of the European Steel Industry." New York: ST/ECE/STEEL 1, 1959.

_____. "Statistics of World Trade in Steel in 1913–1959." New York, 1959.

_____. "Economic Aspects of Iron Ore Preparation." New York: ST/ECE/STEEL/14, 1961.

_____. "The World Market for Iron Ore." New York: ST/ECE/STEEL/24, 1968.

_____. "World Trade in Steel and Steel Demand in Developing Countries." New York: ST/ECE/STEEL/22, 1968.

_____. "Survey of World Iron Ore Resources: Occurrence and Appraisal." New York: ST/ECA/113, 1970.

United Nations Conference on Trade and Development. "A Comparison of World Prices of Iron Ore and Steel 1950–1970." Geneva: UNCTAD/CD/Misc. 58, 1974.

_____. "Iron Ore: Features of the World Market." TD/B/IPC/IRON ORE/2. Geneva: UNCTAD, 1977.

Varon, B. "The International Market for Iron Ore: Review and Outlook."
    Staff Working Paper No. 160. Washington, D.C.: World Bank, 1973.
Villar, J.W., and Gilbert, A.D. "Tilden Mine: A New Processing Technique
    for Iron Ore." *Mining Congress Journal,* 61(1975):40–48.

Index

About the Author

Walter C. Labys is professor of resource economics in the College of Mineral and Energy Resources and adjunct professor of economics in the College of Business and Economics at West Virginia University. He is also visiting professor at the Graduate Institute of International Studies in Geneva and a research associate of the National Bureau of Economic Research in New York. His principal interest is the theory and modeling of commodity markets, with applications in market forecasting, policy evaluation, stabilization, and economic development.

Dr. Labys has served as consultant to UNCTAD regarding commodity model-building, international mineral resources, and the integrated program on commodity stabilization. He has participated in the analysis of commodity problems with the National Science Foundation, the Economic Development Institute and the Commodities Division of the World Bank, the Economic Research Service of the U.S. Department of Agriculture, the Development Academy of the Philippines, the ESCAP, the FAO, the ASEAN Secretariat, the International Food Policy Research Institute, the Southeast Asia Development Advisory Group, and other organizations.

Dr. Labys received the Ph.D. in economics at the University of Nottingham in 1968. A recipient of several academic awards, he received the M.A. in economics from Harvard University, the M.B.A. in economics and operations research from Duquesne University, and the B.S. in electrical engineering from Carnegie-Mellon University. He has written a number of books and papers, including: *Speculation, Hedging, and Commodity Price Forecasts* (with C.W.J. Granger, 1970); *Dynamic Commodity Models* (1973); *Quantitative Models of Commodity Markets* (1975); and *Commodity Exports and Latin American Development: A Modeling Approach* (with M.I. Nadiri and J. Nunez del Arco, 1979).